T0022670

DIARY OF A DYING GIRL

Adapted from *Salt in My Soul*

DIARY OF A DYING GIRL

Adapted from *Salt in My Soul*

MALLORY SMITH

Random House · New York

Text and photographs copyright © 2024 by Diane Shader Smith
Cover art copyright © 2024 by Connie Gabbert

All rights reserved. Published in the United States by Random House Children's Books,
a division of Penguin Random House LLC, New York. This work is adapted from
Salt in My Soul: An Unfinished Life, originally published in hardcover by Spiegel & Grau,
New York, in 2019 and in paperback by Random House, a division of
Penguin Random House LLC, New York, in 2020.

Random House and the colophon are registered trademarks of Penguin Random House LLC.

Contributions by Micah Smith, Jack Goodwin, Meryl Shader, and Maya Humes Markes
are reprinted by permission of the individual authors.

"Clear Lungs" by Jesse Karlan, copyright © 2017 by Jesse Karlan.
Reprinted by permission of the author.

Visit us on the Web! GetUnderlined.com

Educators and librarians, for a variety of teaching tools,
visit us at RHTeachersLibrarians.com

Library of Congress Cataloging-in-Publication Data
Names: Smith, Mallory, author. | Sargent, Sara, editor.
Title: Diary of a dying girl / Mallory Smith; [edited by Sara Sargent].
Description: First edition. | New York: Random House, [2024] |
"This work is adapted from *Salt in My Soul: An Unfinished Life,* originally published in
hardcover by Spiegel & Grau, New York, in 2019 and in paperback by Random House,
a division of Penguin Random House LLC, New York, in 2020"—copyright page. |
Audience: Ages 14+ | Summary: "Mallory Smith shares her innermost thoughts
while living with a terminal illness"—Provided by publisher.
Identifiers: LCCN 2023038500 (print) | LCCN 2023038501 (ebook) |
ISBN 978-0-593-64747-9 (hardcover) | ISBN 978-0-593-64750-9 (trade paperback) |
ISBN 978-0-593-64749-3 (ebook)
Subjects: LCSH: Smith, Mallory—Diaries—Juvenile literature. | Smith, Mallory—
Health—Juvenile literature. | Smith, Mallory—Family—Juvenile literature. | Cystic fibrosis—
Patients—United States—Diaries—Juvenile literature. | Cystic fibrosis—Patients—
United States—Biography—Juvenile literature. | Chronically ill—United States—Biography—
Juvenile literature. | Chronically ill—United States—Diaries—Juvenile literature. |
Chronically ill—Family relationships—Juvenile literature.
Classification: LCC RC858.C95 S65 2024 (print) | LCC RC858.C95 (ebook) |
DDC 616.3/720092 [B]—dc23/eng/20231222

The text of this book is set in 11-point Adobe Garamond.
Interior design by Ken Crossland

Printed in the United States of America
10 9 8 7 6 5 4 3 2 1
First Edition

Random House Children's Books supports the First Amendment
and celebrates the right to read.

Penguin Random House LLC supports copyright. Copyright fuels creativity, encourages diverse
voices, promotes free speech, and creates a vibrant culture. Thank you for buying an authorized
edition of this book and for complying with copyright laws by not reproducing, scanning, or
distributing any part in any form without permission. You are supporting writers and allowing
Penguin Random House to publish books for every reader.

*Tengo que acordarme de todo, recoger las
briznas, los hilos del acontecer harapiento*
(I have to remember everything, collect the
wisps, the threads of untidy happenings)

—Pablo Neruda

CONTENTS

FOREWORD

_____

by Maya Humes Markes

I met Mallory Smith in 2009, at a party in Los Angeles for high school seniors who'd gotten into Stanford University. Two seconds in, we were giggling and bonding over our height; at six feet tall, both of us towered over everyone else. She quickly became one of my favorite people in the world. We decided to room together sophomore year at Stanford, and it was then that I learned she was a writer.

Mal wrote constantly: as she sat through her treatments for cystic fibrosis (CF), before we turned out the lights in our college dorm room, during long stays in the hospital, on cross-country plane rides, and when she wanted to recap a really hard or really good day. She was committed to chronicling everything that went on in her world, and CF shaped so many—too many—of her memories.

Mal was diagnosed at three years old. Her doctors were optimistic that the trajectory for CF patients would get longer with many medical advances in the works, so Mal spent the next two decades doing everything she could to prolong her life: juggling three sports, sticking to a healthy diet as much as possible, trying to get enough sleep, taking dozens of daily pills, and enduring treatments that pounded her chest.

Shortly after we graduated from college, though, it became clear that a bacteria—_B. cepacia_—in her lungs was becoming increasingly resistant, and her survival was at stake. Antibiotics stopped working, and the only option left was a lung transplant. In her final days, Mal gave her mom, Diane, the password to her diary, which was saved on her laptop, telling her mom that she was afraid she "might not make it to the other side." Mal's double-lung transplant surgery was successful, but two months later the bacteria recolonized her lungs. Mal's dad, Mark, arranged for an experimental treatment to fight the bacteria. Called phage therapy, it is now a promising option for anyone battling resistant bacteria. Tragically, Mal got the phages too late.

On the day of Mal's memorial, Diane opened her journal and found 2,500 pages of her reflections over ten years, which she'd begun to write when she started high school. Mal asked her mom to publish the parts of her story that might help others struggling with cystic fibrosis, invisible and visible illness, body image, depression, anxiety, or transplant. You could always count on Mal to dole out sage and thoughtful advice, so it came as no surprise that her journal was chock-full of wisdom well beyond her years. But it was also a devastating reminder of her extraordinary, unfinished life.

Mal wanted to make a difference. She wrote about what it was like to straddle the sick and the well worlds, about living and dying, and about the importance of resilience. She wrote for the people she loved and the people she'd never meet.

I was so, so lucky to know Mallory Smith. I saw her exude warmth and love even as she became unbearably sick, tethered to an oxygen tank and fighting for her life. She faced the overwhelming obstacles of a chronic, progressive illness with immense courage, grace, and dignity. Friends and family marveled at her lifelong commitment to stick to her "Live Happy" mantra despite horrific health challenges. But the truth is that her constant smile and contagious laugh masked many of her darkest feelings and negative thoughts—feelings and thoughts she shared only in the journal she left behind. For me, as a close friend, it was absolutely heart-wrenching to read about the depth of her pain and struggle for the first time.

I've learned that there were countless moments when Mal felt incredibly lonely, hopeless, and terrified of dying. This book—her words—captures that. But her words also inspire and educate as we see her perseverance and discover her powerful insights about everything from love to how to live each day with intention. Mal's journal serves as a reminder that we have to pay closer attention to our loved ones; we have to fight to look beyond what they show us on the surface. Her words urge us to extend empathy and compassion wherever possible, as we can't know all that a person is going through.

Mallory Smith was loving, excitable, goofy, vibrant, brave, brilliant, and hilarious. She was a compassionate listener and the kindest friend. Her illness cut a remarkable life far too short. But her legacy and all she gave to those around her are represented in her writing. The world is a better place because she chose to share her story with us.

The words that follow are hers.

I have big dreams and big goals. But also big limitations, which means I'll never reach the big goals unless I have the wisdom to recognize the chains that bind me. Only then will I be able to figure out a way to work within them instead of ignoring them or naively wishing they'll cease to exist. I'm on a perennial quest to find balance. Writing helps me do that.

I write because I want my parents to understand me. I write to leave something behind for them, for my brother, Micah, for my boyfriend, Jack, and for my extended family and friends, so I won't just end up as ashes scattered in the ocean and nothing else.

Curiously, the things I write in my journal are almost all bad: the letdowns, the uncertainties, the anxieties, the loneliness. The good stuff I keep in my head and heart, but that proves an unreliable way of holding on because time eventually steals all memories—and if it doesn't completely steal them, it distorts them, sometimes beyond recognition, or the emotional quality accompanying the moment just dissipates.

Many of the feelings I write about are too difficult to share while I'm alive, so I am keeping everything in my journal password-protected until the end. When I die I want my mom to edit these pages to ensure they are acceptable for publication—culling through years of writing, pulling together what will resonate, cutting references that might be hurtful. My hope is that my writing will offer insight for people living with, or loving someone with, chronic illness.

Cystic fibrosis is a chronic genetic illness that affects many parts of the body. It operates like this: A defective protein caused by the cystic fibrosis mutation interrupts the flow of salt in and out of cells, causing the mucus that's naturally present in healthy people to become dehydrated, thick, and viscous. This sticky mucus builds up in the lungs, pancreas, and other organs, causing problems with the respiratory, digestive, reproductive, endocrine, and other systems. In the lungs, the mucus creates a warm and welcoming environment for deadly bacteria like *Pseudomonas aeruginosa* and *Burkholderia cepacia*. The vicious cycle of infection, inflammation, and scarring that comes from the combination of viscous mucus and ineradicable bacteria leads to respiratory failure, the most common cause of death in cystic fibrosis patients.

It's progressive, with no cure, which means it gets worse over time. The rate of progression varies from patient to patient, and is often out of our control.

Resistant bacteria does a lot of taking—of dreams, of time, of travel, of friendships, of freedom, of potential, of plans, of lives.

Sitting in a hospital bed, I'm tempted to think about all the things that have been taken from me. More than that, it's easy to think about all the things I want for my future that might no longer be possible, the will-be-takens.

I was diagnosed at the age of three. As a kid, I made plans; I loved getting in bed at night because I had the opportunity to fantasize uninterrupted about whatever I was excited about. Some of what I thought about had to do with the future: where I would choose to live later in life, places I wanted to travel to, what I might be like as a teenager and then as an adult. Mostly, I envisioned other parts of the world—back then, anywhere was better than Los Angeles. The foreign always transcended the familiar. The unknown was brimming with possibility, while the known was full in a less satisfying way; like a big glass of a clumpy protein shake, you know it's good for you but it doesn't rock your world: daily routines, school days spent reading textbooks, long medical treatments I didn't want to do. As Dr. Seuss says, "You're off to great places! Today is your day! Your mountain is waiting, so . . . get on your way!" I believed wholeheartedly in those great places to come.

But for a CF patient, time is the meanest of forces. Just as water steadily erodes rock over the years, causing durable material to crumble with the invisible quality of slow change, my disease erodes the life blueprint I drew as a kid; with time, invisibly but surely, I grow decreasingly confident in the plans that I had etched in this mental map until it's hard to remember they were ever there. Occasionally, I'll remember with a smile the whimsical desires I had as a kid, and how tenaciously I fought for them—the dolphin research trip I desperately wanted to go on (never mind that we'd be living without electricity and I wouldn't be able to do treatment), my water polo team's trip to Hungary that I wished to go on without a parent. Now I chuckle because these fantasies were born out of a sense of entitlement, and I'm thankful to have outgrown that. How many kids, diseased or not, get to go on a research trip to Belize during high school? I couldn't go because I need electricity; most kids wouldn't have been able to go because it's indulgent and expensive.

The things I wanted were never material things, though. For the most part, I wished for a life lived honestly, to do good things, and to be happy. I wanted a career that, selflessly, would help people and, selfishly, would let me work in beautiful places and outdoors. I wanted beauty—not for me, but for my surroundings. Spending so much time trapped indoors has given me a deep appreciation for natural beauty.

A lot of the things I wished for have become reality. I'm incredibly grateful for the health I still have, the people who surround and support me, the time I got to spend at Stanford learning and growing into the person I am today, and the nourishing well of memories

3

I'm able to draw from in times when the new memories I'm forming skew more negative than positive.

But I've also spent a lot more time than I would like wrestling demons, wasting precious energy suffering with problems derived from feeling like a victim. My life is constantly changing, and that's difficult. That's what CF does; like an earthquake, it constantly moves the ground under our feet, so we're always struggling to regain balance, to find our footing. It's hard to look forward when we must always be looking at the ground beneath us; we're more lurching than walking, stumbling to stay upright.

With constant adaptation, though, comes a remarkable resilience. When my original goals become unrealistic, I compromise. When those new goals become unrealistic, I compromise again. When my replacement-replacement goals become unrealistic, I get frustrated. And sad. But knowing that the range of what I'm capable of will shrink, I need to plan a life where my goals do not have to be slashed every year as my health declines. I can be creative with what I'm capable of as the limitations pile on. It's about perception—if careers are a means to an end (in my case, helping people and feeling challenged while making money to support myself), there have to be ways to get there that don't require a strict schedule, hard physical conditions, or sixty-hour workweeks.

Being frustrated and angry that something was taken from you hurts creativity, the very same creativity that could help you reinvent your possibilities and achieve your ends. Understanding this trap is important—knowledge is power.

So yes, resistant bacteria does a lot of taking. It's a complex, unpredictable, irreversible, progressive, painful, suffocating, choking weed, and it's okay to hate it.

At the same time, it does give. It's given me the creativity to reimagine my life, a skill I wouldn't have needed to develop if everything had been easy and nothing was impossible.

It's given me a community of men and women who astound me every day with the strength and endurance they use to ride through daily challenges and life-or-death struggles. We all know this disease delivers both in big doses.

It's given me a way to cut to the chase in my friendships and relationships. Can you hang? Is that same person who's there when I'm laughing and partying going to be there when I'm sick or sedated? It's given me a resounding understanding of the value of a good friend, and my incredible luck in having so many.

It's given me the chance to look normal; not all diseases are so forgiving. It's a blessing and a curse not to look sick—a curse when I need accommodations but am not given them because of the perception that I'm too healthy—but mostly, it's a blessing. I am not branded by illness on a daily basis. If I choose to disclose, it's just that: a choice.

It's given me a second home in the hospitals where I've had some of the best and worst moments of my life. I graduated college, officially (finished my last final), in the hospital. I've spent birthdays and holidays in the hospital. I've had panic attacks in the hospital. I've struggled to breathe in the hospital. I've forged powerful relationships with doctors, nurses, and ancillary support teams in the hospital. I've been grateful for the care I've gotten in the hospital. I've seen the strength of my family tested in the hospital. I've seen my own strength tested in the hospital.

It's given me the mountain that's been waiting for me all my life. The mountain we're all climbing, every day. It looks different for everyone, but we all have our own struggles, every person I see on the street. I have to remind myself not to envy those whose lives look normal, because their mountains do exist, even if they're less obvious than mine.

It's given me empathy, and gratitude, and courage, and humor, and heartache, and happiness.

All that giving balances all that taking and, in the end, I'm still here, in my second home in the hospital, having some of my best and worst moments, feeling at times like I'm going nowhere but knowing that, in reality, like Dr. Seuss told me I would, I'm getting on my way.

—*Mallory Smith*

HIGH SCHOOL

Even though she was two years my junior, I always looked up to my sister. As long as I can remember, she was my mentor, life coach, and hero. With a terminal illness looming over her shoulder, Mallory had no choice but to rise above. And she was wise well beyond her years.

—Micah, Mallory's brother

Thursday, July 23, 2009 (16 years old)

Was talking with my mom today about Britney Spears's younger sister, who will forever be known as the girl who was hidden away by her family when they found out she was pregnant. It led to my mom telling me about when she was pregnant with her third child, my would-be younger sister. The doctors advised her to terminate the pregnancy because the ultrasound showed that she had cystic fibrosis (CF), the number one genetic killer of children in the United States. They said it wouldn't be fair to bring a child into this world knowing that it would suffer and probably die young. I was three at the time.

The next day, I was tested for CF. It turned out I had the disease, too.

Talking about the symptoms and the science doesn't bother me. It never has. But other parts are just too embarrassing to share, so I don't. I think that's why I like writing in this journal so much.

Monday, July 27, 2009

Can't believe I'm going to be a senior soon! I'm feeling a strange combination of excitement, anticipation, anxiety, fear. I made my college list. DEF not going to add any more, but I might take some off if the applications get to be too much. I'm thinking: Duke, Vanderbilt, University of Virginia, Stanford, the UCs, Pomona, USC, San Luis Obispo, Pepperdine, Michigan, UPenn.

Thinking about college apps always leads me back to thinking about what I want. My friends don't seem to go down this rabbit hole the way I do. I think my diagnosis is why I obsess about it. But what is it I do want?

I want to grab life and take it. I want a rich, unforgettable, well-rounded, happy high school experience. I want to fall in love, go to football games, make friends, laugh a lot, cry (but not about how much homework there is, which is the only reason I shed a tear these days). I want to live it for me, not for my coaches, my friends, my parents. I want competition to rear its ugly head only on the volleyball court or in the water polo pool, not in academics. If only. There's just too much emphasis in high school on grades, success, money, the future. It's killing my dreams.

I used to fantasize about EVERYTHING. About traveling, and adventures, and possibilities, and the future! I want to imagine greatness in life. But when you're disillusioned with how life is, how it has treated you—and you don't feel like anything great is going to come your way ever—you stop imagining. That's what's happened to me. My fantasies have been erased—replaced with the mundane things in life, who I'm going to eat lunch with the next day, what I'm going to eat so I don't keep gaining weight, how I'm going to get through all the school commitments hanging over my head. In order to fantasize about exciting opportunities, you have to think, in some small part of your heart or mind, that you deserve these things. I'd like to think I do. But this world has so many problems—death, disease, natural disasters, human cruelty, animal cruelty, racism—why should I get what I want?

I also just want to be a kid again. I moved out of childhood the day I graduated from middle school, and I keep looking back. College is looming large, but I'm still stumbling over vague ambitions and goals, requirements, and standards, as school takes over our brains and we perform rote functions like embedding quotes, improving handwriting, studying for exams, taking standardized tests. I don't want high school to have just been about getting into college.

Tuesday, August 4, 2009
I know this might sound really dramatic, but I feel like the threads of my life are unraveling and I'm standing here helpless, watching it happen, not being able to do anything about it. I'm indecisive, sort of paralyzed emotionally, because I don't trust my instincts, which my mom always says is a sign of insecurity. I think that's what's happening to me. I just don't understand why. The funny thing is that people always call me the Golden Girl because they think I have it all. It bugs me because I so don't.

Happiness is a choice, I know that. And I'm usually good at making the choice. But for some reason I can't get there these days. I've got these internal hallucinations that are so haunting I can't escape them—even when I close my eyes—because the images play on my eyelids as if projected on a movie screen.

Maybe my current angst has nothing to do with my indecisiveness, my insecurities, school, or what other people think. Maybe I'm just mad that Carrie's on the phone with Jay right now and she won't tell me what they're talking about. Maybe *mad* isn't the right word at all. Maybe I really mean *pestered* or *bothered* or *annoyed* or *suspicious* or something else altogether. I don't think of myself as the jealous type, but . . .

She says they're not talking about me, but I don't believe her, and even if it's true, I still don't like it. I just hate that no matter what's going on with us, Jay always brings other people into it, which means other people know more than I do about my relationship. I also hate it when Jay expresses his feelings to me, so I guess I'm just hoping that he doesn't have feelings, which is kind of too much to ask for.

I don't know, something about us doesn't feel right. It used to, but now I don't get excited to talk to him, I don't get excited when he texts me, I wouldn't rather see him than any of my other friends, and I don't particularly love kissing him. It's not bad, I just don't feel any passion. This could be just me resisting a relationship and being screwed up, and I don't want to regret it later if I push him away because I'm scared. Maybe I'm just more of a noncommittal type of person. I really don't like to be tied down to anything. I just get so mad at myself because I've been saying that I wanted a boyfriend for sooo long, but now that I finally have the opportunity, I push it away. What's that about?

Saturday, August 8, 2009
Still trying to figure out what I want. The problem is that I don't know myself anymore. I need to figure out who I am before I can know what I want.

I love to read, but I don't usually finish entire books, because I'll pick one up, then get distracted by another one that I want to read and start that one. I don't finish books because I like books too much . . . that's kind of ironic. Right now, I'm reading *The Idiot* by some Russian guy with a ridiculously long last name. My favorite books are *The Clan of the Cave Bear, Catch-22,* and *White Teeth.*

I love laughing. Duh. It's the only thing that can save me from boredom, sadness, anger, annoyance . . . when I laugh really hard, I am completely silent, but you can see my body convulsing. It's really strange.

When I'm bored, I don't watch TV. I either read Wikihow (you know you secretly want to learn how to make circular bubbles while diving, make a shrimp out of a plastic straw, or attach a garden hose to a kitchen faucet!), read song lyrics, or stare at the ceiling. Just kidding, except for the first two.

I find pretentious teachers really amusing. Although I have to say, most of the teachers I've had in high school have been amazingly understanding and helpful.

I miss a lot of school. I'm not sure what people think about that. But it's hilarious how even though I have only been to chemistry eight times this year, my teacher still reads my name on the absent list every day. I should be on a list when I go, not when I miss.

I can talk for a really long time if I want to (pretty obvious by how long this entry is). I guess I have a lot to say, unless you're talking about the economy, chemistry, or football. In that case I shut up pretty quick because I don't care.

None of my closest friends have names longer than one syllable. I mean technically they do, but I get rid of those names in my head and give them one-syllable names. Same thing with my family, example, Micah is Bridge. I call my dad Pidge and people always think I'm calling him bitch when I talk to him, which I would never do.

I'm really nostalgic. I love to lie on my bed with a cup of tea and look at childhood stuff—pictures, books, letters, TV shows, etc. *Doug* was always my favorite TV show, Harry Potter my favorite book series.

I don't like the number twenty-one. The drinking age should be twenty (or eighteen). I don't like any odd numbers except for nine. They're incomplete, and I like things in pairs.

I get these random ideas, which at the time they come to me seem brilliant, and then I think about it after and realize they're really dumb. I was going to start a company that sells handmade shell jewelry and extra-long jeans (thirty-seven-inch inseam to be precise, for other tall hard-to-find-jeans-for people like me). This is actually really stupid because those two things have nothing to do with each other, but I wouldn't want to sell anything else, and I have no business experience, and no interest in finances. This all means I would suck at having a business!

I hate having political or religious debates because I always think the people who don't agree with me are insane and I don't want my beliefs to disrupt my friendships. I usually feel very strongly about my beliefs, and am not really open to other opinions, because only logical arguments are convincing to me, and I tend to be on the side of logic.

I think the sport of hunting should go extinct ASAP. Hunting is just as bad as serial killing.

I don't smoke (ever). I don't really understand why anyone has the desire to. I don't judge people who smoke . . . yeah that was a complete lie; I kind of do.

I used to think some of my angst was the result of this overwhelming desire I had to be with a guy. That desire wasn't being satisfied because I wasn't hooking up with anyone or going out with anyone. Now I am hooking up with someone (Jay), but I'm still unsure about it. I don't think it's normal to have as little experience as I've had. I mean in some ways I've had more experience than other people because minute for minute I've hooked up more than a lot of other people have, but all the situations have started so unnaturally that I'm not sure they even count. They happened when I met someone new—someone who didn't know most of the people I know, so I got really reckless (because it didn't matter if I got rejected).

I just wish I knew what guys think of me when they see me. Do they see me as pretty? Do they see me as looking old? Do they think I look manly (because I've gotten that before)? The guys that I know from school obviously don't see me as someone to be with and I'm not sure how I got that reputation. Maybe because I'm not sure how to act around guys to make them see me as someone to potentially like.

If things don't work out with Jay, I would like to go for someone I know instead of some random person, but the problem is that the only people I ever like are people that I don't really have a chance with.

Before Jay, I "liked" Terry, who I had only spoken to about three times. How can you even say you like someone that you don't really know? But I always do that to myself, I set myself up for failure by getting obsessed with people who don't have any idea I see them that way and would think it was weird if they did know. This is such a ridiculous thing that I'm writing right now, I want to burn it, because I sound so pathetic and desperate and usually, I get along pretty well without a guy. But now I have a guy, sort of, and am still feeling just as unsettled. I just don't know what to do anymore. Okay, I'm done writing this, it's not making me feel any better at all.

Saturday, August 15, 2009

I woke up today still dwelling on all this. Ruminating actually. I shouldn't settle for someone just because I want a boyfriend, right? When I hung out with Jay two nights ago, I wasn't feeling well and I was really nervous to start double volleyball sessions the next day and I only had one hour to spend with him, so it was a bad situation. But I kept thinking I don't want to be anything more than his friend. How do I know I can trust that feeling? Maybe I just need to get out of my comfort zone. A girl would be lucky to have Jay as a boyfriend because he would be a great boyfriend, but how come I don't want him? Does not wanting him mean I am a bad person? I hope not . . . not everyone is for everyone . . . it's not like just because he has a checklist of amazing qualities, I automatically must like him.

I'm also really bleh right now because I started volleyball yesterday, so I feel like I have no time. I love the sport, but I don't love all the sacrifices I have to make for it. Although I guess I don't really have anything better to be doing . . . it just seems that five hours a day is a little bit much for three weeks of summer. But we have so much potential this year, I think it will all be worth it in the end. In previous years, when we sucked as a team, it seemed ludicrous to put in so much effort when we were never going to have huge accomplishments anyway.

I'm actually excited about this season, so I don't know why I'm saying that I'm bleh. I guess it's because I'm annoyed at myself about Jay. It's kind of ironic, because when I wanted him, he was unattainable (I didn't know why then), and now that he really wants me, I can't make up my mind. It's really easy to admire hot guys from afar, but it's another thing to make them like you, to get them to date you, something which I have never succeeded in doing until now. I don't want to settle, but I also don't want to be a lonely prude old hag who marries the first person with a dick who wants to date her.

Friday, August 21, 2009

What if all my ambivalence about Jay is, in fact, me not wanting anyone to get close enough to see what my life with CF is really like? CF is a bad disease to start with but the layering on of resistant bacteria wreaks havoc in so many ways.

For me, everything changed when I came home from camp the summer after sixth grade. I wasn't feeling great but didn't think anything of it. It was the second day of school; my mom had picked me up to do an errand and we were walking down Sunset Boulevard. I was tracing the lettering on the poster for the next show outside the House of Blues when my mom's phone rang. "Hello?" she said. I was waving at her to draw her attention to something, and she just shot me this look that stopped me in my tracks. She was silent for a while . . . which, if you know my mom, is not a good thing. And finally, she just said, "Oh fuck!" The street was humming with people, but all I could hear was the tinny voice on the other end of the line. That voice belonged to my doctor, and when my mom asked if we needed to come now, he said yes. Right now. I asked her what was wrong, and she made this guttural noise, a noise like when you're just about to speak but the words get tangled in your throat and you can't choke them out. And I asked, "What, what?!"

"That was Dr. Pornchai," she said. "Your sputum culture results came back. You have . . ." And she just looked at me and . . . paused. She couldn't say it.

We got in the car to drive to the hospital, and she cried silently the entire way. We found out that day that my lungs had been colonized by *Burkholderia cenocepacia,* otherwise known as *B. cepacia.* It's the deadliest strain of the deadliest bacteria known to infect CF lungs.

Once I was admitted, they put me in a really stark white room. My mom was freaked out, but my dad was exhibiting an unshakable calm. I could tell it was an act. A lot of whispering took place while I tried to sleep. I was tossing and turning and coughing with a force and depth I hadn't known before. *B. cepacia* can be found anywhere in the natural environment. It's all around us. But it's an opportunistic pathogen, which means it can't derail the lungs of a healthy person. You have to be vulnerable in order to get an infection from it. You have to have something like CF or AIDS or cancer. Fewer than 3 percent of people with CF have *B. cepacia* in their lungs, so my question was, why me?

That year at camp, I had been irresponsible. I was just being a kid. I didn't like the food, so I subsisted on bread and salad and the occasional chicken tender. My cabinmates and I would stay up every single night whispering in our bunks about our counselors' secret lives and which girls were mean to us and who kissed who after the nighttime *Siyum* song session. During my treatments, I would talk while I was inhaling medications through the nebulizer, which meant losing some of the lifesaving meds into the surrounding air. I'd shave ten minutes off each treatment to make the next activity on time. And when you're not vigilant with CF—the lesson my mom says she will take to her deathbed—when you are not vigilant every second of every day to keep your body strong, anytime something touches your mouth it's a potential encounter with a dangerous pathogen. The infection entered the microbial ecosystem of my lungs uninvited, waiting until my body was vulnerable to make its move. Microscopic armies of bacterial cells marched in and set up camp, creating colonies that no drug in existence can evict.

During that admission, everyone was trying to put this weight on my shoulders and make me feel it, make me wrap my head around it and understand what it meant to have bacteria that was known for its resistance. But I couldn't. How could they explain to a twelve-year-old child that she might never be able to get a lifesaving lung transplant? That once she reaches end-stage disease she probably won't get the second chance at life because her strain of *B. cepacia* is the strain most associated with rapid decline, high virulence, resistance to antibiotics, and high post-transplant mortality?

I didn't realize that my chance encounter with an opportunistic pathogen at camp, the safest place in the world, was like walking up to the devil's vending machine—I gave up my life as I knew it, and in return, I was left with the sinking and undeniable reality of my mortality. Null and void. Erased.

Until then, lofty medical terms and distant notions of death were just words. I didn't want to think about any of that and I didn't

19

want to know. I just wanted to be a normal teenager with all the ups and downs that entails. Is that really possible now that I understand exactly what it means to have *B. cepacia*? Could that be the reason I keep pushing Jay away?

Saturday, August 22, 2009

During lunch yesterday I found out that there are now three volley-ball captains, and I'm not one of them: I was actually crying, which really surprised me because I totally thought I didn't care. But it's humiliating since I'm the only person on the team who has been a starter for three years, and I was captain last year. Also, I was named Female Athlete of the Year at Beverly Hills High School three years in a row. Now I'm wondering if they gave it to me out of pity. Or maybe because I'm one of only a few who play three sports.

It's Micah's birthday today—he's having a party at his frat to-night!

Friday, August 28, 2009

I got good numbers at the doctor today, so that's one good thing. Dr. Pornchai told me two weeks ago that if my numbers didn't go up then I'd have to go on IVs, and I would have lost my volleyball season if that had happened. I'm really relieved about that. I also wrote a rough draft of my college essay last night, and even though it's corny and doesn't really make sense, at least I have a draft down. It was starting to hang over my head. I'm gonna stop writing and go pee now for the millionth time today. I swear, during volleyball season I drink more water and sweat more and pee more than a giraffe. No joke.

Sunday, September 20, 2009

I can't believe I'm a senior in high school!! Last night we got dressed up and went out with a random crew. And I just decided to drink because I hadn't in a while and I felt like it. The people we were with were drinking, too. I started out having three shots but then I ended up having five. . . . Badddd Mallory! It was all Patrón and that's why

I had so many—because Patrón tastes so good! Later in the night, we decided to drink water and eat bread and stuff so we could sober up before we went home, but we ended up staying out until 2:30(ish). And I asked my mom if I could sleep over at Jay's house (realizing I need to write more about him/us since it keeps changing), but she said no because then other people would think I was a skank (my word, not hers), which I totally think is true now that I'm home; it would have been extremely awkward to wake up in the same house with his parents and have to explain why I slept over! He did ask me to be his girlfriend and I was like, Ahhh . . . finally! I'm ready! And then a little later I went home.

Tuesday, September 22, 2009

Today my mom asked me if I had landed on any colleges to apply to. The conversation got me thinking about my GI issues. I don't know if my inability to go to the bathroom in other people's houses is mental or physical. But college will be a huge problem, a big dilemma. In fact, it will be a catastrophic situation. Even now it prevents me from wanting to sleep out and even from going to school sometimes. This is the one secret I have kept from every single person except my mom. I hate admitting it—even to myself—because it's so pathetic. I tell myself to grow up. I can't live at home forever.

Will I need to stay close to home because of CF? I hate exposing people to the truth about how I live, what I have to do each day to stay alive.

Saturday, October 3, 2009

I had the cutest day today, I slept in and had breakfast with my mom and then did yoga with Tamara and then did college stuff and some homework. Then Jay came over and we had a really good time tonight—everything's good now. He's really good-looking and funny and smart, so I'm kind of starting to like him more and more. And I'm getting more used to having a boyfriend, it was really weird for me in the beginning. I was sooo not used to it. I sound like a broken record. He didn't sleep over. I'm NOT ready for that.

Sunday, October 4, 2009

I woke up today after sleeping for twelve hours, completely exhausted. I had chills, hot flashes, really bad chest pain, runny nose, sore throat, and fatigue. I pretty much sat on the couch staring at the wall for an hour. Turns out I had a temperature, and Mom has swine flu, so I was scared that I had it, too. I went to Starbucks and Koo Koo Roo with Pidge once I was feeling a little better. The wild thing is that Jay is sick now, too; he wasn't feeling well when he left last night and ended up in the ER with some virus. I feel like sickness is invading everywhere and it's so hard to avoid it.

It's kind of funny that it's now Sunday night, I've played six volleyball matches this weekend, and I haven't showered since Friday morning.

I was kind of depressed all day today, but I think it was just because I was feeling so sick earlier—I'm feeling so much better now.

Thursday, October 8, 2009

The past two days have been so intense and good. Yesterday was our home game against Santa Monica. We'd been building it up to be the biggest match of our season and expecting/hoping to win for so long that I had been anticipating it and anticipating it and I didn't know what to think about it, but when it came it was absolutely amazing. It reminds me why I play sports, for that feeling I get when I play well, and the team plays well, and we win. It was a home game, I had friends and my mom and dad and my grandparents there watching, we had a lot more fans than usual, we were all PUMPED for the game, the warm-up was amazing, I slept well the night before, and I just wanted to win so bad and knew we could win. My defense was really good in the game, and so was my serve-receive . . . it wasn't absolutely perfect, but I was being really scrappy, helping out, and being really involved in every play, whereas sometimes I freeze up when I get nervous. But I was just putting everything onto the court, and I was 100 percent zoned in, I didn't even see the sign that Becca and Maria and Natasha made me, and I didn't even notice that Jay was there until I was sitting on the bench during a time-out. The first game we won 25–14, and the second game we won 25–23. I served on game point of both games and didn't miss my serves, and we were all so confident and loud and excited and zoned in that we were just unbeatable to Santa Monica, and they looked like they had no clue what to do. It was a complete reversal of positions from last year, when we looked like deer in headlights against their amazing team. But now we're the amazing team and they are the one that sucks. It's pretty awesome.

After the first two games, I was a little nervous because a lot of times we win the first two games and play really well and then let the other team come back in the third game, but in the third game we beat them 25–14 again! And I served nine points in a row and about half of them were aces and that's how we got so far ahead, and then I got a kill on match point. So all in all it was awesome, and apparently it'll knock them out of being ranked in the top ten and put us there, which is what we've been aiming for all season but has continually eluded us.

Saturday, October 10, 2009

This morning was the SAT. It's been a year since I took it in October of junior year, and since I scored really high, I didn't take it again until now. I think I did really well! And Jay tested at Beverly, too, so I got to see him before the test. I was wearing a Marist T-shirt from Michelle and my UCLA sweatpants (haha!) so I was really decked out in college gear, which is pretty appropriate for taking the SAT. I am so relieved that it's done, and that I took my math test yesterday and got a 98 percent!! Everything's turning out nicely this weekend. Plus, it's my birthday Monday and there's no school so I'm super excited about that. And tomorrow I'm going to brunch with Becca and Michelle and Natasha in Santa Monica and we're going in pajamas because I'm surely going to be too lazy to put on real clothes, and then we'll probably see a movie. Today after the SAT, Jay came over for a little while, and then he left and I wrote one of my college essays and then wrote a list of all the books I can remember reading since seventh grade . . . it's like seventy or eighty books.

Tonight I went with Becca and Natasha and Michelle and we hung out at Becca's and then we went to dinner really late at Islands, so now I feel kind of sick from the French fries but it was worth it because I haven't eaten them in forever. And sometimes you just need to eat what you want; I can't deprive myself all the time. I love hanging out with those juniors—it's nice to get away from the college app pressure and hang out with people who still are in high school mentally and act like they're in high school, because we are (still in high school) but seniors always forget it. And they're all so sweet, like planning stuff for my birthday and getting me cards and presents and stuff, and they're just so thoughtful and nice and fun to hang out with. I just want everything to stay the same and to have another year of high school after this one. But that can't happen, and I don't want to stay here once everyone else moves on and be the only person still living in the past, so I guess I just have to accept what's coming and get on with my life. I'm going to miss my family, including Maria, who has lived with us since I was five—and my dog, Dewey, and Millie and Grandma and Grandpa. And what if Grandma or Grandpa dies when I'm in college, or what if Maria moves back to El Salvador? I'd be seriously depressed. Because everything's pretty good right now and I want it to stay how it is and not change.

Wednesday, October 14, 2009 (17 years old)

I'm so completely overwhelmed right now. It's like my whole life is in overdrive and the more I have to do the more I procrastinate so everything builds up and I just feel like I have no time for anything and I'm running late constantly and I'm always needing to figure out what is the least important thing, so I don't have to do it. I haven't been to physics or physics lab in days, and I'm so behind and I missed a quiz, and I don't even know what's going on in the class. In English, I am six days late in taking a huge, huge test on the whole Bible and mythology, which I know nothing about and didn't study for enough. I missed the National Honor Society meeting, so I don't know what happened. I've missed government for the last four classes and the economics part is hard for me to understand, so reading the book really isn't enough. I still have more college essays to write, and when I have a ton of stuff to do (like tonight), instead of doing it, I sit here and write about what I'm NOT doing in this journal, which is not productive. But I think it helps me mentally.

DISCLAIMER: If future Mallory is reading this, don't think I've spent high school being sad. I just don't write in my journal when I'm happy. And I need to learn how to block the negative from my mind. I need to make a list of things that make me happy and do at least one of them every day. But right now, I need to finish reading . . . and pray that my teacher doesn't check my math homework, which I'm not doing.

Thursday, October 22, 2009

Gaby came over today; she was here when I got home from volley-ball at 6:45 and I ate dinner and then she told me about her trip to Mexico this weekend. She's gonna stay and do homework with me! I also need to work on college apps. Trying to decide if I should apply for early decision.

Sunday, October 25, 2009

I had a little problem with Jay tonight. Overall, our relationship has been going well, at least I thought it was. Normally, I see him once, maybe twice a week, but we talk on the phone every day. I felt like that was good enough and I don't feel like I see too much or too little of him and I still get to see my friends. But tonight, when I was with my friends and I didn't want everyone to have to make their plans revolve around me getting to see him, he got really pissed off and frustrated and he felt like I blew him off. And I get why he feels that way, but still, I feel like he's overreacting. So, we talked about it and it's kind of hard to talk to him when we disagree about something. I guess I need to remind myself that overall things have been going well. I like our relationship and it's so unbelievably nice not to have to worry about finding a guy, or to have to be sad that I don't have a guy. But I wonder how long it'll last . . . maybe another few months? He's a very good guy, he's nice and he's smart and he cares about me,

I think, but he seems a little guarded now. Like he doesn't seem as open as he used to before we were going out, which is kind of odd. We do have fun when we're together, and I can talk to him about stuff, and he's attractive, so it all works. But I wouldn't marry him or anything. I'm not in love, obviously.

Thursday, October 29, 2009

They weighed me in clinic last week and I was under 150 for the first time in a really long time! Being six feet tall, I always weigh more than most girls my age, but I'm never really happy about it. It's confusing/frustrating because on the one hand, I want to look thinner, and I like to be thinner, but on other hand, my parents and doctors tell me it's not good for me to be so thin. And even though I felt good the day I weighed under 150, I have to admit, I don't really think it's working out for me because when I weigh less, I just have less energy. This all means I've failed. I need to figure out how to eat well to feel okay. I need to stop writing because I have to sleep before my big game tomorrow!

Sunday, November 8, 2009

I had the best day ever today for some reason. And kind of a wild week . . . on Monday I was sick with a fever so I didn't go to practice. Then Tuesday we had our last home game, and it was our senior day, so we all got tiaras and flowers and Coach Weiss said something about each of us over the microphone, and the thing she said about me was actually really nice. She mentioned that I'm the go-to player and that I'm one of the best all-around players in Beverly Hills High School history. So that was pretty cool.

Then on Tuesday and Wednesday I started getting this awful inflammation in my lungs that prevented me from being able to cough deeply so I just had this persistent, dry, unproductive cough that made me lose my voice! UGH. It was actually horrible and every time I did treatment in the morning no mucus would move, it was completely trapped, and the airways were so constricted that I couldn't get to them, and it was hard for me to breathe when I was playing, and I was extremely worried for the Thursday game against

Torrance. And during treatment I would cough so much and so hard trying to get a deep cough that I almost threw up. So, on Wednesday I had my mom call the doctor because I was still worried, and then I just had to do a ton of Xopenex breathing treatments and stay home from school. AGAIN—literally my teachers probably think I'm SUCH a hypochondriac drama queen!

But then Thursday came . . . and it was our Culver City game, and I was sooo excited, and I think adrenaline kicked in and we got on the court all pumped up to play and beat them. And we beat them in three! I got some pretty good hits but mostly our middles did the job, which was good and took some of the pressure off me and I didn't have to work that hard, which is good because I was way more tired than usual because of the asthma inflammation stuff.

I actually played great defense (my defense is getting much better) and I think it's because I'm stretching so I'm more limber and because I've lost weight so I'm quicker and lighter on my feet. Or . . . maybe it's just desire! All I know is I've really stepped it up in the last week or so and my playing has improved sooo much, especially starting at the last tournament and continuing until now.

But then in the third game, something happened to Syline. She sprained her ankle and she had to be carried off the court and taken home. It was really sad, because she's had all her shoulder problems, so she's had a pretty disappointing season already and then this happened. . . . I just hope she's better for the CIF tournament (California Interscholastic Federation) because we need her. But then after our game we were sooo excited because we found out that we won the coin flip and got first in league!!!!! Yayyyy! It was actually amazing, because four of us seniors have been playing together since freshman year and all of our hard work is finally getting us results and rewards and we're ranked ninth in the division and in general our prospects are looking good, and we have a home game on Tuesday for the first round of CIF! Which is a must-win. I'm much more confident now so I'm getting less nervous because I feel like I know what I need to do to play well. So anyway, we were all freaking out when we heard about the results of the coin flip.

Friday, November 13, 2009

The more the doctors tell me that I need to put on weight—and the more they say it—the more I just want to lose it. I can't tell if feeling accomplished that I lost weight makes me a sick person. I just think I look sooo much better when I'm thinner, and I hated my body before and now I hate it much less. I think if I were at 140 that would be a perfect weight for me, and I would be the happiest with my body. I hope it doesn't all sneak back on . . . that would be sad. It's weird because I have mixed feelings about it. It's not all just a vanity thing WHY I like being thinner, I actually FEEL better. I don't know why but I do. I feel lighter, quicker, springier, more energetic, prouder, more in control; it's emotional and physical and mental and everything. It's kind of obsessive in a way but I've always struggled with food issues so it's not like it's a new thing. It's just that I'm writing about it now because my parents are trying to fatten me up at the same time I'm trying to keep slimming down so it's complicated. I just hope that if I don't put the weight back on they don't decide to do something wild and annoying and weird like appetite pills or a feeding tube or something . . .

Sunday, November 15, 2009

I'm in such a bad place right now. In just a few short weeks so much has changed, starting with my emotional status and outlook on life. I was happy, excited, confident. Now it seems like life is a chore, I trudge through every day looking forward to going to bed, waiting for the weekend. In just a few short weeks, school has become overwhelming. There are not enough hours in the day to get through all the work. It seems like I have lost all semblance of my youth, surrendered it to the monster we call society. Or maybe it's more accurate to say reality. What happened to the concept of free time? I don't have time to do the things I want to do: hang with friends, take a moment to breathe, to watch *Gossip Girl,* to finish reading *A Confederacy of Dunces.* There's no time to watch the sunset (what little can be seen through the layer of air pollution that also contributes to my lung function decline).

Monday, November 23, 2009

I'm in Hawaii right now! I'm obsessed and so happy! Every time I come here, I feel amazing because the magical combo of salt and sea clears the mucus in my lungs. I really think I could live here for a year and be very content. The only good part about having CF is that Hawaii is healing for me so my parents bring me every time they can. My mom jokes that she works full-time to support my Hawaii habit!

I'm going to swim laps in the pool in Kihei right now, so I'll write more when I get back.

It's nighttime now. Doing treatment and watching *School of Rock*. Too tired to write more but still can't believe that last Saturday night I went to Josh's bar mitzvah and Jack Black was there! Jay says he's going to miss me while I'm away. He's so sweet!

Sunday, December 6, 2009

Dear Mom,

DISCLAIMER: You're going to think I'm ridiculous after reading this.

I still have a fever of 104 and a pulse ox on my finger to measure my oxygen saturation level, so I can't think—or write—very well. I wanted to let you know that even though my CF team says I don't have an eating disorder and I don't think I do, either, I counted calories very carefully for the last few months and it was part of my daily routine. Sometimes you told me to write down what I was eating so I could see what caused acid reflux or whatever, but I was already doing that for a long time.

I don't think I am anorexic; I just think I used to look bad and now I look good. When I was in eighth grade, I weighed 136 and was five eleven and had a BMI of 19. Two weeks ago, I was six feet and also had a BMI of 19. And I wasn't comfortable with my body in middle school and this entire year until now. That's why I didn't care about fashion and hated shopping, because I hated my body and couldn't control what I was eating and just gained weight year after year.

I know I sound ridiculous. That's why I never talk about this to anyone. When everyone told me I was skinny this year I took it as a compliment because I felt and thought I looked so much better. And people finally told me they thought I was pretty and thin, and it was the only part of me that felt good because my lung function was horrible, and I couldn't control that. Then I got braces (AGAIN . . . ARGH!!!), had an ugly smile, and had a PICC line. And I thought I looked worse in every way but one, so I didn't want to gain weight again and go back to how I used to be. Because I used to hear from people periodically that I looked like a man, or I looked really buff, or I was really big. I heard that so many times and people didn't describe me as thin, they described me as athletic, and I hated it. Examples: 1. Kevin saying, "I don't know her, is that the girl that looks like a man?" 2. Everyone describes me as having an athletic body type, when it used to be a slender body type. 3. Jay constantly saying I look "buff" and that I was buffer than him.

So then I got skinnier, and I didn't feel like I was bigger than everyone I knew, and I was finally comfortable with myself in that area.

I know I wasn't fat before. I never really had any fat to lose. I would actually prefer to have more fat, but I know that's never going to happen with my body type, it's either buff or skinny. And I choose skinny. I look at pictures of myself in a bathing suit from last summer, and I don't think I looked good at all. And I understand that it's affecting me negatively now, but it's extremely annoying that I'm not allowed to be both healthy and comfortable with my body. And it's one of the many frustrating things about CF, that *if I were a non-CF person, I would be considered to have a very healthy body. But I'm expected to be bigger to fight the bacteria. And I know now that it's important, which is why I eat much more than I used to and why I'm not fighting the lipids, because I don't want to be sick anymore and I'd rather dislike my body than have to miss out on my life because I'm on IVs.*

I never even wanted to weigh 140. I wanted to weigh about 143 and when I did, I was happy with that. But that's when the acid reflux thing started, and it wasn't like I was choosing to eat healthy and less. I actually HAD to in order to not feel horrible. But then my period stopped and Dr. Pornchai said to gain weight, so I tried and am still trying. I just wanted to explain what has been happening, so it doesn't seem like a huge mystery or like it's your fault.

Love, Mallory

Monday, December 7, 2009

Today I got called into the principal's office for the craziest thing. The home health company gives me these little pumps with my IV meds in them, so I don't have to hang them from a pole like I do when I'm in the hospital. Which makes it easier to do at home or school. Anyway, I'm on IVs now and was infusing during lunch today on the front lawn. When it was done, I did what I always do . . . cleaned the tubing, injected the heparin flush to be sure the meds were done, and then disconnected myself from the medication ball. But today I must have forgotten a flush, or a syringe, or an empty medicine pump on the grass, because someone showed it to the security guard on campus and then the guard probably thought someone was a heroin pusher and turned it in.

When I walked into the office, the staff started laughing because the situation was so ridiculous, but Susie said, "Mallory, we know you have a lot of IV paraphernalia to keep track of . . . try to make sure you get it all in the trash because other kids are starting to get ideas." My mom always says, if you can't fix it, feature it. This whole thing led to me naming my IV pole "Sexy Pete" and dressing it up!

Tuesday, December 8, 2009

Dying is really a weird thing. And it's scary. At least to me it is. But I don't think that people who believe in the afterlife find it weird or scary. It's a strange phenomenon because the world has been around for billions of years and will be around for billions more years. Since the concept of a billion is too hard to imagine, it's easier to think that people have been living and fighting and having sex and being human for thousands of years, and while so much has changed, so much doesn't change. And we're here for this tiny, tiny, tiny part of it, which feels sooo long to us. It's this sense of "long-ness" that makes us feel important. But we're not important. The world doesn't need the human race. It just keeps spinning and would be so much healthier without people who destroy it by how we behave.

The problem is we think we matter because we feel like we're here for so long and we think we do so much in that time. But so much of what we do is just filler . . . filler to alleviate boredom. Boredom because everything we've invented has made our lives easy and given us free time and allowed us to live lives that don't resemble those of hunter-gatherers. Back then, they didn't sit around. If we were programmed to understand innately how fleeting a lifetime is, maybe we wouldn't strive to survive (our most basic instinct). Maybe we wouldn't care to work, to make money, to feed and bathe ourselves. I can't decide if understanding how short life really is would make us apathetic? Or if it would actually make us more motivated to make the most of the time here?

I think everyone has this feeling at least once in their lives, but there's no way to hold on to it. Because it's unnatural. I have it right now and I'm writing it down and tomorrow morning I won't remember. I won't remember to laugh at myself for complaining so much about my strep throat and how much it hurts. Or to realize how pointless it is to worry about what I got on my math test. I find myself asking: "What am I going to do on this earth that gives me

32

the right to beg—every year—for my community to donate their hard-earned money to the Cystic Fibrosis Foundation so that I can live a longer life?" We raise more than $100,000 every year! Why should they do that unless they know that I'm going to do something big? Which I can't do because nothing we do can be that big. Our brains, our conceptions of size, cannot handle how huge the universe is, how small we actually are. Even as I'm writing about this, I can't imagine it. Humans are just so pretentious, thinking we can solve every mystery and acting like we know everything.

I want to send out a message saying: Attention, all arrogant people! Please stop thinking that you know everything because you read it in a book, and you believe everything you read. Think for yourself for once. Take an astronomy class and look through a microscope and see how fucking big and complicated and beyond-our-capacity-for-understanding the universe is. And then take a prehistory class, or a geology class, and figure out for yourselves that the world moves and does its own thing regardless of what little drama we're acting out down here on Earth.

Maybe there's another way to look at all this. Maybe if we thought our time was fleeting, we would go the other way instead and try to make the most of it. And maybe that's a different reason why people like me fear death, because an eighty-year life is so short already, that to cut it down even more takes away valuable time and makes it even harder to do anything special. It's selfish thinking, I know, but it's natural. We're wired to want to stay alive. I don't want to die.

All that said, I still wonder why I fear death. Because when I actually think about it, if I were to die, since I don't believe in the afterlife and all that, I would cease to exist. There would be no more of me. Yes, I would be missing out on things I could have done, experiences I could have had. And the me that's alive right now writing this is aware of that and sad about it, even though it's a hypothetical situation. But the dead me in the hypothetical situation would not be conscious of the fact that I'm missing experiences, etc. The only thing I should actually fear about death is how it will affect my friends and my family. How it'll make them feel the same way I felt tonight. I actually don't feel that way anymore because of this long-winded epistle.

I see the outpouring of love for people that die and I'm thinking, *Of course it's kind; of course it's a natural reaction; of course I would want that for myself if I were to die.* But it wouldn't matter to me if I were dead because what happens after is just a way for the living to bond with others. Because the way I see it, no dead person is hearing the thoughts, prayers, and loving wishes those left behind are sharing. If I die, I'd want a celebration of my life so my family and friends would have each other instead of having me.

I know this sounds like I'm trying so hard to be philosophical, but my thoughts just carried me here, carried me in circles, and I had to think it out loud (well, write it actually), and I'm no less confused by death than I was before. This entry started with me thinking I was going to write about being sick, and how amazing Jay's been to me in the past few days by coming to visit me and bringing me tea and cuddling with me even though I'm contagious.

Friday, December 11, 2009
I got into Stanford!!!! All my hard work paid off!!!!

Friday, January 1, 2010
It's 3:00 in the morning on New Year's Eve. Well, technically it's the first day of the new year in 2010. Jay and I broke up. It happened earlier tonight. We never got the balance right—he always thought I prioritized my friends. I thought he didn't understand. There was a lot of drama, but I don't feel like writing about it. Sadly, I don't think I will remember the good times we had because I've written mostly just the bad stuff in this journal. But there were good times. Very good times.

New Year's resolutions for 2010:

— Be kind; work on myself as a person. Be considerate,
   thoughtful, approachable, fun, easy to talk to, etc.
— Make the most of the rest of senior year; have fun at

all the senior activities, don't stress, do fun things, be
with friends, etc.
— Have an amazing summer after graduation
(Lifeguarding? Working? A program in another
country?).
— Start college and try to adjust and be happy.
— Figure out stomach issues; ridiculously enough,
oftentimes my mood during the day depends on if
I've eaten healthy and if I've gone to the bathroom.
Figure out how to make those things happen every
day in college.
— Get to a weight of 142, maybe 144. Somewhere
around there would be okay. As always, I'm just
happier when I'm thinner. It's one less thing to worry
about if I don't have to dislike my body.
— Figure out how to stay in touch with people when
they/I go to college.
— Work on style.
— BE HAPPY; LIVE HAPPY; make a conscious effort
to do something every day that will make me happy,
or to think a happy thought. Too many days go by
where I'm too stressed to be happy. Need to work on
thinking about good memories, listening to a song I
love, walking outside on a crisp morning, stretching,
making a really good meal, being nice to someone,
talking to friends, etc.

Sunday, January 10, 2010

I have a lot of friends but I often feel left out and alone because managing my disease and battling the *cepacia* takes so much time that it takes me away from my life. I'm not part of the memories created when I'm not with them. Not part of their inside jokes. The rhythm is different.

Despite how I feel, I always try to be nice. Being nice to people (whether they are friends or not) is a choice, not a disposition. If everyone made that choice, the world would be a much more civil place. A lot of people use the "I'm just not going to be fake" excuse as an excuse to be bitchy. Personally, I think that just because you don't like someone doesn't mean you have to be rude . . . I kind of believe the thinking that if you don't have something nice to say, don't say it at all. And no, I'm not a kindergarten teacher.

Sunday, January 17, 2010
During treatment I was looking through the Los Angeles guidebook and thinking about stuff to do now that I'm a second-semester senior! (I know, I always make lists of things to do and then never do them but hopefully this time I actually will!) Here it is:

> — Go to the Science Center (see an IMAX movie).
> — Go to the Long Beach aquarium.
> — Go sailing (not sure how to do this one).
> — Go to Angel's Gate Recreation Center.
> — Go to Griffith Observatory.
> — Hike at Griffith Park.
> — Go to a concert.
> — Go to Calamigos Ranch.
> — Go to the Getty Villa.
> — Go to the Autry Museum of the American West.
> — Go to the Craft and Folk Art Museum.
> — Go to the Natural History Museum.
> — Go to the International Surf Festival in Manhattan Beach at the end of July/beginning of August.
> — Go to the Sunset Junction Street Fair.
> — Go to the LA County Fair.
> — Go to the Eagle Rock Music Festival.
> — Go shopping on Abbot Kinney Boulevard.
> — Go to Redondo Beach for the Riviera Village Summer Festival (June 27 to 28, summer concerts on the pier).
> — Go to the farmers market.
> — Take surfing lessons.

— Go to Hermosa Beach and Manhattan Beach for the day/for beach volleyball.
— Hike at all the places in the hiking book!
— Go horseback riding (another that falls under the heading of not sure where).

Okay, now I'm actually going to go to bed. I have to wake up in less than eight hours.

Tuesday, January 19, 2010

I'm not writing anything right now except for food resolutions (because I ate shitty food today, so now I feel like shit):

— No more soda (not even diet soda).
— No more chocolate chips (not even in my oatmeal! I end up eating like five handfuls of them).
— No random snacking. I should be able to remember everything I ate in a day.
— Go back to being thoughtful about what I put in my mouth like I used to be.
— No muffins or other super-sugary stuff for breakfast.
— Make a daily eating plan.
— Eat smaller portions!!
— Never finish a meal feeling heavier than when I started. That's my biggest problem!
— Eat a good breakfast, coffee, and water in the morning. Drink green tea.

Saturday, January 23, 2010

I'm back in the hospital, having been admitted after a massive episode of hemoptysis (coughing up blood). It has been a few days since the episode, and I haven't been allowed to do the breathing treatments because they can irritate the airways and cause more hemoptysis. I feel short of breath, fatigued and nauseous, with coughing spasms so intense they made me vomit.

My nurse, Keith, knowing I was having a rough time, came to check on me yesterday whenever he wasn't with another patient. When he came in to bring me some nausea medication, he sat down, talked to me for a while. He treated me like a real person, not just a patient or a number. When my mom stepped out of the room to take a work phone call, he asked me, "What's your life philosophy?"

I asked him what he meant, and he said, "You know, what's your motto? How would you sum up what you live for?" I was taken aback that one of my healthcare providers would care enough to ask. I told him I wanted to be happy. To Live Happy.

He said he wanted to help people. He jumped from job to job because he was trying to figure out which profession would give him the greatest ability to make the greatest difference in the greatest number of people's lives. As we talked about it more, I realized that what I hoped for most in a profession was to be able to help the world in some way. Though it sounds trite, since I was a little girl, I've known that whatever I end up doing, I want it to help move the needle on something that's important. But I also realized that I would never be able to do that unless I took care of my own health first and foremost. A dead person isn't a very helpful person. I had to do the hard things now, to ensure my body would work well enough to support my endeavors later.

I have big dreams, big goals.

On a more mundane level, my braces are hurting a lot and I sort of feel like I'm thirteen again. I never thought I would have to go back to braces EVER. But life is unexpected, that's definitely something I've learned through experience.

It's so easy to feel sorry for myself. But when I do, I think about my mom's bout with breast cancer, my dad's struggles with depression, my grandma Ronnie's alcoholism. And then I move on to think about cruelties on a broader scale; I picture a child losing his father to war, someone getting ridiculed for their race, a homosexual being laughed at on the street. When I feel like the world is crashing down on me, I cry because of my disease but also the iniquities of the world, which I carry deep within me.

Sunday, January 31, 2010

Had SUCH a fun night last night. The plan we had was kind of a failure, but it worked out in the end. We went to Becca's and Talia, Blair, Michelle, Erica, and a bunch of other girls came over and we got ready for the party. And then some guys came over and when we were done getting ready, we started drinking. Vodka and Crystal Light lemonade, not the most delicious combination. The guys left to go get beer because they wanted to play beer pong and the girls basically had a dance party in Becca's living room. Her parents were out of town, so she just invited random people and didn't really care who was there. Then at 11:00 a cab picked us up and took us to the Mark on Pico, which is where the party was, but when we got there, we went in for five minutes and they turned off the music and shut it down. So, we were basically there for twenty minutes, I saw a million people and said hi to everyone, and then we left and walked back to Becca's. Actually, we ran because we didn't want the cops to pull us over and give us a curfew ticket. And I was barefoot because the shoes I was wearing gave me blisters so I was running down Pico holding them in my hand and it was really funny. And when we got to Becca's again a bunch of people started coming. Oliver brought his two limos there and word got around, so pretty soon there were like a hundred people in her house. And we were dancing, and I was talking to people, and Gaby came, and Tamara and Julia and a bunch of other people, and it was really so fun. It was mostly people from younger grades, but I honestly don't mind because I like hanging out with random funny people as long as I have a few close friends with me, because those are the funniest times. The only problem is some of them were smoking weed—which makes them so NOT interesting. So yeah, really fun night!

Eventually we went to bed around 4:00 a.m., after I ate a bunch of food and drank a lot of water, and I slept on the couch with Natasha. And the randomest people were sleeping everywhere. Michelle, Blair, Andre, and Zach were in Becca's parents' bed, Becca and Erica were in Becca's bed, Nicole and Tammy were in Amanda's room, Andy and Daniel and some other guy were downstairs in the guest room, and me and Natasha and some other guy were in the living room. I got woken up at 7:00 because everyone was running around the house making noise and watching TV, so I just got up and then we ate pancakes and hung out. And I wasn't hung over! Surprisingly, I feel really good! I've honestly become so much more responsible this year. Every time I stay up super late, I feel REALLY guilty about it, both because I think I'm gonna get sick and also because then I know I'll sleep really late the next day and miss out on the day. Like if I had woken up at noon today like I expected to, the only thing I would have done all day would have been to go to the doctor.

But I do *always* feel guilty after I drink. I have fun when I do it but then I feel bad the next day. I shouldn't really feel bad about it because everyone drinks in high school and I'm not the kind of person who gets to the point where I throw up, and I don't think I'm an embarrassing drunk. The wild thing is none of the parents know their kids drink. I heard Shelby's mom telling my mom her daughter didn't drink (LOL!). Anyway, I have to go do treatment, and I'm going to watch TV, which I haven't done in a very long time!

Sunday, February 14, 2009
Today is Valentine's Day! And I don't have a valentine . . . surprise, surprise. It's okay, though, because I'm spending the day with all my friends who also don't have valentines! So it's all good. And it's a day for love and I love my friends so it's perfect. We're meeting at my house at 12:00 and then driving to Temescal Canyon to go hiking, then going to bake cookies at Tamara's. Tonight, my mom is doing a family dinner with the Sunday night water polo crowd.

Dinner was really fun! Coach Bowie stayed after everyone left so my mom could pack up leftovers for him. I swear she does these dinners to feed him! He asked how long I'd have my PICC line in, when I could get back in the water. I really miss it and want to get myself on a good footing again. I'm going to take really good care of myself and get my lung function up and go back to water polo and excel at school again (I've been having major senioritis lately, but I've been working all weekend on projects for government so hopefully I'm getting back on track) and find a new boy I like and who likes me. Okay, so the last one is kind of a long shot. It's a little too much to ask to find two guys in one year who really like me.

Tuesday, March 2, 2010
So now it's Tuesday, and I've been on IVs since Friday. I didn't write for a while because when I was off them, I was having SO much fun. It's hard to describe how I'm dealing with it this time. I'm taking it a lot harder emotionally than I have in the past, I think. I'm not sure if it's because I'm a senior (so I realize that I'm wasting at least one whole month of my six remaining months before college) or because I was so motivated for swim season after finally getting back in the water for the second half of water polo season. But it's just really hard to be living your life and then, as it always happens, be derailed, completely thrust out of the swing of things. It's enormously frustrating to be cooped up at home, spending four to six hours a day doing treatment on my couch, i.e., completely incapacitated, when I feel completely fine.

After a busy weekend, on Sunday I just crashed. I had been in high gear when I was supposed to be lying low, basically living my life normally but with the addition of four treatments a day and three rounds of IVs. Since the treatments are supposed to be spaced four hours apart, and there are four of them, that leaves me barely eight hours to sleep. Also, my dose of metoclopramide was increased from 5 milligrams three times a day to 10 milligrams four times a day, and since that drug makes you tired, the combination of everything left me able to do nothing on Sunday but sleep. I woke up to do treatment, ate breakfast, and fell back asleep. Then I woke up to do a second treatment and fell back asleep. Then I woke up and did a third treatment, then ate, then did a fourth treatment, then fell back asleep! Basically, I've just been sitting on my couch, going from treatment to treatment, staying in my pajamas, and watching *The O.C.* I hadn't touched any of my books (until about an hour ago) . . . so I was feeling extremely unproductive. But I couldn't deal with home-work because it was too connected to my ACTUAL LIFE, WHICH I'M MISSING RIGHT NOW. I just needed to detach and remove myself . . . so I turned to *The O.C.* It's funny. I feel like I have my actual life, and then I have my side life. My actual life is being a senior, having my friends, my sports, my homework, all that. My side life is doing treatment and dealing with medical issues. Sometimes my side life interferes a lot with my actual life, and sometimes it doesn't. Right now it is interfering. My bacteria is rearing its ugly head and prevent-ing me from doing what I want to do. It's holding me back when I feel so able to just go forward. That's what is so wild about all this. I feel completely healthy, my lungs don't feel that congested at all (not any worse than they usually do), I feel good at the weight I'm at (for once). I was swimming well and was in good shape. I was happy. It's funny how I'll be so in the swing of things and then I'll just get ripped out of my life so abruptly. I should have seen it coming. My numbers were bad for a month and I got tested every week but they kept rising and rising every week and I was working so hard and sleeping and doing three treatments a day and I was just so hopeful that they would keep going up and that I could stave off IVs for a long time, and I just wasn't even considering any other possibility, and then they went down. It's a complete mystery! I mean, why are my numbers so bad when I feel FINE?! It makes NO SENSE! Shouldn't my lung function numbers be an indicator of how my lungs are doing, and shouldn't how I feel be an indicator as well? Shouldn't they match up? Always in the past I would feel it when my numbers were declining, but this time I can't feel it at all. And now that I'm on IVs I can't tell if I'm get-ting better, because I felt fine in the first place. But if I don't get better by Friday I'm going to be admitted to the hospital.

Saturday, March 6, 2010

While Stanford is obviously an extremely prestigious institution, there are other reasons why it's the best college choice for me (even though I don't really want to go there). One of these is the caliber of the Stanford Medical Center. I have intermittently been under the care of Dr. Cornfield, Stanford's pediatric cystic fibrosis director. That's because I got really sick last year and Dr. Pornchai had to leave unexpectedly to go back to Thailand so I had to see a replacement doctor, who wasn't very good. Dr. Cornfield took over my care; I trust and consult with him as often as possible. Since my protocol calls for monthly visits to monitor my lung function and to prevent progression of the disease, it will make my life much easier to be on campus with him for the next four years. I am also having recurring hemoptysis (SO gross when I cough up blood), which I now understand can be life-threatening and will quite likely require embolization. Dr. Cornfield sent me to Stanford's interventional radiologist, Dr. Sze, who is considered to be one of the top specialists in this field. I know it's the right place for me but I always thought I'd go to UCLA since my mom, my dad, and my brother went there.

Friday, March 12, 2010

I'm sort of having a weird "midlife crisis" . . . more like insecurity issues where I think about something and then I start freaking out because I put myself in hypothetical situations where I just can't see myself succeeding. Example: getting a job this summer. I'm not really qualified for anything, especially a job as a camp counselor, which is what I think I want to do but I'm really not perky enough or good enough with kids and kind of just not fun enough. And I've been rather moody lately.

I can't make decisions about my future because I don't know what I want, but I know I'm not happy with things right now. I don't see myself at Stanford, but I can't not go. I can't see myself finding a guy again because every time I look at myself in the mirror and smile I think I look disgusting because of my braces. My teeth are pretty yellow since I can't whiten them because of the braces.

Another problem is that I don't have the personality to attract a guy right now, even though I really (for some non-understandable reason) want someone. But it's not going to happen. Especially since when I do emerge from my house, it's usually as a greasy-hair-ridden-depressive-itchy person (the grease because I don't shower enough because of my PICC line, the depressive because I can't get myself out of this funk that I'm in, feeling sorry for myself and being sad about my situation, and the itchy because of my goddamn dressing, which I just want to rip off because it's destroying my skin underneath/I feel it crawling/it just drives me insane).

So I barely do emerge from my house, I basically spend my time (STILL) watching *The O.C.* (surprise, surprise!). And I'm not on track in school, and all I can think about is two things: 1. How depressing the "moral of the story" of my week was. I worked my ass off, stayed home from school all week, rested, did all my treatments, ate healthy, exercised a reasonable amount, and slept enough. And despite doing all that, despite working so hard to the point that my life for the week was simply figuring out what I could do to pass the time between treatments, I got WORSE. My lung function was 3.3 last Friday, and Dr. Pornchai (THANK GOD HE'S BACK) said I could back off a little, do only three treatments a day instead of four, and that if I improved more by next Friday (today) I would get off IVs. It would be two weeks. My personal record of shortest IVs, I think. But I got my hopes up WAY too high and too soon because instead of improving, which I naively thought was inevitable given how much effort I was putting into it, my lung function decreased to 3.17. The acid reflux is driving me insane; no matter what I do and how correctly I take all the medicine and how perfectly I eat, it's incessant belching. And that's somehow affecting my lung function and making my infection worse or maybe my infection is making my lung function worse. I'm not really sure but I want answers and I want results and I'm not getting either of those things. There are just more mysteries about my health, and more validation of the concept that I'm utterly unable to control my situation. Which leads me to wonder if I should just forget about working so hard (since it doesn't make a difference anyway) and just live to have fun in times like this instead of living to get better so I can get back on track. Because when I start working so hard, I expect to see results, and then I never get what I want out of it and I'm disappointed. And I just can't handle another one of those situations where every single

Friday I expect to get the PICC line out and to go back to my life and to being a normal girl and it keeps getting pushed back and pushed back. I just feel like it will destroy my will and my sense of control over my health and my body if all of these mysterious factors continue to cycle around with each other and fuck with my health and prevent me from getting off IVs and out of this house!!

My mom is trying to make me feel better by saying we'll have O.C. marathons and I'll have time to hang out with my friends, but the truth is my friends are living their lives and I'm stuck at home. Working away on something that is unyielding and unforgiving and unrelenting. Trying so hard and putting so much of my heart into it and getting nothing, nothing back.

Friday, March 19, 2010

I JUST GOT MY PICC LINE OUT! And I'm sooo happy. Well, I'm 90 percent happy and 10 percent nervous. . . . With CF it's always about my FEV1 number (which stands for forced expiratory volume in one second). It didn't go all the way up to where it should be (it's supposed to be back at 3.35 to 3.45 range), and today it was 3.22. But since the acid reflux is probably what caused this whole thing, Dr. Pornchai decided I don't need to do IVs anymore, so we pulled the PICC line out! But I have to pretend like I'm still sick this week and do three treatments a day and exercise and eat and sleep a lot, and if I do badly this Friday then I have to go back on IVs after Hawaii (which would be horrible because I'm running out of veins). So he told me that I was taking a risk to pull it out today but that he thinks it's going to be okay, so I'm going to do everything I can to not have to go back on IVs again in two weeks. Basically . . . hard-core swimming, sleeping, treatments, minimal school, etc. I'm ecstatic!

Monday, April 5, 2010

Things I'm thankful for:

    — Selflessness of my parents
    — A comfortable home

— Improvements in energy
— Time spent in Hawaii
— My best friends
— Love of Maria, Micah, Dewey, Millie
— My education and opportunities
— Remaining at 50 percent FEV1
— Height and past athletic ability
— Kindness/compassion
— My brain
— Books
— Amazing doctors
— Love for yoga
— Living somewhere where I can go outside in winter
— Having people who love me

So I wrote that out on the plane home from Hawaii last night, and it sort of did make me feel better to write down what I was thankful for when I knew I was heading home and straight into the hospital.

Tuesday, April 6, 2010
Hard to type because of IV placement in my hand this time. So . . . short writing. Home from Hawaii on Sunday night. So sad to come home. Fastest trip I've ever had (don't know why it went so fast). So fun: beach, blasting music and stalking people on Facebook in our room with the amazing view, lying in the cabanas by the pool, swimming in the ocean, training with Rich at Kihei pool and playing water polo with locals, hot guys, great food, laughing, drinking with the Canadians we met, and more. Very good trip, very happy I went, it was an island of happiness during this frustrating and sad time of being sick for so long. I got sick so long ago (like maybe halfway through the water polo season?) and have been struggling to get better for so long that I can't remember not going every Friday to do a pulmonary function test (PFT) and worrying about it, etc. Worry that everything I tried to do (extra-hard treatments, exercise, sleep,

Hawaii, swimming, eating) didn't work. All over again. Sadness about what I'm missing out on while I'm here in the hospital (got admitted right after I got home) and that it will take another whole month or longer for me to finally get better. I think maybe Dr. Pornchai is right about the weight. I've done EVERYTHING, tried EVERYTHING, to get better. Went on IVs for three weeks already, did three to four treatments a day for countless weeks, went to Hawaii, where the salt water thins my mucus and I am able to bring up so much . . . so there has to be something else making me sick. Maybe I do need to gain weight. I just miss my life . . . my regular daily life . . . morning swim practice, drinking my coffee in the morning on the way to English, going to all classes, practice, hanging out with friends, interacting with people (my age) all day, dinner, homework, etc. The stresses of life, the pleasures of being out and just going about my day and doing my thing. Funny I'm listening to a song that just said something I know is so true: "And it's funny how it's the little things in life that mean the most" (from "Chicken Fried" by Zac Brown Band).

I wish I wouldn't have to be torn away from my life all the time. I wish I could just worry about stuff like school and prom and boys. . . . I do worry about that stuff, but I have so many other worries layered on top. Worries that disrupt me and confuse me and make everything so complicated. ALWAYS.

I'm back in the hospital because Dr. Pornchai says no more home IVs because they aren't working, I have to get a PICC line again, which is bad for my veins; I'm here for at least two weeks, so bye-bye swim season and bye-bye getting to know Dillon (my secret crush) and bye-bye enjoying second semester of senior year. After Dr. Pornchai told me I had to be admitted, I went to school to tell my teachers, then went with some of my teammates to get coaches' gifts (we talked about where everyone is going to school and how weird and sad it is that everything is coming to an end so soon), then hung with Talia, then went to the water polo banquet. So fun and so cute, good memories of season and last four years. Coach Bowie started crying when he said goodbye to the seniors; it made me tear up. He's been such a part of my life since I was thirteen.

Weird how I'll probably not ever see him after high school (except when I come back to visit). I know I'm moving on to bigger things (Stanford) that may be better, but I'm so happy with things now. . . . I don't need to move on. My life is insane. I mean it's weird how I can be Mal, senior captain and a friend and the co-MVP and nice, and then drive straight to the hospital to go through hell. It's like a double life . . . that only my closest/oldest friends know about. Wish I had a boyfriend right about now so I wouldn't feel so alone and pathetic. It's easy to be happy when I'm in Hawaii, with three of my best friends having an amazing time, but how to be happy when I'm in horrible circumstances is something I need to figure out. I used to be okay when I would come to the hospital. I didn't really mind it. That was before the disease got scary and debilitating . . . before it really affected my everyday life. Before I had to think about every decision and how it would affect my health . . . back when life was simple.

Back then, if I got sick, I went on IVs and got better. Easy. Not so anymore. I hope I have lots of visitors and do lots of homework, so this time goes by fast. And then when I'm out I want to find a gorgeous prom dress so I can come back after no one's seen me for a month or two and look amazing. And a gorgeous prom date would be nice, too, haha (or at least a funny/nice one).

Friday, April 16, 2010
I've been in the hospital for a while now, and it's really not that bad. They moved me yesterday from the pediatric floor to the adult floor because they needed my bed for a young pediatric patient. The peds floor had so many cool photos of animals but the adult floor is STARK WHITE and so depressing.

I had sooo many things done the morning after I was admitted . . . CT chest scan, CT sinus scan, PICC line put in, chest X-ray, and more that I don't really remember because they gave me some drug before I got my PICC line in that makes that day seem really blurry.

One of the nights last week was really bad. Dr. Pornchai said I had something called transient bacteria (sepsis), which basically means that some of the bacteria from my lungs got into my blood-stream. Apparently, my fever got really high, so they drugged me and did a procedure. But it's all a blur. Micah was there and I heard he was freaked out by the state I was in. I think he thought I was dying. My high fever lasted pretty much the whole night, and I had a mon-strous headache because I was so dehydrated, so they gave me a lot of fluids through the PICC line.

All I remember is that it felt like I was being burned from the inside out, like the infection was raging around inside me like a Tas-manian devil and I had to shake it out of me. But on the other hand, I had the out-of-body sensation of sitting off to the side.

As I was pondering all this, I noticed how extremely tight my chest was. . . . I couldn't (and still can't) take a deep breath, my coughs are shallow and apparently there is so much mucus, but I can't get to it because it's deep down and my airways are so irritated. I thought it was just irritation from the bronchoscopy, and they put me on oxygen for a while, but now it's been two days and I'm still needing the oxygen (because my O_2 sats aren't staying consistently above 92 percent), so they got worried this morning and rechecked my chest X-ray from after the procedure and the radiologist realized that I have pneumonia. Pneumonia on top of everything else . . . I've been doing four treatments a day and doing the best I can even though it hurts to breathe, and I am short of breath and have low energy and get winded and it's strange because I've never felt this way before. But then again, I've never had pneumonia. I've always felt fine whenever I was in the hospital; this is the first time I don't feel well. But I'm also pretty much stuffing my face, on top of getting 1,500 calories a day through my PICC line. So I also feel disgusting in that way.

Besides how I feel, I don't have anything to complain about. I've had so many visitors every single day, my social life is bigger when I'm in the hospital than it is at home. I've had Talia, Marissa, Nata-lie, Natasha, Becca, Erica, Maria, Oriana, Jodie, Ben, Stacy, a bunch of my mom's friends, Eileen, Don, Rob, Micah . . . it's been pretty much constant, to the point where I haven't done any homework at all yet and haven't watched any movies or read any of my book. All of the nurses are incredibly nice and caring and attentive, the doctors are amazing (especially Dr. Pornchai), and I'm really not having a bad time. When I think about what I'm missing at home obviously I get sad, but I'm not really thinking about it often because I'm so busy and I feel like I'm away (which I am). I almost prefer being in the hospital to home IVs because I don't have to worry about anything, they just worry about everything for you, and I feel like I'm sick and like I should be on IVs and not at school. Whereas when I'm home I just feel like I should be at school and going to swimming and going out and all that. So it really doesn't lead to me getting better. Although ironically, I'm here now and I've never felt sicker. But I know that's just because of the complications of the bronchoscopy. . . . I just hope I can get better soon because I'm ready to go home.

I have to miss the Taylor Swift concert. . . . I cried a little when I realized that. And I have to miss Jason's play, *Curtains,* which I was really excited to see because I've never seen him act. And I'm pretty much giving up on swim season because by the time I get back it'll be basically over. So if I were home I would be sitting there depressing myself about all this all day, but when I'm here I'm surprisingly happy. Even though I don't sleep well, I'm in a hospital on IVs all day, I don't feel bad. It's really really bizarre. Also, everyone notices when you're in the hospital and they've brought me enormous amounts of amazing food, movies, books, cards, clothes. . . . I kind of realize how many nice people I have in my life every time I come to the hospital, which I don't always think about in my daily life.

Sunday, April 18, 2010

I'm not getting better. Early on the doctors were hopeful and optimistic that I would get better quickly. But after what happened, no one is sure of anything. Dr. Pornchai came in today and after listening to my lungs and talking to me, he still seems really worried. There are so many different issues going on, so many more issues than I've ever had before: blood sugar/diabetes, possible sinusitis, pneumonia last week, *B. cepacia* taking over the *Pseudomonas* (a different bacteria) and the entire lungs, too-high hemoglobin levels, weight loss, and other things I can't remember. Every day the doctors traipse in, starting when I wake up and pretty much continuing the whole day . . . infectious disease doctors, GI, child life specialists, respiratory therapists, pulmonologists (Dr. Pornchai and Dr. Ischander). It's very disconcerting because they all have opinions, some of which are directly in conflict with others. For example, Dr. Ischander was adamant that I start on vancomycin, because she thinks my hemoptysis could be a result of a staph infection in my lungs, and she wanted me to stop all these medications for two days after the hemoptysis. But Dr. Pornchai, who sees me every month and knows that I cough up blood on a monthly basis, doesn't think it's a result of *Staph. aureus* and doesn't see the point of putting me on vancomycin when it does nothing to combat *B. cepacia*. So if Dr. Pornchai had been the one on call, he wouldn't have put me on it, but since Dr. Ischander was on call, she and the infectious disease people decided to put me on it. When Dr. Pornchai was on vacation last week, though, Dr. Ischander was very thorough and caring, and she came to my room twice each day and stayed for a long time. They're very reassuring but different in their personalities. She is very perky and happy, and he is very kind and genuine and sweet. And together, they've always given me hope that everything was gonna be fine, even when I wasn't feeling well after what happened last week, because they would say they were positive that I was going to get better. But today, for the first time, Dr. Pornchai said, "I have to be honest with you, I am starting to get worried because things aren't turning around." My white blood cell count is so high and I am still getting fevers (which means the infection isn't under control at all), and I've been sick so long, and I'm not feeling as well as I did when I got here, and the *B. cepacia* has taken over both entire lungs (and kicked out the *Pseudomonas*, which sounds good because there's only one thing to deal with, but *Pseudomonas* is actually easier to treat).

So now it's about 2:30 a.m., before when I was writing it was like 7:00 p.m. I've had a pretty rough night. . . . Becca and Natasha and Matt and Kara came to visit, and it was fun, and I laughed a lot, but then when they left I went straight to bed at 11:00, and at 11:45 I woke up and coughed up so much blood. Clinically it's not enough to be worried about, because it's less than a cup, but it will set me back like another week with IVs and in the hospital because I have to stop airway clearance for a few days when it happens. So I have to back off and then the mucus accumulates and just makes me worse and worse. It's the vicious cycle I've always dealt with of infection and bleeding, then backing off treatment, which makes infection worse, then more bleeding. They're pretty sure I have diabetes now, which I believe, because I literally can't go five minutes without water or I feel so dehydrated I can't stand it, and I pee everything out. Every time I pee, which is pretty often, it's 1,000 mL, which is over two pounds. So now they have to start checking my blood sugar five times a day, which isn't really that bad, it's just I don't need another thing to add to my list of things that are wrong with me. But diabetes explains a lot . . . why we can't get the infection under control, the drinking and peeing, the tiredness, and the inability to gain weight even though I'm eating like a wild person and having 1,500 calories a day of lipids through my PICC line.

The nights here are pretty unbearable. The days are fine, they pass quickly with treatment and visitors and all the doctors, but the nights just seem interminable. I wake up basically every hour and stay awake for long periods of time. I'm never rested when I get up in the morning. I'm always hooked up to a million cords and contraptions so I can't sleep in the position I want to sleep in. Right now, I'm hooked up to pulse ox, the heart monitor, oxygen, and IVs. Which comes out to like fifteen cords and drives me insane. Add to that the stress of being here and having everything go wrong over and over again, and it doesn't really equate to a good night of sleep.

When Dr. Pornchai said he was worried today I started crying a little bit. He said I was his favorite patient and when his favorite patient is sick, he feels sick. And he literally looked sick to his stomach when he looked at me and saw that I was upset. He just looked so nervous that it made me scared and made me realize that no one can ever just fix this, the doctors don't have a magic wand, so much of my care on their part is artistry and experience and good decision-making and luck. It's a science, but not a perfect science, because there are no definitive answers, and so all we can do is try things and hope they work. Especially when we're running out of options, like now. Aztreonam is pretty much our last gun, which I'm starting tomorrow.

School is a distant memory. When I try to remember my routine before everything was just about health, it just seems like a different lifetime, like I was a different person.

I'm not sure how much of what's going on with me to share with my friends, or how much they even know. Like do they realize that this time is so much worse than any other time? They couldn't possibly understand how I feel physically . . . they see me as an athlete, someone who does sports just like them or maybe better in some cases, and then they see me here. And I've always maintained that I felt fine, and I did. But now I don't, and I don't really bring it up and when people ask how I feel I say a little better than yesterday even though I've pretty much just been declining in how I feel since I got here. Oriana was here today when Dr. Pornchai was here and when I started crying, my mom asked her to go outside. And I just want to know how much my friends understand about it, because they act like everything is fine, which thank God they do because they're the only ones keeping me sane and making me feel like I'm not dying or something. They're used to me being in the hospital and feeling fine and then coming home and then getting all better, and it must all look really easy and routine and simple. Which is how it was supposed to be. I guess my main thing is that if I start telling any of my friends what's really going on, not the extremely condensed version, then there are probably several people I'd have to tell or more. And then it makes it more real . . . and it makes me think about things that I could have done to make me less sick now. Because as I get older, I realize it's so much better to sacrifice in the short term than the long term. Like I should have realized as a kid that this was serious, but when it's not serious yet you can't treat it like it is. I remember camp, when the most important thing was staying up till 4:00 every night, talking and laughing and having an amazing time. And then I'd wake up at 7:00 and do shitty treatments because I just wanted to get them over with. That's when the *B. cepacia* invaded my lungs.

Imagine if I had been able to see then that what I was doing could literally chop years off my life. I used to think that it was better to live life 100 percent to the fullest and do every single thing I wanted to do, and if I didn't live as long then at least I would have lived well. Now I think that it's length that matters. I want to extend my life as long as possible, because dying is a lot worse than the alternative of having to give up a few fun experiences or having to modify my lifestyle a little bit or having to accept certain limitations. Example: I'm starting to consider getting a single for college.

I'm attaching the message Talia sent me, which was so nice I want to save it forever. It really made me smile:

> *Hey, so I just tried to record you two videos but neither of them worked. But I guess that's for the better because they were really long and boring. I decided to write you instead so I could keep it condensed and still say hi.*
>
> *I heard your procedure didn't go as planned. I'm so sorry and I hope you're not feeling too bad. You're such a trouper for hanging in there and I know you'll hate me so much for saying it, but I cannot even tell you how much I admire and respect you and your ability to stay so relaxed and positive.*
>
> *On a brighter note, you have so many yummies to look forward to you won't even know what to do with yourself. I already made one of the things on the list, and I can say, after having about fifty pieces, it is amazing. In addition, my mom is making you a chocolate chip challah for tomorrow since you're so religious and all :). Lots of people are asking me about you and they all want me to let you know that they hope you feel better, but I just told them to come visit you :). Aisha and I are planning on coming tomorrow after school if you're feeling up to it. She*

is bringing a special treat. I bet you know what it is. I miss
you so much because our last forty-five-minute encounter
was definitely not enough, considering before then I hadn't
seen you in like two years.

Anyway, I hope you're feeling better, and I love you
sooo much!!!

Tik/takua/til

So now it's after 3:00 a.m. I'm gonna try to get some sleep, even though the effort is doomed from the start.

Wednesday, April 21, 2010

It's Wednesday and I'm going home tomorrow!! I had the quickest turnaround. On Saturday, Dr. Pornchai basically thought I wasn't going to get better, but then I started gaining weight like wild and my lung function went back up and apparently, I look and sound better and so now I'm going home! I had my lung function test this morning and my number was 3.14 . . . which is a little better than when I got here. Thank God, I'm finally getting better. It is weird how it does seem like everything gets better when I weigh more . . . and now I can go home and get back to my life and then I'll deal with how I feel about it later. Dr. Pornchai still wants me to weigh 155 minimum. I'm not really down for that.

My life is such extreme highs and lows! This hospitalization was stretching on, and I couldn't see the light at the end of the tunnel. I never expected to be getting out, because I felt so horrible, and now all of a sudden, I'm leaving tomorrow morning before 9:00! I wasn't optimistic at all, but Dr. Pornchai was—and the test was good, so yeah. It's happening. And I'm going to Stanford this weekend for Admit Weekend! I didn't think I'd make it but I'm going.

Monday, April 26, 2010

I finally have time to write about Admit Weekend! It was not at all what I expected. Best part was the Club Fair. About four different people from the crew team came up to me to tell me I should try out. They all seemed really enthusiastic, and it sounds really fun, so I might consider trying out for it. Plus I think I'd be good at it because I'm a swimmer and crew is all upper-body muscles. Although I'd probably get pretty buff, and I wouldn't be able to do it on IVs. And they have morning practice and apparently, it's cold on the water so might not work for me. But we'll see, I'll figure it out next year. There were probably over a hundred clubs represented there . . . religious ones, sports ones, and then the randomest ones you could imagine (bread-baking club, Asian queer club, Stanford eating club). The other highlight was playing an icebreaker game thing that was kind of like tag, but I was failing miserably because my IV was hanging out and making me scared to move quickly or push off that arm and stuff. Then we walked to the quad and talked awhile and started playing ten fingers, which is really hilarious to play when you don't know any of the people because some of the people were saying really benign and uninteresting things like "I have never eaten potato salad" and then there was one guy who said "Never have I ever had sex with two people in one night." So there was definitely a wide variety of responses, but the people were all nice and it wasn't awkward. Then this hot guy named Andrew that said he was a profro (that's what they call prospective freshmen) but didn't look like one came up on a bike and said he had biked to campus because he lived nearby.

The last few months have been such a whirlwind . . . I went from my first round of IVs, during which I was basically doing nothing and watching TV all the time, to getting off and swimming in invitationals, then straight to Hawaii, then the day after I got home from Hawaii I went back to the hospital, then the day I got out of the hospital (last Thursday) I went to Stanford. So last night was the first time sleeping in my bed since before spring break, so my first time since March. It's now almost the end of April. And the AP tests are literally in one week exactly!! WOW! I have been out of school for a very long time. Today was like my debut back. But I only went to one class (government) and then ten minutes of math. Oh, I also forgot to write about Dillon walking into my hospital room with flowers to ask me to prom. I still have no idea how my mom, Rob, and the nurses worked this out. I'm not sure I really want to know. But I'm stoked we're going to prom together. And Jan bought me a dress!!

Wednesday, May 12, 2010

I've had such a busy last few weeks that I sort of forget I'm on IVs. It's not really interfering with my life that much anymore because swimming's over and I'm going to school, and I'm off tobramycin (TOBI), so I only have three thirty-minute treatments a day (as opposed to one thirty-minute and two ninety-minute ones). It's life-changing to be off TOBI.

It's so funny to think that when I was eleven (in 2003), I went and spoke to people who work at Novartis. That's the company that makes TOBI. I told them how hard it was to do TOBI because of how long it took. Apparently, they were working on a new delivery system for the medication, a faster way to inhale it, and wanted to hear how it might help patients. I told them it would make life sooo much easier.

I went to get PFTs yesterday, and my number was 3.08 (the week before it was 2.94 and the week before that 2.69). So it's slowly going up!! I'm very happy. I think it's because I'm finally exercising every day. I ran three miles yesterday with Talia! We planned to run from Beverly to El Rodeo and back, but then we ended up running from Beverly to Holmby Park. We walked the hills, though. But still, that's the most I've done in a really long time. I'm happy to be getting back into shape. I'm starting to catch up in school, too. Which is pretty funny since it's almost the end of my high school career!

A Pablo Neruda quote inspired me to audition to be a graduation speaker: *Tengo que acordarme de todo, recoger las briznas, los hilos del acontecer harapiento.* The translation is "I have to remember everything, I have to collect the wisps, the threads of untidy happenings." It made me want to capture what high school has meant to me. Writing my speech will force me to focus on what the past four years have been about.

Wednesday, May 19, 2010

I wrote my graduation speech earlier this week (it's Wednesday today, it was due yesterday). I think it's pretty good. I talked about the duality of the experience of graduation, how it emphasizes both the past and the future. So my closing quote was, "Farewell . . . hello . . . farewell . . . hello." I don't know if a lot of people will understand it, especially if they drift off during the middle of the speech while I'm talking about the past/future and closing one door and opening another.

I don't even know if I'll get picked because a lot of people submitted drafts. Actually I think I probably won't get picked because so many people are trying out, and a lot of them are really creative and probably came up with way more interesting and unique things to say than I did. Mine is more of a traditional graduation speech despite it being deeply personal.

Tuesday, May 25, 2010

The craziest thing happened I forgot to write about. I was voted Prom Queen! After languishing in a hospital bed for so many weeks on end, I was grateful to be out with friends. It was an incredible evening until the after-party, when someone threw a smoke bomb into the venue. It was so scary!!! My throat started to burn, my lungs were searing, my eyes and nose were watering, and then I coughed up blood. It was awful. At least Dillon was really sweet. We left and sat on the sidewalk and then went to a coffee shop, where we talked for hours.

Terrifying moments like this have given me a profound understanding of how lucky I am to be alive. How precarious life is.

Tuesday, June 1, 2010

Completely random tangent, I keep winning all these awards and it's insane. First I got the graduation speech, then Prom Queen, and tonight at the Quest Awards I got Hall of Fame, Female Athlete of the Year, and the Sue Jones Memorial Award (that comes with $1,500 to use for college!). It was like whoa. I kind of feel like a cheater, taking so many awards for myself, but then I think about everything I contributed to sports during high school and how much I pushed myself in everything, how I put sports before school and social a lot of the time and they rewarded me for that.

Friday, June 11, 2010

I'm not worried about making friends in college, I'm just worried that I'm going to be comparing them to all my friends at home and feeling like they don't measure up in terms of how much fun I have with them. Like all the people I met at Stanford's Admit Weekend were perfectly nice and really friendly, but I can't imagine being silly with them and running around doing the shenanigans that I do with my friends now. I just can't imagine being able to be myself around all these new people, and finding friends to replace my old friends, and keeping in touch with all my old friends while I'm gone because I want them to stay current friends, not old friends. But I also want to live in the present and enjoy college, so it's just weird.

Communicating long-distance just ALWAYS gets hard, becomes a hassle, never feels normal to me, no matter how close I am with the person. Because I get so frustrated with technology and it can't replace face-to-face time. It's going to be weird staying in touch with my parents and Micah, too. Like I'm going to have to call them to chat. Now I talk to my mom about plans and where I'm going and what I'm doing and what I'm eating and stuff, but next year it's going to be to tell her about my life.

This week I've gone to school every day! Every class, every day, except I did PFTs on Tuesday, which took a few hours out of the day, and today I skipped sixth period to go to Dr. Pornchai. But it's been so chill this week because we're done for the year, so we're not really doing anything at all. But since it's my last week of high school, I want to be there, and I want to have a lot of people sign my yearbook (something I never really cared about before). My PFT was bad and they basically determined that the IV antibiotics are doing nothing, because after twelve weeks I'm exactly the same as when I started, and I just keep going up and down and up and down, so they're perplexed. But they did pull my PICC line that day. It's sooo nice to do everything with no PICC line: showering without my DRYPRO cover!!, putting on and taking off clothes, sleeping, living my life in general, etc. . . . . it's amazing. It really makes you appreciate your arms. Mine are just so weak now, so I have to get them strong again because they're awkwardly too skinny and non-muscular when the rest of my body isn't.

Friday, June 18, 2010

I GRADUATED FROM HIGH SCHOOL TODAY! I woke up early on my own. My mom's friend Linda did my hair and makeup, and then we rushed over to school at 8:00, got my robe and rose, and went to the room with the people who were sitting on the platform. It was weird to see my teachers on the day of graduation, as a final goodbye. But there were a lot of teachers I wanted to see before graduation and say goodbye to that I didn't get to. The graduation itself was really short. I thought I would cry but I didn't. It hasn't really hit me, I guess. I said my speech early on in the ceremony, which was good because I was nervous beforehand and after that I just got to relax. I wish I could have written more about the last few weeks of high school but I just didn't have time and it was all so exciting and so much fun and I can't believe high school has come and gone.

After graduation I went to lunch at Talia's house with both of our families, then went and hung out at Jason's family lunch thing, then packed for Hawaii—so excited Talia is coming with us—and then at night went to a bonfire with Amanda, Becca, Mich, and some other people at Dockweiler Beach. We just chilled and sat on the beach in front of the fire, had some s'mores, met some hilarious guys we flirted with, then went to Urth Caffé at 10:00 for food.

Saturday, July 3, 2010

Got back from Hawaii on the 29th of June. IT WAS SO MUCH FUN. Probably one of the craziest weeks of my life, but truly incredible! We were scheduled to leave on the 26th but my mom decided to leave Talia and me behind in Hawaii and she and my dad went home.

It was incredible. We were on our own, independent, able to do exactly what we wanted when we wanted. It gave me a little taste of college and made me really excited. We hung out on the beach, found hot guys, drank a little. SO amazing to be without my parents hovering!!!

Tuesday, August 10, 2010

Today is my mom's b'day, my dad's is on Thursday!

Fun summer seeing lots of movies (*Toy Story, Iron Man,* Twilight Saga). I got back and started working at Motive Marketing with Talia. It's been good so far; I work from 11:00 to 5:00 on Tuesdays and Thursdays. One of the days I wrote a summary of a conference call, one day I got contact information for a bunch of organizations, today I sent an email blast to a bunch of people and made phone calls. It's cool because it's not a very formal work environment, like I can wear jeans and stuff, and most of the interns sit in the conference room together and do our work there. If we were all separated it would be much more boring. There's one really hot intern, which is cool because it gives me a reason to look presentable when I go to work. He's more than hot. He's beautiful. I'm debating if I should add him on Facebook right now. His name is Pete and the weird thing is that when he told me his last name, I realized that I'm friends with his sister on FB. No idea how or why . . .

Wednesday, August 25, 2010

As college gets closer and closer, it seems farther and farther away. Which might not make sense, but I just can't imagine living there in a few weeks. I haven't even started packing, I don't know who my roommate will be, I've barely even thought about it lately because every time I do I get stressed. I am just so worried they're going to pull a bait and switch and give me a single, but I'm simultaneously worried that if they don't, I won't have enough space and I won't be able to live. I spent a lot of time explaining to the housing office WHY I don't want to be in a single, why I don't need to be. But I think they think my lifestyle (my treatments and medical equipment) will be "too much" for the average freshman to handle.

But if they do give me a single, I'm going to have a heart attack and be lonely and isolated and depressed. But enough about that. It's just so weird that my friends are already in college (besides Gaby and Talia, who are on vacation because their schools start later). I'm actually excited—finally—to move out and be on my own and do whatever I want and have new experiences. Yay. I say finally about that, because during the year I was like no! LA is fun, I want to stay! But now I'm ready to move on.

Monday, August 30, 2010
I'm kind of depressed right now. I just feel restless and kind of lonely and aimless and like I'm in this weird interim where nothing is going on at all and I don't really have anyone to hang out with. And I know that's just because I'm in limbo because Stanford starts so much later than other schools—so I feel really detached with everything that's going on here. Or maybe it's just because it's late at night and I didn't go out.

COLLEGE

When she wasn't winning sports games, academic awards, or service accolades, Mallory made time for the people she cared about. This came in the form of countless adventures, deep talks, and late nights of life advice. Mallory seemed to always have the answers to life's toughest questions.

—Micah

Saturday, September 18, 2010

I'm here at Stanford! It's so beautiful, no wonder they call it the Farm. There's so much to write about because so much has been happening and it's so fun!!! The first day I met this soccer player named Adrian who's in Ujamaa dorm (I'm in Lagunita) and we've been running into each other, and he is sooo beautiful. He's athletic and he looks exactly like Zac Efron and has an amazing body and he's nice and he's shy! Aka perfect for me. So I'm working on that . . .

What else has been interesting? I like that I run into people I know on campus. I had to make a list last night of everyone I've met because there are so many, and I was afraid I'd forget. It's finally getting a little bit less busy, but I'm still really torn about classes. Basically my dilemma is complicated; I want to take a third class so I need to pick one, but Spanish is during lunch every day and I'm gonna sleep through breakfast, and physics will probably have too much work. I wrote down a list of classes that are three-unit classes (so that I end up with a total of less than twelve units—it will be less stressful, and I'll get a tuition reduction), but if I do yoga that will be exactly twelve units and then I don't get the reduction (I think). And I just keep going back and forth between Spanlang 15 and Physics 15 and a history class and an anthro class.

I love my roommates—Sabrina and Adele. Both are premed,

both seem to understand my needs. It's wild/amazing how Stanford paired me with people who would "get" me . . .

But anyways, yeah, I signed up for Spanish and I'm going to sign up for yoga and just see how it goes. If I want to switch, I have two more weeks before the deadline.

I'm getting to know people better, there are a lot of cool girls on our floor. Marushka, Judy, and Zoe are in a triple together and they are so nice. The RA (Anthony) is sooo cool, and we have Ingrid and Lyric (who are so fun to hang out with) in our dorm. We finally met the football players on our floor, at least a few of them. One of them is almost next door to us and his name is Jordan and he's pretty cute. Yesterday I did a million errands, met with Teri Adams at the Office of Accessible Education, got my parking permit, went to the history open house, went to the bookstore, got a book, a calendar, and a planner, etc. The more places I go, the more times I have to find my way somewhere, the more I understand how to get around campus, which is good. I should probably find my classes today or tomorrow so that on Monday I'm not freaking out about where to go and getting lost when I'm late.

Tuesday, October 12, 2010 (18 years old)
It's my birthday!!!

Sunday, November 7, 2010
Last night we drank in Chris and Daniel's room with everyone from the dorm plus Ali. So much fun, didn't eat too much so felt the alcohol pretty quickly. Then to Sam's room to say hi for a bit, then went to chase down the bus to the Mausoleum Party. Such hilarious drunkenness all around me. Got to the party, stayed with Ali because Lyric saw some friends and left to hang with them. We got home late, chilled in the hallway and talked for a while, then went to bed at like 3:00. Today, went to brunch, chilled, ran six miles on treadmill!!! Yayyyy. Need to start studying for physics . . . def procrastination to the max!

Thursday, December 9, 2010

My brain is kind of in a shambles. I haven't been able to focus AT ALL on anything school related this entire week, starting over the weekend. It was like after I turned in my essay for Intro to Humanities (IHUM) on Friday, my brain stopped functioning. And then over the weekend I was supposed to study soo much for physics, but I literally ended up studying for one hour on Sunday night. And it was very unproductive, but that turned out okay because I ended up getting a 58 out of 60 on my midterm! Yayyy! I don't know when I'm going to learn to not stress and just get my shit done. Because I seem to always get it done, at least that's the pattern. And I'll think, *Wow, this is the time when I won't get it done, this is the time where I'm going to completely mess up and my brain just won't get it and I'm going to fail.* And maybe that stress is necessary in order to force me to work. Like if I weren't stressed out and I thought it would just get itself done, then maybe I wouldn't feel the pressure to do it. I don't know. But anyway I haven't read this story for IHUM called "Sorrow Acre" that I was supposed to have finished reading by Monday, and there have probably been at least seven times when I've sat down at my desk and said I'M GOING TO READ THIS STORY NOW AND FINISH IT but then instead, I go check my email, or I start texting, or I go on Facebook, or I start writing to-do lists, or I clean up and start organizing. I just get so creative with my procrastination. And I skipped IHUM lecture both days this week because I was sleeping.

Saturday, December 18, 2010

I used to have fun, be fun. Now I'm afraid of EVERYTHING, of being myself—but also of losing who I am. That the choices I make are going to cut my life short. All the IVs I do are very hard on the liver, so drinking is a big risk, which layers on the fear that if I can't drink anymore, I won't enjoy college because everyone drinks. I'm afraid that I won't ever be truly happy, won't find a long-term significant other. Sex with a PICC line and an IV drip? UGH. I'm afraid that I'll always just be "that sick girl."

Sunday, January 9, 2011

Back at school. The break was a really nice combo of seeing family and friends, sleeping.

Went to brunch, which was so fun except I ate pancakes and soooo much coffee cake, and coffee, and afterward I just felt like I was going to puke. Why didn't I just order an omelet? I was bad last night, too. There was this hot amazing peach cobbler in the dining hall, and so I just felt like I HAD to try it because everyone was saying how good it was. But then when I ate a piece, I wasn't satisfied so I ate more. And the whole dining hall eating style—with good food put in front of me—makes it hard NOT to eat. I really do hate my body right now at this point. It was so easy to stay at a low weight in high school because exercise was a huge part of my day, every day. Because school and sports kept me so busy, the amount of time I would spend eating was very small. It's so different here. Dinner is from five to seven, approximately. So, when I get out of physics at 4:30 and then have to do treatment, I have to go to dinner right after that, otherwise I won't get any. In an ideal situation, I would be able to go work out after treatment, and then have dinner after. But I can't, because it's over, and after I eat dinner I can never work out because I'm too full. I just feel like I'm so out of control of my eating and it's disgusting.

It doesn't help that my skin isn't good, so I'm not sure how to fix that, and I have that weird fungus thing on my hands where my palms look all weird and get so pruny whenever they get wet, plus I have that discoloration on my arm from when I was on IVs that probably won't go away unless I laser it off, and it's really noticeable whenever I wear anything short-sleeved or sleeveless. I wish I could be happy with my appearance naturally so I wouldn't have to think about it. Because it just wastes my time and it's such a stupid thing to think about. I'm at Stanford, I should be thinking about intellectual things and be excited about going to class and about doing my work.

Thursday, March 31, 2011

TODAY WAS SUCH A GOOD DAY. It was so sunny. Absolutely stunningly beautifully sunny. Basic rundown of the day: breakfast,

IHUM lecture (wore a really cute outfit I got over break), then SWIMMING conditioning (really cute guys in this class haha), then lunch at Lag, then photo class, then talking to Talia, then going to Neurobiology of Relaxation class (hot guys in this class, too!), then going to dorm barbecue, then volleyball, then fountain hopping with Erin, Karen, and Linh, then back to Lag for late night with Lyric, Adeeb, and Tyler. Best part of all this is that I was outside so much. A lot of times in the winter I was in my room during the days, which gets depressing.

So many good things happening. I got the job at Shoreline Lake!!!!!!! I'm going to be president of club volleyball next year!!! Marcus told/asked me tonight.

Tuesday, April 5, 2011

My photography class is SO cool. I learn things in class that I don't fully understand and every time I'm at my computer I just start looking up what I learned, rereading it, so I can understand it. It's fascinating and POWERFUL (what you can do with a camera). And I think it would be amazing to be able to develop a talent at photography and be able to use it either professionally or just as a hobby in life. I'm SO drawn in by aesthetics and a beautiful image is more moving to me than almost anything else. Beautiful images (in photos and just in life), beautiful music, all those things are just so stirring to me. That's how I know that if I had developed it earlier in my life, I could have been artistic. So I think it'll be a hard class and I'll definitely have to work! But I want to put in the work because I *care* about the subject.

Monday, April 25, 2011

I'm having a very good day and I had a very good weekend. Thank God I quit my job at the lake because now I'm actually able to get my work done, enjoy myself and have a social life, and not worry that I'm running myself to the ground and will have to go on IVs. Today I woke up at 10:00 after going to bed at 12:00, so I was rested, and I had breakfast and did treatment (started TOBI today, which is great because I'm sooo sick of cleaning the machine I use for Cayston three times a day—such a bummer it needs its own machine), and did all my reading for Prussia, which made me feel accomplished. Then I went to the pool and swam and had a good workout. I'm able to be happy after I finish swimming now because I've lowered my expectations for myself. I realize I'm not a competitive swimmer anymore, I'm not swimming eight months a year for two to three hours a day, plus I'm in a long-course (fifty-meter) pool instead of a short-course (twenty-five-yard) pool, so I can't expect myself to swim nearly as much or as fast. And it's also fine, because this way I can stay in shape, and get to swim and be in the water, which I love, but I won't have to feel like I look like a body builder. It's nice to find that balance of moderate exercise that's enjoyable and good for you.

Then I went to my Prussia class, which is probably the class I've enjoyed most here at Stanford so far. I'm never bored, even when the professor is lecturing, and especially when we have discussions about what we read (except when I don't do the reading, but even then I'm usually engaged). The class is full of interesting people that I would totally be friends with outside of class, and that's unusual because I haven't really felt that way before about a class. There's a really hot guy in the class named James who is a senior living in SAE frat house, and I saw him at SAE on Saturday night and we talked. He's really nice and smart and athletic (in addition to being hot), which is a good combination, but he's also VERY shy so I don't think anything will ever come of it. Actually I'm fairly sure of that. I don't want to ever get my hopes up about a prospect of a guy, I just have to let things happen naturally, but also do my best to be friendly. Anyway, there's also a guy named Paolo who is a complete character. He's a European hipster who went to boarding school in Europe and is fluent in German and he's very well read in philosophy. He's just a funny person in general. And a guy named Daniel, who is going out with Brett (this really nice guy in the FloMo dorm who I know through Devanshi), is hilarious and really interesting to talk to. It's just such a better humanities experience than IHUM because the people all chose to be in the class, so everyone is interested in it, and everyone just seems really smart. Not to mention how adorable and sweet the professor is (Adrian Daub). He also happens to know everything there is to know about Germany.

Today we tried to reproduce German eighteenth-century salons in class, so we sat at tables in small groups and discussed the reading and anything else intellectual. Our professor also got coffee and tea and desserts delivered, so we just sat around and ate and drank and discussed interesting things. The TA Leela was at my table and she is just so sweet and adorable, and Daniel was also at my table and we had a good discussion about the value of intellectual labor and whether that's something that is good for society, and when people got up and rotated tables James and Paolo were at my table and we had another interesting discussion about sexuality in Europe at that time and how emotions were suppressed in favor of reason. It's just a weird concept to think that I enjoyed myself in class.

Wednesday, April 27, 2011

Spring quarter has been so fun lately! It feels like there are no consequences to my work anymore. I'm not sure if that's a good thing or not, but at least I'm seeing the big picture (that education should be about personal growth and learning and development of the brain for your own interest and hard work, and not doing it because that's what you're SUPPOSED to do in order to SUCCEED).

Whenever I get stressed, which I definitely do when I have an overwhelming amount of stuff to do, I just think about the fact that I don't care about my GPA and none of this is consequential, and the only reason I want to make sure I pass all my classes with good grades is for my own pride. But with this mentality I can actually try to enjoy my classes without stressing about it too much. Right now the only thing I'm worried about is my midterm because I definitely need to pass that class to get the engineering requirement. But yeah. Life is good.

Everything has just seemed a lot like summer vacation, with some added responsibilities to keep things interesting. I get up and have breakfast, put on a nice cute springy outfit, go to class, usually go swimming (and have a nice, quick forty-five-minute workout where I feel good about myself but don't kill my body), then have more class (or take a nap), then do whatever I'm doing at night (meetings, dinner, hang out, homework, etc.).

Tonight I saw Nnamdi and David at late night! And it was sooo out of context. I went to Open Gym last night by the way, and it was so much fun. It was me, Karen, and Lara (we were the only girls), and then some of the guys: Josh, Andy, Greg, Alec, Becker, Nicholas. We were all just being ridiculous, and I think I got more exercise from laughing than from playing. But it was super fun. This weekend is Admit Weekend! So I think I'm going to see Josh. And also the girl Emily from Buckley who played volleyball at Sports Shack, who came to visit Stanford. I ran into her a few weeks ago.

Also the other thing I want to say is that I sometimes just have the most INTERESTING conversations, and it makes me think that I want to stay in humanities. Like today when we were discussing Hegel in Prussia class, and I didn't even do the reading and I was interested, and same with IHUM where we were discussing *One Hundred Years of Solitude*. It just sucks because I actually LIKE reading but because the assignments are so big, I don't feel like there's a possibility that I'll ever be able to do them, so I just don't even bother starting.

Also, I think Hawaii is finally getting finalized! I believe I'm going from July 6 to August 22 to do summer school!

Saturday, May 7, 2011

I was trying to write an essay last night, which was about "what does pursuing further education mean to you" and it was sooo hard. I had all these ideas, but I just couldn't put them onto paper in a way that didn't sound pretentious and abstract and wordy. Sometimes I feel like I have this inner voice in my head that has a style of writing, but I just can't bring it out onto paper. It's so frustrating.

I used to want to be a writer, but I definitely don't want to do that now because it would just be way too frustrating. I enjoy writing when the limitations of proper, formal structure don't apply (e.g., in a journal). And I wish I had more time to actually write serious things about what I'm thinking, and not just chronicle daily events. There are so many times, actually, pretty much every night before I go to bed, where I lie there, and I think about things and get really pensive. And I have tons of memories that I want to write down, because they make me smile. And things sort of fall into place and make sense, or I have these broad life questions/worries, and I wish I could get them on paper so they could be recorded. Because *that's* the stuff that actually matters, the stuff I will want to reread later.

I think that's why I write so much more often when I'm upset, because then I'm writing about my thoughts and emotions, whereas when I'm just happy and content, I'm usually just writing about the activities that fill my day. And I don't want to think that my brain is regressing into triviality, focusing on the mundane. I like to care about things, and to think about things that matter, like how I treat people, or what my purpose is, or what anyone's purpose is, or why we interact how we do, or how I feel about certain people in my life, and why I feel that way, and how I feel about myself, and what I wish I did with my time that I don't, and what kind of a person I want to be. I have substance and depth, I'm a complicated person, and I like to try to understand myself better. But I need to cultivate this substance and depth, and writing helps, and reading for fun helps. But just reading alone isn't enough. I need to read and then think about it/reflect on it in some way. So I have a few new goals:

> Do more pleasure reading of GOOD literature . . . *God's Debris, The God Delusion,* poetry, more Douglas Adams, *The Gospel According to Jesus Christ, The Omnivore's Dilemma* . . . I have so much that I want to read.

> Read instead of wasting hours on Facebook and webmail.

> Start doing yoga again (I had to do it for the Neurobiology of Relaxation class and I was really

reluctant and didn't feel like doing it at all, but I felt sooo good after that I can't believe I ever stopped doing it).

Continue working on photography and actually TRY hard on the assignments, be creative, etc. . . . don't just try to get through the assignments to fulfill all the requirements.

Sign up for one of the noncredit photography classes in Hawaii in the summer (it will help build my portfolio before I start taking Conservation Photography in Arts Intensive).

SURF this summer—no explanation necessary. Four times a week, I hope.

Learn how to cook and be more mindful about food (constantly working on this).

Keep my mind grounded in things that matter, maintain *perspective* (so easy to get caught up in stupid little details).

Hike more often. I miss it! Both in LA, and in Hawaii.

Continue to work on pushing myself out of my comfort zone, always being friendly and meeting new people.

Monday, May 16, 2011

Everything has been really fun lately, and I've realized how much I love all my friends here at school and how much I'm going to miss them this summer. It's hard to have two lives, my life at home with my family and my life here at school. I don't miss my really close friends from home because I talk to them (Talia, Becca, Natasha, Jason, Michelle, Gaby) but I really miss Maria and I do miss my parents. I just feel guilty that I'm going away to Hawaii this summer for seven weeks and then I'm coming home for about a week, then going back to school again for Arts Intensive (Conservation Photography . . . so excited!). On the topic of photography, I think I'm going to register for this noncredit class in Hawaii this summer called Great Moments in Great Light. I just want to get as much experience as I can, because I love feeling like I understand the camera and how to make beautiful images.

Apparently, the geology class I signed up for is going to be canceled because of low enrollment, which sucks, so I have to find a new class. And it sucks for a few reasons. Geology is something I need for earth systems and it's the only class I could take there that would go toward that major. Also, it was going to meet only three times a week, from 4:00 to 6:00 p.m., so I'd actually have like the entire day to surf, swim, go to the beach, etc.

Sunday, May 29, 2011

I've come to the conclusion that I am HORRIBLE at attracting guys for dating. I can figure out how to get a guy to hook up with me easily, or I can make them think I'm cool and make them be my friend, but guys that I hook up with NEVER want anything more. EVER. It's kind of annoying. With the Morgan situation it's a little bit more understandable because we met at Exotic Chaotic and that's just one of those nights where it's kind of like everyone on campus agrees that anything goes. And everyone is always sooo drunk at Exotic Chaotic and nothing is ever like a strings-attached hookup. So I understand why he didn't want anything to come out of that, but he still could've responded when I texted to say hi and done the nice thing and just said something considerate but to the point like, "You seem like a really great girl but I'm not looking for anything right now but it was nice meeting you" etc. Why is that so hard for a guy to figure out? Why do they always think that ignoring you is the better route?

Monday, June 6, 2011

I'm leaving this week to go home for the summer! I can't believe the end of this year has come sooo fast. That I'm going to be a sophomore in college. So much happened and it does feel like forever ago that I was in high school, and that I lived at home, but it's just still weird that the year is over. There's always that weird duality with things ending where they went by so fast but at the same time you feel like you've always been there and can't imagine being anywhere else. I'm just so used to doing what I want to do now, making my own decisions, planning my life, taking care of my responsibilities, etc., and not having my parents be involved, that I can't imagine what it's going to be like to not have that be the case. I think it's good that I'm only going home for like three weeks because I won't get sick of being home and feel that urge to get out that a lot of people feel. I'll have a nice relaxing time at home, then I'll go have an amazing seven weeks in Hawaii, then I'll be home for one more week, then I'll be back at Stanford for Conservation Photography! One thing about moving around so much is that that's what I naturally am inclined toward, I have total wanderlust and I always have, but I've never actually been able to do it because it's so hard with treatment and everything. I'm healthy when I have a stable routine, and I'm in one place, and have my whole setup and everything constant, but this summer is just going to be a whirlwind of moving around, which could be hard. I just have so many possessions, and I hate the fact that anywhere I go no matter what I automatically have like twenty pounds of medical gear I need to bring with me. It really prevents me from doing what I always yearn to do, which is just to be spontaneous and travel around, do what I want, just GO.

I shouldn't complain. I'm actually very grateful for the fact that I made it through this ENTIRE year without a hospitalization or any real sickness (I'm sure it's the clinical trial I'm in that PTC Therapeutics is doing with the drug ataluren) and that I get to have this amazing summer, which I would never get to do if I didn't have CF. I hate the word *blessed* because it's not about anything spiritual, but I just feel sort of overwhelmed with gratitude at times when I think about everything that I have, all the opportunities. The fact that I'm in a position now where I get to DEFINE what kind of life I have and what kind of person I am. So yes, I have this twenty-pound weight around my neck at all times, and a minimum two-hour-a-day medical regimen I need to do in order to maintain these opportunities and a stable lifestyle, but everyone has something. CF in some ways is a negative, and in some ways it's just neutral. But it's actually a positive in other ways. I don't want to sound philosophically arrogant in any way, but I feel that I have a really deep and true understanding of what life is about, and I have a perspective about what matters and what doesn't that no one else I know has. And most people don't understand it, and they think it manifests itself in weird ways, like excessively taking naps, or going to Hawaii for the summer instead of dedicating fifty hours a week to researching molecular genetics, or being completely fine with a C in a class as long as I feel like I learned something and got something out of it, etc. People don't understand the way I feel about the world and my life and what it means to me and what I want to do with it. I don't inherently believe in external measures of success; that's why I'm not motivated by grades, networking and connections and money, I don't feel the need to over-schedule myself insanely so that I feel useful in society, etc. People don't understand that THERE'S NO POINT IN ANYTHING IF YOU'RE NOT HAPPY. There's no point in studying for hours and hours and hours, and not sleeping or seeing your friends, and sacrificing your emotional and physical health, just to get one stupid A. There's no point in FREAKING out about other people thinking you're a slut. There's no use in being a bitch to anyone because we're just all here living our lives and figuring out what we want.

That was a rant. But the point of it was that I just have this existentialist view that there's nothing after this, *this is all we're ever going to have,* so if you're not actively pursuing happiness then you're insane. And I don't think I would have this perspective if I didn't have resistant bacteria that will likely kill me. Obviously, I can attribute it to other things as well, but I just don't think other people think about this stuff a lot, but I do. It's what I think about when I lie in bed at night, and when I hear about other people's lives and think about my own decisions and theirs.

On a side note, it's so weird how so much of who I am is related to the experiences I've had, and a lot of my maturity comes from the fact that I've always had to weigh options and make sacrifices and figure out what's most important to maintain my health. I've had to be happy even when I'm in the hospital for three weeks and then on IVs for nine more, missing my sports, parties, friends, etc. But that sort of feels like a different life at this point. It's contributed to how I look at the world, but I can't even imagine that happening right now, which is kind of scary. I need to always be prepared; I never want to be blindsided.

Recap of what's been going on here:

Last night after my final I came home, and I was skipping because I was just happy and sentimental at the same time, haha. But I was just relieved that it went well and proud that my studying pretty much worked and then I came back to Lag and Lyric and Ali and Zippy gave me a mixed drink and we got dressed to go out to a Nomad party. We went to Nomad with a bunch of Lag people; it was really fun, and I ran into Nnamdi, which was actually very very awkward (he said to me, "You look beautiful tonight, but I know that ship has sailed . . ." LOL).

Later at the quad I ran into Zach, the guy from my IHUM section, and we ended up staying together and went away from my friends and we walked around and were hooking up and then we went to Lake Lag and were hooking up there, but it was too public so we decided to go back to my room but when I opened the door I saw Adele and Sameer in there, so we just left. Then we ended up walking all the way back to Larkin, where he lives, but it felt really short because we were having good conversations the entire time we were together. I felt like I could really talk to him about real things, because he's just kind of a nerd at heart and likes to talk about nerdy things like I do, haha! So we were hooking up at Larkin but then he started to take it farther and this was going on for quite a while and I realized again that I didn't want to lead him on and I didn't want to do anything else that night. I just wasn't down for a whole situation of clothes removal, giving him hand or head or anything (and sex was completely out of the question), etc. So I just told him I thought I should leave, and he was really nice and understanding and didn't push it at all, and we ended up talking for a while longer, like maybe fifteen minutes, then he walked me home all the way back to Lag, which was very nice and unexpected. I really don't think anyone has ever actually walked me home before after we've hooked up. So I had a pretty good night and I'm happy that I just followed my instinct and didn't force myself to do anything because I felt too uncomfortable to speak up and stop it. And I've been attracted to him this entire year, ever since fall quarter, and we'd always see each other and flirt at parties, but this is the first time anything happened.

I need to now go figure out transfer credits for my summer geology class and finish my Prussia paper so I can actually be done!

Friday, June 10, 2011
Got home tonight at 1:00 a.m.! Kind of had a packing fiasco where we couldn't fit everything in the car once we had packed it all into bags, so we had to unpack everything basically this morning (today is Friday) and repack it all and figure out what to leave at my uncle Danny's for the summer, so we didn't end up leaving until about 4:00 p.m. I'm SO lucky he lives close to campus. Then we had to stop multiple times for food and drinks and rest because we were tired, etc. But I'm very happy to be home! Can't believe it's over. But I've said that a thousand times and it's still just as weird so no need to reiterate. Moving out for good was the weirdest, seeing the room completely bare like when we moved in.

Friday, June 17, 2011
I have these weird moments where I visualize myself dying in really weird ways, and how everyone else would go about their lives with me gone, and what would be different about their lives. I don't have a fear of dying, I don't get a bad feeling when I have these visualizations necessarily, it's more of just an eerie type of thing and I don't know why I always do it. It used to happen a lot when I'd run on the treadmill for a long time. I'd imagine myself having something really horrible happen to me, like getting sepsis and spiking a fever and

dying, or getting horrible hemoptysis and losing too much blood and dying. And I'd picture the news story about it and try to imagine how everyone would feel. IT'S SO CREEPY AND WEIRD and it's insane because I don't feel like I'm one of those people who wants attention or would want something bad to happen to me so that I'd get more attention.

Friday, July 15, 2011

So much has happened since I last wrote. I'm in Hawaii now living with Mich!! I think I've been here nine days now. Quick recap of home: It was a blur seeing people, trying to unpack and organize myself, getting ready for Hawaii. On the Fourth of July I went to a party with my mom and met a really cute nice cool guy named Eric (my mom is friends with his mom). He's twenty-four, I think, and living in LA so there's absolutely no chance . . . nothing. So maybe we can be friends in the future. Then went to Stanford to go to clinic before leaving for my trip. I spent the night at Danny's and flew straight to Hawaii the next day instead of flying home first.

It's amazing how I came here, and I immediately started feeling better. I started feeling like myself again. I sort of lost myself for a while during the year, I changed in a lot of ways that were good (probably becoming more outgoing, more open, discovering what I want to do with my life and what my passions are, figuring out what kind of people I want to surround myself with, learning how to take care of myself and deal with all the medical stuff and be independent, etc.). But in some ways that were not good (coming to dread exercise, feeling bad about myself every time I would finish a workout). I had no control over what I was eating even when I knew it would make me feel sick. And that continued into LA a bit but got a little better when I started doing yoga.

It sucks because I'm so torn in two directions. I want to feel good and feel strong and healthy, and I feel that way when I'm in good swim shape and I do great swim workouts. But when I start doing that, I notice myself bulking up and I realize that in some ways I feel better about myself when I'm more feminine and not so buff in the upper body and athletic and boy-looking. And then it's like I try to lose weight and eat healthy and all that (not a lot of weight, just like five pounds would be good)—but then if I start to feel sick in my lungs like I'm getting a bit of an infection, or I'm more irritated than usual in my coughing, then I'll eat because nutrition is therapeutic and fat fights infection.

I'm constantly going back and forth about what I want and what is more important to me. It's not even between appearance and health, because if it were that simple, I like to believe I would just choose health and learn to love my body whatever it looks like. What makes it hard is that I actually *feel* better with my gastrointestinal system when I'm thinner and eating less (I don't get acid reflux, I don't get blockages, I'm not as fatigued, etc.), and I'm able to exercise more, which also makes me feel better. It's really not just about looks. But then again when I'm bigger I feel better in my *lungs*. It's a hard trade-off.

But back to the point, I just LOVE being here because it's amazing how quickly I see the benefits. On Friday, when my mom and Cathy were still here (Cathy is Mich's mom), we went to the north shore and rented surfboards and surfed for a while, then chilled and swam in the ocean, then went paddleboarding. And I felt sooo good that night. I was bringing up so much mucus, feeling so clear, not waking up in the middle of the night unable to breathe. That's probably the worst part of my lungs is when I wake up in the morning and I feel like I can't even stay standing long enough to eat breakfast and brush my teeth and stuff, I mean I do but it's kind of hard. And I don't have that problem as much here. But then when me and Mich were volunteering this week (Monday through Wednesday, with CampUs All-Stars, a three-day summer camp for entering ninth graders at risk of dropping out of high school to teach them the importance of education, high school/college, etc.) we didn't get to the beach for three days because we also had class and studying, and I felt sooo much worse. My stomach was worse, lungs were worse, mental state was worse. There's literally nothing comparable to the ocean for me in how instantly it works.

I bought a surfboard on Saturday, too! I bought it from a woman named Joey who is a local here. She's a surf instructor, I found the board on Craigslist. It's a $400 epoxy ten-foot, two-inch longboard that I got super cheap. I love it! It's big to carry but at least it's a little lighter and makes it easier to catch waves. We drove out to Kailua to get it from her, which is an amazing neighborhood—I love it there. The beach is ranked top ten in the world! And you can kayak there. Anyway, Mich and I went with her on Sunday the next day to White Plains Beach after our moms left. Cutest beach, all locals that are super nice/welcoming and friendly. I got hit on a lot by people I was definitely not interested in, but it was all innocent. We literally surfed all day . . . got there at noon and left at like 6:00 pm. And I brought up a flood of mucus and felt amazing that night. Such a great experience. I wish I were taking more pictures to document this stuff, but I just like to be in the moment and not worry about having my camera out and I also don't like to have a lot of valuable possessions with me because I don't want anything to get stolen.

The house is perfect! I love my room, it's very college-like, fully stocked with kitchen stuff and towels and even a cat!! The cat's name is Rusty . . . he's actually wild. We have my surfboard laid out on the couch and he always walks on it and looks so cute, so I call him Surfer Kitty or Skitty, haha! It's appropriate because he's also very skittish. And very playful and just psychotic in general.

I've been going to bed between 9:00 and 11:00 and waking up between 7:00 and 8:00 every day. Until last night when we went out to Waikiki and stayed there until 3:30 in the morning. But we met some cool people, especially this guy named Josh who is a musician and is living here for the summer. We're going to go snorkeling with him on Tuesday at Hanauma Bay.

Sunday, July 24, 2011
There's so much to write about it's overwhelming. We've been all over the island at this point, driving everywhere, meeting people. . . . I feel like I've been here for a while but at the same time I can't believe I'm ever going to be leaving and going back to Northern

California because I feel like this is the place for me to be for so many reasons. . . . I just admire the people who live here so much for how little they worry about *anything*. I'm definitely not a worrier in comparison to most, I generally think of myself as having a really good perspective about what's important and knowing what things are just not significant enough to warrant my worrying about them, but the people here take it to a different level. I just think it's awesome. . . . It's sort of my first reaction to judge some of the people I meet as weird (sometimes), but then I remind myself that the culture here is completely different, everyone was raised so differently, that sometimes I can relate to it but sometimes I just don't understand.

For example, last night this girl who looked like she was sixteen but who was actually twenty-one told us she's getting married in like a week, and I asked where and she was like, "Oh, I think we're going to do it on this beach. Everyone is invited, by the way!" It was just so interesting to see a wedding planned (or not planned, I should say) in that way, when everyone I know is all about the ritzy expensive showy weddings that you plan for a year. And this was just basically that they decided they wanted to get married, and the act in itself is what's important to them, not the party, not the guest list, not the dress. It's very refreshing to see that.

I basically see some qualities that I have in myself in the people here, but I see them taken to an extreme. But I think if I lived here, they would be more developed. I would have no schedule, I would do whatever I wanted, I would have some random job to pay the bills and spend all my excess time hanging out with people and getting to know them and being at the beach in the water and exploring the island. Which is kind of what I'm doing here now.

And in a lot of ways, I can see myself living here, but probably only for a few years. I think it's an amazing way to figure out who you are, get closer to nature, do exactly what you want to do and just focus on connecting to people and yourself and the earth, but then I think I could potentially get sucked into it forever, and sort of drift away from everything that has been my life up until that point. Basically, I want to live here for a few years in my twenties, but I want to make sure I do move back to the mainland. I might want my kids to live in Hawaii when they're little, to grow up with the same appreciation that I have for it . . . to have the opportunity to start things like surfing, hiking, etc., when they're really little and make it part of their lives forever.

I'm just so incredibly lucky to be here, though. I think about it every time we're driving somewhere, and the breeze is blowing and it's warm and we have the sunroof down, and we're playing some bomb country music and singing to it or laughing about a text from some guy we've met, and looking out at the mountains or the ocean or the green or the cute houses or whatever it is that we're seeing that's so beautiful always. I sort of feel like I've been plopped into a life that could be mine sometime in the future, or that should be mine right now, or that's someone else's that I would really enjoy. It's just sooo different than Stanford or LA. I love all three places, but for different reasons. And there's nothing like getting up and being able to drive twenty minutes to a stunningly beautiful beach with amazing weather.

Thursday, August 11, 2011

We're leaving in six days. It's now Friday morning at 5:40 a.m. . . . . We had our last day of class today (I guess yesterday) and went out tonight to an eighteen-and-over club and it was kind of hilarious. Kind of wild and made me realize that's just not my scene at all. Like being drunk and dancing is fun . . . but I'd so much rather do something real, and meet people in a real way, where they can get to know me for who I am and not for this random wild person I am when I'm drunk. I mean I am myself, but I guess it's also that I'm just kind of over random hookups for now, I don't find them enjoyable anymore, so the whole thing is just kind of pointless to me. I'm looking for a connection with someone. And I'm not like sitting here itching to hook up with someone every day . . . I'm more comfortable with the idea of being alone. I don't feel like I need to hook up with people in order to validate myself feeling pretty or desirable anymore. Maybe I only feel this way because people find me a lot more attractive here than they do at home, and it's obvious to me because they make it obvious. I seemed to have the identity in high school (that I couldn't break out of) that I didn't date anyone from Beverly, or even hook up with them! (Until Dillon. LOL!) And then I went to college, and I could be whoever I wanted to be, but between figuring out school and everything else, I didn't make myself the person I wanted to be. And I think now that I've had some time to think a lot, read some books, get back to what I really love, experience some real interactions with new guys in the real world (outside of a college frat party setting), I've learned a lot about myself. For example, I have no moral qualms with people having one-night stands if that's what they want. That's just not what I want or need right now to make me feel good emotionally.

I want to look for someone good and worthwhile. I don't want to waste my time trying to hook up with as many people as possible, which I think a lot of people do. They think it means that they're a desirable person if they hook up with more and more people. . . . I used to think that way and I guess to a certain extent it's true, but now I've had enough of that.

Thursday, August 18, 2011
I'M HOME! It's literally so weird to be home. I miss everything about summer (except maybe the ants in our apartment). I miss even the stuff that I originally thought I wouldn't . . . having only one suitcase of clothes, having to market and cook for myself, being away from all my family and friends at home. It was literally just like a hiatus from everything in my life. That's kind of a good way of thinking about it, a breath of fresh air (or fresh salty water . . .), and a break from stress, business, obligations, everything that could overwhelm me, even clutter! It was minimalist in a lot of ways. . . . I mean obviously I had a lot of stuff but not anywhere NEAR all the stuff I've collected that is now in my room at home. It was minimalist in terms of friends because it was me and Mich, so we had that comfort zone of being with someone we knew, but other than us we just branched out and met ALL new people. All different kinds of people. . . . I

really do feel like I learned so much about the world and myself. There was so much less attention on image, status, stupid hookups, clothes, social drama, what other people think, etc. . . . stuff I always knew didn't matter but it was impossible still to not let it affect you when you live in the midst of it and you can never get away. But there it was just like . . . freedom. Freedom to choose what to do every single day, freedom to take only one class and actually focus on it and do the reading, freedom to not be stressed, to eat whatever I want, to exercise and play as much as I want, to be in the sun whenever, to sleep whenever, to meet anyone and to be anyone.

So, yeah, I really miss it. Even though it was really nice to see Maria, and Millie and Dewey, and it's been nice to be reunited with the family minus Micah, who is still away. But beyond that I just want to go back. I want to be able to jump in the ocean anytime I want. To go out and take a walk and not run into everyone I know. Sometimes that's nice, but sometimes exploring a new neighborhood is so much more fun. To be out in the waves on my surfboard, getting pummeled and looking at the sky. To meet people who want to hang out with you and are not afraid of making that clear. To focus on myself, my health, my happiness, my sanity, my goals, my daily desires, my weight, my education.

I could go on about this all day. It's so weird to be home. Weird to have a fridge stocked with food. Weird to have SO MUCH STUFF around me, stuff that I just can't seem to get rid of. I think it all has a purpose . . . but is its purpose just to sit in my room? I don't need it when I'm away so why do I need it here? I don't know, it's a mental block. But I love getting away from it. Weird to get back to the routine of calling people and making plans. Too much choice is overwhelming, too many things to do. Don't want to think about this right now, I'm exhausted completely. Horrible headache. Funny that I come home, and right away I have a headache.

Spirometry test tomorrow to measure my lung function (spiro). I better have improved, otherwise I'll feel like a complete failure, now that I know for sure that I'm on ataluren, the actual PTC drug, not the placebo, and I do Pulmozyme twice a day and I've been in Hawaii for six weeks. Really inconvenient that I didn't sleep all night on the red-eye and I was already feeling like I had a cold, and I've been having stomach issues so I have skipped some treatments. But we'll see. If it's not better, that doesn't mean it wasn't worth it because I *felt* WAY better, and that's what counts. Going to organize my pictures now and then crashhhh.

Wednesday, August 31, 2011

It's going to be September tomorrow. When did it become true that 2011 is three-quarters over? I guess tomorrow.

It's actually turned out to be nice being home. I was totally dreading it, thinking it was going to be the typical wild business, doctors' appointments, plans, millions of people to see and please and feel guilty about if I couldn't see them, etc. But that's actually not how it has been! I think the main thing is that most of the people I know are already gone back to school or are away so I didn't have to worry about scheduling and craziness. Which was a great change . . . not that I didn't want to see those people, it's just so nice to be able to focus on a few people and spend a lot of time with them. I spent sooo much time with Mich initially when I got back. . . . I think I was the only person she wanted to be around because I understood how sad she was feeling to be back, and all she wanted to talk about was Hawaii and Hawaii people and she can do that around me but that's boring for other people. But then I started going to volleyball every day with the other Michelle, and training some freshman girls in volleyball, and doing a lot of stuff with my mom, so I haven't seen her as much.

Sunday, October 9, 2011

I haven't written anything in over a month since I've been back at school. It's been a complete whirlwind that I can't even begin to describe. I moved into Toyon on September 16 with no help from parents, which was difficult. My mom really wanted to come with me, but I said no. Good/bad . . . happy I don't need her anymore but I def do better with her help. Didn't unpack for an entire week, which was stressful. Wasn't sleeping a lot, wasn't doing a lot of treatments at all. Stomach problems. It was weird to be back with my friends here (kind of) after being home with other friends for so long and then being isolated in Arts Intensive, where you go to school before school starts and focus on a single art-based project. Missed a few days of Arts Intensive actually!

Weird adjustment going from my friends at home to friends here. Ali is a really *really* good friend to me. And I LOVE rooming with Maya and Makiko—we have an amazing setup. Toyon is the best dorm on campus, I'm convinced. I'm actually much happier to be living here than in a house, even though I originally wanted a house.

The new dining hall opened—the food is actually pretty disappointing after all the hype about how it was supposed to be award-winning menus, chefs, etc. But I'm so happy it's continuous dining, so I really can't complain.

I live next door to three Otero boys on one side (John, Miles, and Brendan) and three Otero boys on the other side (Andrew, Michael, Jason). Michael is Jewish, and I had dinner with him at Dr. Cornfield's house on Rosh Hashanah randomly. Brendan is actually kind of cute. I realized a few days ago that I met him the first week of last year when we were both really drunk, and both of us don't really remember. I only remembered because Ali told me. He saw me doing treatment one day and came in and sat down and was asking me about it, and he seemed genuinely interested/concerned, which I thought was really nice, because people usually just walk by wondering what the spectacle is or what all the equipment is for. He's from New Orleans and he had to move schools and houses like four times during Hurricane Katrina (that's a random fact—it's just what we were talking about when he was in here hanging out with me).

My dorm's Peer Health Educator (PHE) is also really really hot. . . . I was kind of obsessed with him for a little bit, but that's definitely toned down a lot now that I realize that every other girl is obsessed with him, too. He's very good-looking and endearing, genuinely enthusiastic about things, fun, super smart, outgoing, nice, etc. He's from Los Gatos, he's a swimmer, I feel like we have a lot in common and get along really well. We actually went swimming together today, which was so cute (he asked me if I wanted to go this morning so we finally did—we'd been talking about doing it for a while), and when we got back, he said he wants to make it a thing to go every Saturday and Sunday. I'm not obsessing about him anymore, just curious to see if we become better friends/if it goes anywhere.

I'm doing so much more exercise these days. Maya inspires me at the gym because when she goes, she runs for like forty-five minutes on a higher speed than me, so it makes me want to do more and more.

I always wrote Human Biology (HumBio) off as the premed major—so not for me—but now I'm excited about switching to it. I was also originally hesitant because it's so popular as a major it's like a cliché, and I felt like I was just jumping on the bandwagon, whereas earth systems is a much less common major, so I felt like I was forging my own path and it was unique. But it's great to be able to study with so many people and go through it together!

Saturday, November 19, 2011 (19 years old)

I'm happy to be home for Thanksgiving break. I haven't been writing in my journal at all during this month even though it would have helped me to get things off my chest. Instead, I've just let my negative emotions build up and go away or fester, I'm not sure which. Probably fester . . . because I'll feel strong emotions, and then think they go away, but then randomly I'll start crying when my mom tells me my room is messy (which she did today) or when I think about everything I can't do. Which shows that the emotions are not going away but are just waiting for me to pay attention to them, to give them space and flesh them out, to dwell in sadness for a little bit.

I'm reading a really good book called *Pigs in Heaven,* by Barbara Kingsolver, who also wrote *The Poisonwood Bible,* which I love. It's so nice to read for pleasure again. I want to do that a lot for the next six months while I'm on IVs, and I also want to do some type of art . . . maybe learn how to play the guitar, which I've always wanted to do but never had time.

Friday, December 30, 2011

I'm starting to think about New Year's resolutions. The briefest summary of 2011 I could possibly compile:

Starting out the new school year great after trip to Hawaii—regrounded

Spring quarter

Depression about not being able to do sorority rush because it conflicted with my volleyball tournament

Nationals 2011 in Houston—so much fun

Getting into photography; visual communication, oceans, marine conservation

Nnamdi

First (and hopefully last) drunken moment with swimmer Morgan

Amazingly fun last quarter of freshman year

Clinical trial using ataluren

Summer in Hawaii; meeting amazing people (too many to list), reevaluating what I'm about/what I stand for

Anti-drinking feeling, anti-hookup feelings, desire for low-key down-to-earth people

Trying edibles for the first time at Kyle's house

Calling the police multiple times over the summer

Country music

Appreciating family more than I ever have

Nervous apprehension/excitement about sophomore year

Arts Intensive—Conservation Photography

Starting off the new school quarter on a shaky foot

Beginning to have more anxiety—paranoia, especially at night

Health and fitness goals, began to achieve them (masters swimming, running, etc.)

New roommates, new friends, trying to branch out, reevaluating last year's relationships

Questioning some friendships, trying really hard to form new ones without always being conscious of that effort

Very late nights, and early mornings; reduced compliance with treatments

Feeling overwhelmed

Panic attacks—late at night, crying, set off randomly, extreme mood fluctuations, feelings of despair, fear, worry

Switching major from earth systems to human biology

Going into hospital on November 4; two weeks, needing my parents and accepting that

Out in time for Thanksgiving, sick all of Thanksgiving (still my favorite holiday)

Back in hospital for five days; bad prognosis; four weeks of IVs

Back for checkup; decision of three to six months of IVs (no volleyball this year, no masters swimming, no drinking, more emotional stress, reduced course load, etc.)

Passing all my classes—two As and one B! But STRESS

Winter break—Hawaii trip canceled; stayed in Malibu house

Walking on beach, sunshine, coming to terms with where I am with my health

Goals for every day:

Stretch

Eat healthy—avoid feeling sick, be in control

Stay on top of homework, be in control

Call friends—keep in touch

Feel happy every day

Fight stress—peace of mind, acceptance

Goals for the year (ongoing):

Surf all summer

Start writing a book?

Learn to play guitar (while on IVs especially)

Improve Spanish (to be able to talk to Maria and call her often)

Goals for winter quarter:

Figure out something to do in Hawaii for summer—job, internship, research, class?

Build relationships—don't withdraw from people because of stress/fear/sadness

Track the natural cycle of ups and downs week to week

Watch symptoms/signs of serious underlying issues that
are dangerous and seem impossible to overcome

Tuesday, January 3, 2012

I feel so so so so tired. I don't want to look at the sun because it's too
bright and it hurts my eyes. I don't want to move too much because
it's too hard. I don't know if it's the meds that make me feel this way,
or if it's the fact that my sleep is interrupted all night, but I'm not
myself. Sometimes I still feel the desire to do something fun, to act
like a normal nineteen-year-old, to do something other than invite
my friends over to sit on the couch and talk or watch a movie, but
then I just get *tired* and decide not to. This is just so not me . . . normally I'm so down to adventure, to try new things, to go out, have
fun, meet new people. Now I have no desire to hang out with anyone
except for my very closest friends because there's just so much effort
in seeming perky, making conversation, telling people that I'm good
when they ask "how are you." So I've just been ignoring people and
putting it off when they ask for plans. I'm trying to adjust to the
long-term IVs and getting used to the idea of not playing volleyball
(sad as it is that I'm never going to see any of those people I love
all year, that I'm not going to be able to go to nationals, etc.) and
not swimming. But the adjustment that's much harder to make is to
thinking I might not have fun the whole quarter. I need to prevent
myself from just being depressing, though, or I'll lose all my friends.
I feel like I have to pretend to be happy, pretend that I'm okay with
all of this and that I'm going to make it work, but how can I do that
when I don't even feel well enough or myself enough to want to go
for a walk, or go out at night?

I wrote in my scholarship application for the Boomer Esiason
Scholarship that compliance is a *bargain;* it's a trade-off. I give up
hours of my day and in exchange I get to feel good enough to try to
live a normal life the rest of the time. But now, even though I spend

so much time doing medical stuff (probably about eighteen hours of my day I'm thinking about health or doing something health related, including sleeping), most of the time I don't feel well enough to do anything that I would normally do (swimming, volleyball, hiking, gym, going to the beach, going to parties, meeting new people, etc.), and even when I do, I'm not really allowed.

Friday, January 20, 2012

It's halfway through January, the second week of winter quarter. I'm taking HumBio 3a, HumBio 3b, and an intermediate oral Spanish language conversation class. I might be taking a class called The Rise of Indigenous Communities. The first week was so much fun, which was surprising given how worried I was about coming back. But other than having a persistent cold, it's been fine! I've been able to go out with people and have fun sober (which I didn't necessarily think I'd be able to). I just have to be smart about what kinds of events I go to because some things can definitely be fun sober, others NOT. Frat parties, for example. If you're not drinking, you realize they are crowded and disgusting and everyone is sweaty. The biggest problem is that when I'm sober it kind of makes me look down on them in a way. Sometimes, I'll think people are being annoying or obnoxious, when I know I'd be acting the exact same way if I were drunk (and I would be drinking if I could be, so I really shouldn't be judging). It's just hard not to realize how stupid the whole drinking culture is when you take a step back from it. And it's funny because I'm starting to realize that like 80 percent of my hookups last year were drunk (and then I wonder why they don't lead to anything despite the fact that they don't start from anything other than two drunk people at a party!). I'm just kind of over it and I don't really miss it. Specifically, I have no desire anymore to throw back shots and stumble around and dance while trying to look sexy with a random person.

Monday, January 23, 2012

I applied to be a PHE! In case the doctors won't let me go abroad next year, I thought it would be fun to be on staff somewhere, and

I even put the freshman dorms (Wilbur and Stern and Cedro) as an option, which was a totally spur-of-the-moment decision.

Saturday, January 28, 2012

It's 1:00 a.m. and I need to wake up in seven hours, and I really had wanted to get a good night's sleep tonight (I didn't do any homework whatsoever tonight, so I really could've gone to bed). But I have a lot on my mind, so I decided to watch *How I Met Your Mother* to relax a little, but the second I turned it off I started thinking about everything again, which is why I'm not sleeping—and writing here instead.

Sunday, January 29, 2012

I'm pretty happy right now. I think I'm in a good place mostly. I'm not really upset about volleyball anymore, and in fact I'm remembering last year winter quarter how all my weekends were consumed by it, how I would be exhausted, not get enough sleep. I was getting up so early in the morning, wasn't getting my work done, etc. When I think about all the times last year that I considered quitting, it makes me feel a little better about not doing it. I definitely miss it and the girls, and just playing a sport instead of having to go to the gym all the time, but there are certainly some advantages that aren't lost on me now, and I really appreciate them. It's funny but sometimes when I go on IVs I get to live a little bit more of a normal life in some ways (SOME), just because it makes me take away some of the busyness that I always have and give myself a little more time to just spend with friends and hang out.

Friday, February 3, 2012

It's 3:00 a.m. . . . I had the worst night. No particular reason really, just my outlook, I guess. I just freaked out, felt like a fly on the wall, like I don't fit here, like I'm just watching everything unfold and I'm not part of it and don't want to be part of it and it's not me and what is this that we call college life and what's the point of it and why am I not happy with it and why do I always think about everything so much when I'm sober and everyone around me is drunk and why I can have fun sometimes and then sometimes the smallest things will just set me off. And why I keep having these images in my head of me when I'm X age, whatever it may be, thirty, forty, twenty-two, of not being able to do anything without oxygen, of being pent up in my house, of being even less normal than I am now, and I can't even enjoy what I have now and the semblance of normalcy that I do have (because when people can't see my IV and don't literally see the treatments they think I look fine) because I just feel so NOT normal and so separate from these carefree people who pound shots and don't sleep at all and pull all-nighters because school and grad school are their biggest concerns. Why is it that when I should be enjoying this, the only time in my life I'm ever going to experience college life, I just have scorn and contempt for it, like I'm hardened about it and I think no one is genuine, no one wants to really connect with people, they just want to say hello and nice to see you again and how is your quarter going (if that at all), and if not they ignore you like they've never met you, or they're too drunk to realize that it's rude to not introduce themselves when they're standing next to you talking to your friend for twenty minutes. And why is it that in trying to just be classy and cool and have fun sober at a party I just seem bored, or boring, or at least not interesting, or maybe just not pretty, or just neutral to the point where people don't think a second thought about me either way. Is it really the case that for people to realize you're there you have to be stupid and drunk-looking and scantily dressed, you can't just meet people and have fun and have them look you in the eye and actually talk to you about something substantial, maybe take some interest in you however slight that may be, why is it that that doesn't happen at frats. In fact, all you can do is push your way through the sweat and the grime, holding the hand of your friend because you don't want to get left alone because otherwise you'll just stand there looking around for people you know to talk to, because let's face it no one wants to really admit to themselves that they're not self-reliant, that they're not comfortable independently, that they NEED people to be there with them or they feel stupid, they need people to understand them. And when you don't have those close friends reading the same page of the book you are, when you are ten pages ahead because your life has always been in fast-forward, all the time, even when I'm not conscious of it it's molding the way I live, at least I think, I wouldn't know for sure because as I said I'm not usually conscious of it, but then when I think about males and I think about commitment and I think about the utter impossibility of any guy having a normal relationship with me, because they wouldn't even be able to get to the point of getting to know me and liking me as a normal person without seeing me as some type of sick person, with something wrong with me, and the fact that I can't drink, and my arm is bandaged, and I am so fucking out of breath all the time. I wish somebody would just care enough to be like woah what's the deal with her that she looks strong but she's actually not, is she actually sick? Does she have cancer? Is she like dying or something?

I was crying tonight but about what, specifically? Was it about being a fly on the wall? Or is it more about being a spectacle that people are so confused about that they don't see me as a normal peer? Or is it anger at myself that I can't have fun when I'm not drunk and that I overthink every single thing all the time when I'm in those types of situations, and it prevents me from living in the moment.

Having a disease and resistant bacteria has changed me so much as a person that I don't think I'm recognizable to how I was at thirteen, for example. I prided myself on being chill, and tonight I freaked out because someone knocked over my nebulizers and then tried to cover it up by putting them back in the same tray they were in, but I knew because they mixed pieces that didn't belong together, but if I hadn't noticed that I would've gone ahead and done treatment, and I would've inhaled some hard-core filth from the carpet where the nebs fell, where shit's been growing disgustingly because people don't have the consideration to realize that I need it to be kept clean, and I don't have the balls to say anything about it because I don't want people to think I'm anal, or I have a stick up my ass, and I don't want to impose on people and make them change their lifestyle for me (because what if they'd just rather me not be here than have to change their lifestyle?).

I don't know why I can't talk to my parents about this. I think it's because whenever I have a breakdown like this, they say I need to change something, they don't realize it's temporary and I'll go back to being carefree in a matter of how many hours, and they'll freak out and want to fix things. So that's why I don't.

Sleep time now so necessary.

Thursday, February 16, 2012

This past Tuesday was Valentine's Day. I didn't have a valentine, obviously, so it was kind of depressing, but then at night I was in my room and Makiko randomly told me she needed to take me downstairs and outside, and the Fleet Street a cappella group serenaded me! I was super confused because I didn't know who would be sending me a serenade, but it was funny because I know so many of them! It was SO cute, though, and it really made me happy. It turned out that Andrew sent it. Apparently they serenade their own girlfriends and close friends, so he picked me. And it just reminded me that I really do have good friends that care about me and that's better than some random dude buying me chocolate. Oh, I forgot to write about going off IVs!!

Wednesday, March 14, 2012

Summary of the sex part with Rob . . . since I guess that's kind of important. I was kind of expecting it to happen—I just didn't know which night. It was good, but I wouldn't say pleasurable exactly. Like it certainly did not feel amazing, I felt good after, but during it was a little painful some of the time, and mostly not painful but just kind of uncomfortable and different, I don't know how it's supposed to feel exactly, I don't know if it's just because I haven't had sex, or if it's because there's something wrong with me and I just don't get pleasure from sex. . . . I don't think that's it, though, because someone touching my skin and kissing me makes me feel good, so I'm assuming it's just because it's somewhat new that it doesn't feel good yet. Then we cuddled in his bed and spooned and talked, we told each other our first kiss stories and then almost fell asleep but I was trying not to because I knew I needed to go do treatment and wake up in my own bed for tomorrow morning. I didn't want to walk home alone so he walked me, although I knew he really just wanted me to stay over because he didn't want to walk all the way to Toyon at 3 a.m. We ended up getting a Zipcar and he drove me back. He's really sweet with me so I don't regret that it happened. I would write more but my computer is about to die so I need to close this window, because it would be very embarrassing if I left this open and it popped up next time I opened my computer. Kind of a big fear of mine.

Thursday, April 19, 2012

This week's journal assignment for my IntroSem was hard for me at first. I didn't think I could do it because I'm in the hospital, so I was originally thinking that I don't have people to interact with to develop an awareness of my connection with others. But the longer I'm here, the more I realize that I do have plenty of interactions with people, they're just different types of interactions, with different types of people.

I worked on being more aware of how I was interacting with people, and that was an interesting experience, especially with nurses and nurses' aides. Normally, my interactions with these people have tended to be patient-caregiver interactions, but sometimes I connect with a nurse in more of a friend-to-friend way, and this is something I can consciously cultivate if I'm aware of it. For example, Martina, the housekeeper who has cleaned my hospital room the last four times I've stayed here, came into my room today and for the first time, I made eye contact and had a true conversation with her instead of resuming my homework or other activity. She told me that she has three kids, one of them my age. We talked about her husband . . . where Martina is from. It was one of those moments that made me realize how many people I miss out on meeting and getting to know because I just don't even think about putting in the effort to talk to them when I actually could. This is an environment that makes it very easy to only talk to caregivers, and to only talk to them about a few very specific things, letting all other conversations fall to the wayside because they seem unimportant.

This is a recipe for losing sight of the outer world and becoming unhappy. I'm very appreciative now of the relationships I've formed in this hospital because it makes it much more pleasant to be here. Every time I walk down the halls here, I run into respiratory therapists, nurses, doctors, and housekeepers who know me. This feels like a "second home." It's sad to come here because it draws me away from my "real" life, but if I have to be in a hospital, it's nice to be in one that's familiar, where I trust the people and the people know and care about me.

In terms of my ability in general to make connection with others, I think that I do best with others when I'm happy myself. When things are going very wrong in my own life it's hard for me to relate to other people, and that's something I need to work on . . . not shutting out my friends and family when I'm going through a hard time and opening up to them only if they ask me how I am and I'm not actually "good."

On the other hand, I think I'm pretty good at being aware when something's not right with someone else and trying to let them know that I'm there to talk to. I just don't necessarily let other people do that with me. It's important to know which people will be there for you no matter what and which people won't be, but now that I've figured out who those dependable loyal amazing people are, I need to let them in and let them be there for me when I need them. They try, but if I shut them out, they might think I don't need them, and I really do. I'm not the kind of person to ask for help, and I keep a lot of my thoughts to myself, which can be harmful if my friends don't understand what's going on with me and I can't relate to them. This is something that I'm trying to work on: not masking my emotions, opening up to my close friends more, and not trying to pretend like everything is okay 100 percent of the time.

Monday, April 23, 2012

This hospitalization has been rough. Once a pathogen like *B. cepacia* colonizes the lungs, the body has to wage a constant battle to limit the numbers of bacterial cells in the colony. When my body slacks off in the fight, the enemy gains ground and sets in motion a vicious cycle: the thick mucus already present in my lungs creates an ideal environment for a *B. cepacia* population explosion, which makes the inflammation and scarring of my airways even worse, which leads to even more mucus production and often, pneumonia. Anything can set this in motion and lead to an exacerbation of the disease: a pharmacy not sending a prescription on time, a night of sleeplessness, skipping a few breathing treatments, being exposed to someone else's cold, or just the mysterious physiological happenings within my body that no one fully understands and I don't fully control.

Healthy people have thousands of bacterial species in their lungs. It's a microbial ecosystem that remains healthy because the diversity of species means no individual bacteria can gain too much traction. But cystic fibrosis makes this type of idyllic polyculture impossible, by making me susceptible to virulent pathogens that outcompete all other bacteria and resist eradication by even the most powerful antibiotics.

In my lungs, the healthy bacteria present in a healthy polyculture were long gone. I am stuck with a monoculture perched atop airways that are growing increasingly fragile from the endless assault.

In the years since I found out I had *B. cepacia*, I've actually been relatively lucky. Some people who get *B. cepacia*, especially my strain, quickly get what's called cepacia syndrome, a rapid and progressive pneumonia that's untreatable. It can come on at any time and usually leads to death within a matter of weeks.

I've never had cepacia syndrome, but that March night at UCLA hospital back when I was in high school—when my friends were worrying about spring break and prom—my parents and doctors thought I did. They thought this unimaginable night was the beginning of the end. Asking my body to fight *B. cepacia* in the lungs is one thing—it's almost a fair fight. Asking my body to fight a septic infection spreading throughout my body is a whole different story.

Wednesday, April 25, 2012

I'm finally leaving the hospital tomorrow and I'm so ready to go back to my life. It's hard to adapt psychologically when things change drastically in life but somehow it always happens faster than I expect it to. Being in the hospital is nothing new to me, and being on home IVs for a long time with no help from my parents is something I'm totally used to by now, but I'm not used to feeling sick all the time and having to try to keep up with everyone around me. It's easier if I don't even try to keep up, if I accept my limitations and come to terms with them before going back to campus life and having to realize the hard way that living like everyone else lives doesn't work when I'm sick. When I am sick, though, I appreciate small things so much more, like days when I wake up feeling well, or sunny days, spending time with friends, a long shower, etc. And right when I come off IVs (which probably won't be for a long time so I'm not holding my breath waiting for that day), every single thing I get to do feels like the most amazing experience in the world, and a lot of people don't get the chance to feel such intense gratitude so regularly. For example, each time I finish a months-long course of IVs, the first time I jump in the pool or ocean after I get my PICC line out is like being reborn.

I've been thinking a lot about forgiveness lately and I find myself thinking about Jay, my high school boyfriend. I realize I am angry because there was a lack of closure in our relationship (for me, anyway). The time he was in my life was a bit of a roller coaster—we met at the end of junior year through a mutual friend, and immediately connected more than I had ever connected with a guy before. I've decided I'm going to write this out in excruciating detail here because it's better for me to do that than to write him a letter. For some reason I just need to get it out.

Here goes: Our first week of knowing each other, we talked three to four hours a day nonstop and got to know each other (or so I thought) really quickly. It didn't occur to me that we wouldn't get into a relationship immediately; it felt as inevitable as hitting water after jumping off a diving board. But then, after two weeks he told me that he liked me a lot, but couldn't date me, and wouldn't disclose the reason why. Eventually I learned from our mutual friend that he had originally said that because people always made fun of him for dating girls who had "something wrong" with them (one was depressed and cut herself, one was extremely emotionally needy and unstable), and he had found out I had a serious illness. He didn't want to prove everyone right that he had a pattern of finding girls with problems so he could be the hero who saves them. Because I didn't know the reason at the time, I figured he just wasn't ready to jump into another relationship when he had just broken up with his last girlfriend a few weeks before, and our connection was so strong that we became very good friends. That summer we hung out almost every day when we were both home, and when he was traveling in Europe for a month we kept in close touch. My family thought he was great, and nobody understood his mixed signals—choosing to spend all his time with me in intimate situations, introducing me to his family and inviting me to dinner with his grandparents, and treating me like a girlfriend while telling me that he couldn't date me.

By the end of the summer, there was still a lot of sexual tension, but I was no longer obsessing over why he didn't want to date me. I went to Hawaii with my friends and met other guys, which apparently made Jay extremely jealous because a few weeks after I came back, he asked me to be his girlfriend. We were already hanging out a lot, the only difference was that this established us as exclusive. I was ecstatic in the beginning to be with him, because he made me laugh, I was comfortable with him, and he was perfect on paper (brilliant, tall, athletic runner, musically talented jazz piano player, motivated and disciplined, caring, etc.).

Over time, though, I became less and less attracted to him; his quirks that were initially so endearing became annoying. He wanted to get more serious, and I did not want to let him in, because I knew our relationship had an expiration date and I didn't want to put a boyfriend over my friends in my senior year. As I pulled away, he became clingier, and somehow, I came to dislike him mainly for how much he liked me. The tension erupted on New Year's Eve. Looking back on the situation, most of the fights that we had during our relationship came down to one basic thing: I didn't like him enough and was trying to push him away without even realizing it. He was amazing to me during our relationship (of course I realize that now that I've seen how most guys act on the opposite end of the spectrum) so it seems odd that I'm thinking of him as the person that I need to forgive. The reason I have ill will toward him and want to work on forgiveness is because of how he acted after we broke up; he completely severed all communication with me for so long that by the time we talked again it was like the relationship never happened. I know you can't have your cake and eat it, too, and I was completely in the wrong to think that I could treat him so poorly and then expect him to be able to be friends with me right after. But the things he said the night we broke up ("You're a heartless bitch," and "You're incapable of allowing yourself to feel emotions") really hit a nerve and I wanted to believe that he didn't really think those things.

If we had talked a few days (or even weeks) later, had some closure, and stayed friends (or at least kept in touch occasionally, cordially), I would have been able to believe that those were just meaningless insults thrown around the room in the heat of the breakup. But since he refused to talk to me for so long, I wasn't able to forget what he said about my character, and those things are now nagging shadows that follow me around. I know I'm not a heartless bitch, but the accusations that I refuse to let anyone in, that I turn on anyone that tries to get close to me and pick out their flaws, that I care more about playing (and winning) the game than loving, and that I'm scared shitless what people think about me . . . those have stuck with me to this day.

If I *were* to write him a letter, I would first ask him for forgiveness for the way I treated him, and then I would say that I forgive him for shutting me out of his life and ending our relationship (and a really close friendship) on such a sour note. But I'm actually somewhat thankful that I had to let those accusations marinate and fester within me for so long, because it forced me to really think about what had gone wrong and accept some of the blame. The night we broke up I was convinced that he was a huge asshole, but by this point I realize how distorted that view was; he was just a guy so frustrated and exasperated by my coldness that one day he snapped. If he had been willing to be friends soon after we broke up, I could have continued falsely thinking that I did nothing wrong. So, while it was uncalled for—him being so harsh—I think it has ultimately made me much more self-aware in my relationships since then.

Thursday, May 10, 2012

When I'm on top of my workload and my time management, the vitality and energy of the students at Stanford are amazing. Much of the time I feel so lucky to be at a school where people are so talented across the board, because it exposes me to so many different types of interesting and high-quality incredible people. But the pressure, personally, to live up to that expectation that everyone else also has of what students at Stanford should be capable of accomplishing (and should desire to accomplish) has definitely drained me at times. There have been many times that I wonder if a school that so values accomplishment, busyness, and having secret superpowers that enable you to squeeze forty hours of extracurriculars, classes, and socializing into a twenty-four-hour day is the right place for me. Being at Stanford, while engaging me intellectually and socially and spiritually, has also made me realize that I'm different than many people here (or at least than the stereotype of people here): less focused on accomplishments and the future, more laid-back, and more concerned with whether I'm enjoying myself along the way as I pursue "success." So, when I have a manageable workload and a manageable set of extracurriculars that I enjoy and that provide me with a balanced schedule that leaves me enough time to relax and reboot, I find Stanford to be all the things it's cracked up to be: stimulating, challenging, rewarding, drawing me in to feel connected to the energy and vitality of the people on this campus. But when I take on too much (which I often do because there are so many opportunities that it's hard to say no and hard to realize how much is too much when other people seem to be able to handle so much more than I can), I get drained. I forget what I'm here for. I'm aware now that taking a typical path and losing sight of my health could shave decades off my life. I don't think it's worth sacrificing my present for my future or doing anything that's not fulfilling.

To keep myself from falling into that trap, I need to be aware of how much is too much. Accepting my limitations is probably the biggest step I need to take in ensuring that my mental health is stable so that I can stay connected to others and be a dynamic PHE next year assuming I get chosen. It's a supercompetitive job I'm trying for and the application was INTENSE. But since this is the first time in my life I've really struggled with any significant mental health issue, and my dad's family history of depression is starting to show up in me, I figured it was a good thing to do.

One of the biggest reasons why my depression is happening now is that my typical expectations of what my life should be like (which are based on how my life has been in the past) don't match my reality, which may be my reality for the rest of my life. Things have changed as my disease has worsened and although people always say you can accomplish anything if you set your mind to it, I'd rather not continue chasing dreams that aren't feasible. Psychological adaptation is something I've always been good at and adapting to my new set of limitations (instead of trying to crush them) will allow me to embrace everything that I do currently have instead of being unhappy and trying to gain back the life and health I used to have.

I am choosing to practice the PHE protocols I'm learning about on myself, because I am lacking a healthy balance right now. The first step was realizing I had a problem, and actually, the depression quiz that I took from *The How of Happiness* was my first clue. I was working so hard to suppress so much frustration and fear that I had no idea how beaten down I was. Once I saw that I tested as depressed on the quiz, things started to make more sense—not wanting to go out with friends at night, feeling distant and isolated from people who I used to be close to, having panic attacks, being constantly fatigued, having nightmares, lacking motivation, and feeling apathetic toward things I used to enjoy. I had been attributing those symptoms to just being physically sick, and while I certainly was physically sick, many of those symptoms were caused or exacerbated by depression.

Admitting to myself that I had an emotional problem was one of the hardest things I've ever done; even though I wholeheartedly believe that depression is nothing to be ashamed of and is outside of our control, for some reason I felt like that didn't apply to me. My entire life people have praised me for being resilient and never letting anything get to me, to the point where I thought I could never break down; I felt like if I got upset about my situation people would think I was weak or be annoyed that I was wallowing. Keeping my disappointment and fear in for an entire year took a toll on me and started to manifest itself recently in strange ways that I didn't recognize, like the panic attacks and dreams I've been having. This is something I'm working on, and I firmly believe (as do my family and doctors) that I have situational depression instead of chronic depression, but I started to see a psychiatrist during my last hospitalization and I'm excited to get my happiness level back to normal!

Thursday, May 24, 2012

There are probably a lot of areas in which I'm more silent than I should be. But right now, the most pertinent situation that that applies to is my relationships. I'm not in a formal one, exactly, but I have been seeing Rob for over three months and have never really felt like I've been able to be completely honest or speak my mind. I do feel somewhat "bound by a silence" in the sense that I've told myself multiple times that I'm going to talk to him about one thing or another, and then can't seem to find the words, can't figure out the right moment. Because of this I'm always second-guessing what we are when we're not together, but then when we are together, I feel fine about it and just feel like everything's fine because he treats me really well when we're together.

But then when he's gone I think about things that bother me and don't have the courage to say them to his face. For example, the fact that it's important to me for sex-safety reasons that we be exclusive. When I'm with my friends and talk to them about it, they tell me that of course I need to bring that up and make that clear. But when I'm with him, I just have a feeling that it's something that's mutually understood, and I don't need to say anything.

It feels relevant to what my prof was talking about in class the other day. Someone brought up that guys get insulted if you say something that might insinuate that they could potentially have an STI, and this is so true. Obviously I should have the mentality that a guy that would be insulted by me being concerned about my safety/health isn't worth it. But in practice it just doesn't pan out that way and I'm working on it. We always take precautions by using condoms and are smart/safe, but it's still concerning if you don't know who else the other person is sleeping with. I KNOW I shouldn't be bound by silence and should be able to speak up to clarify that exclusivity is something I expect.

Thursday, May 31, 2012

This quarter continues to be really interesting, and I've learned a lot from it. It seems like serendipitous timing that I am taking this PHE class, that's so focused on psychological health and well-being, at the same time I'm going through so many difficult life situations. It's helped me realize that my happiness was lower than my set point; it functioned as a stress-relieving part of my life; it assigned work that actually improved my mental state by forcing me to reflect on a lot of things I might not have otherwise thought about instead of things that stress me out; it really helped me to maintain perspective and understand that my health is the most important thing right now, and everything else can wait until that improves.

The self-change project I'm doing got interrupted because a lot of it had to do with daily routines, which obviously had to change when I was off campus in the hospital for a long time. But my view that mental and physical health interact powerfully has been confirmed. In the last two weeks I've had such a drastic improvement in my mental and physical health that I feel like I might be finally accomplishing my goal of finding balance and warding off stress. A new antianxiety medication may also be playing a role in that.

I started to feel physically better at the same time I started to finally get caught up with school, and at the same time I also started a new medication. It might be the combination that has me feeling so much happier and more relaxed. But it might also be what I'm learning from the PHE training. Some of the factors were in my control and some were not, but I think that my desire to regain control over my life was instrumental in bringing me back to normal (so it wasn't completely external factors).

I have learned much more about well-being and campus health than I can write here during treatment. One of the most important things is that personal change is a work in progress. Perfection is impossible to achieve but just being aware of wherever we are in terms of well-being at a given moment will make it that much easier to strive to be more self-aware, compassionate toward others and ourselves, and confident/secure. I've also come to believe that happiness comes naturally to some and for others it takes effort; and maybe for some that it comes naturally for, when external circumstances become more challenging, it stops coming naturally. There's a whole spectrum of how people respond to the challenges and changes of daily living and learning how to allow the waves of change to roll over you while maintaining emotional stability is extremely important.

This is something that I hope to be able to help my freshmen with next year, since freshman year is a time so rife with enormous life changes that can be hard to adjust to. Being at an age where we're grappling with our identities and figuring out exactly who we are, at the same time we leave home and suddenly have to grow up and deal with academic and social (and maybe also financial, medical, sexual, etc.) stresses, means that a lot of issues will come up for the first time ever. It seems the ultimate goal of the job is to help them make their way through their first year of Stanford with as little stress and turmoil as possible.

Tuesday, June 26, 2012

Sophomore year ended quickly (as every year seems to do) and now I'm here in Santa Barbara! Blue Horizons is actually a perfect summer program for me even though it wasn't my first choice. I had planned to work in marine biology but now realize that the field of conservation is in desperate need of a makeover, and it's work I can do. It needs writers, photographers, and filmmakers to make conservation appealing and sexy to a public that currently doesn't understand why they should care about the bleaching of coral reefs or the increases in dead zones. It's sort of funny. My mom is a communications professional and has always tried to get me to go into PR, but I was always sooo against it. Now I see that communication and messaging are two of the most important, but sadly often overlooked, components of the environmental movement. So far the program is amazing—so much information has been squashed into the first three days of the program. And now we have so much to do, starting with a core idea and story line that we can weave through a fifteen-minute film!

Tuesday, July 3, 2012

Turns out Nate (one of the guys I'm doing my project with) is not only cute, but he's really cool, he's from LA and went to Loyola actually, and he just graduated SB. Today I went with Nate and his friend Blake to the beach, and we jumped in the ocean. It was so amazing to be back in the water—it's been so long. It reminded me of how therapeutic the ocean is. But this entry is going to be about Nate. He's pretty hilarious and easy to talk to. One night at Blake's house (the other guy in the group), some of their friends were smoking mugwort (a plant people collect at Coal Oil Point, part of the University of California's Natural Reserve System, that Native Americans use to smoke for "respiratory health" and that gives you really vivid dreams). It's bad when people smoke around me, but I didn't want to make a scene. It's been a busy, wild week with program stuff in the day and lots of hanging out. By the end of the fifth or sixth night, I decided I definitely like Nate because he makes me laugh a lot.

Yesterday, Mom and Pidge came into town, and it was really nice.

They brought me so much food, so now I'm eating like my normal self again, which is great after spending multiple days just eating restaurant food or the only thing we had in our home—peanut butter and carrots. Today, Pidge had to work so my mom and I went to a yoga class. I've realized that when I do yoga, I feel so much better physically in ways that are hard to describe. . . . I stand up straighter, I feel limber and agile and more graceful and coordinated and balanced, I'm more relaxed, I feel strong, my core is strong, etc. I wish I could do it three to four times a week, but it's hard because yoga is expensive, it's not like running where you just put on your shoes and go anywhere anytime. I've been thinking that I would love to devote six months of my life to studying yoga and then become an instructor. It would be so awesome to have a part-time environmental job and a part-time job as a yoga instructor, because then I could get my fill of intellectual, changing-the-world kind of work, and also do work that would allow me to be physical and stay in shape and maintain a practice.

Sunday, July 8, 2012

UGH . . . I coughed up a little blood last night and had to go to the ER—to a random hospital where no one knew me. The doctor on call asked a few more perfunctory questions about my medical history, took notes as I talked . . . but he didn't really engage. It's shocking to me—when a doctor doesn't seem to care. I'm sure he does. Otherwise, why would he be a doctor? But he never looked at me. Spent the entire time typing in his computer. He said the amount wasn't enough to admit me. Sooo grateful—it would have been AWFUL to be stuck in a hospital where I don't know anyone.

Tuesday, July 10, 2012

I'm thinking a lot about Nate . . . wondering if he thinks of me as his girlfriend or just a hookup for the summer. I have a feeling it's more the former than the latter, but I just don't want to assume anything and then be sad if that's not the case. I'm just gonna go with the flow, not try to push anything forward but just keep hanging out with him when I can and feel it out.

Thursday, July 12, 2012

Finally. The other night Nate and I went in my room to "cuddle." This happened because when we were out on the porch talking about how tired we were I was like, "I just want to get in my bed and cuddle," and Nate was like, "I'll cuddle with you, I love cuddling," and then I knew he was interested. Throughout the night I kind of thought I had been wrong, and he wasn't . . . to be continued later, my mom just got here to bring up more meds.

Continuing . . . so, I thought I had been wrong and started to second-guess whether he liked me, but then he would do things that were sweet and made me think he did like me again. We lay in my bed cuddling and talking for a really long time before he eventually kissed me. One thing he brought up was, "Do you think it's weird that we hang out like this?" (Or maybe it was, "Do you think the group will think it's weird?") and we talked about how it was unprofessional but not bad. The bottom line that I took from that little conversation was that it's okay for us to hang out like this and hook up as long as we don't have some awkward falling-out or bad situation before the film gets done. About the "cuddling." He was a really good kisser, and his body just feels right with mine because he's the right height and everything. We were also in my bed; I was comfortable with the situation. People often assume that I'm an introvert or opposed to partying and drinking—that I don't drink much and never have and am awkward at parties or something like that. I can't explain to them what's really going on . . . that my medications interact with alcohol and make me feel exhausted and nauseous after one or two drinks. That one night of partying can lead to seven weeks of IVs if I'm already run-down. That this lifestyle is what led to my 30 percent decline in lung function over two years. That I could be looking at a lung transplant and possible death within five years if I continue to make those kinds of choices. They have no way of comprehending that, and it's not possible for me to explain it without sounding super dramatic and making people uncomfortable. If anyone asked me privately why I don't like to drink or party anymore, I would tell them. But when it's 11:30 at night and everyone's drunk and rolling out, I just say I'm tired and have to get up early.

Wednesday, September 12, 2012

Back at school. So happy to be here but I need to recap the rest of the summer since I got so busy and didn't write enough:

Nate and I ended up deciding to be exclusive, we finished the film (*Silver Bullet*, about whale strikes). Funny side note: I was interviewed by the local paper in SB and they quoted me in print saying, "I learned more from this summer program than I did in my two years at Stanford." Taken out of context it sounded really bad and isn't how I really feel. What I meant was that Blue Horizons is an incredible program and I learned A LOT.

I also need to recap what happened when I got back to Stanford. The night before I was supposed to start my classes, I was still on IVs from the hospitalization that started when I got back from Santa Barbara. The program was really fun, but I was sooo run-down at the end from all the late nights. Anyway, I had gotten all ready for the first day of school—written down all the rooms and buildings of my classes, gathered my notebooks and pens and binders in my book bag, even laid out my clothes so I wouldn't be late for my early-morning econ class. But at 1:00 a.m., I woke up from a deep sleep to cough and stained my new white comforter with blood. Each breath brought more blood, so I grabbed the roll of paper towels I always keep at the bedside and rolled onto the floor. My lungs bled for twenty minutes, and I lay there on the floor alone, collecting the bloodied paper towels so I could measure the quantity for the doctors. I called my parents in LA and asked if they could come up. I knew it was bad. And then I called 911 for an ambulance. It took twenty minutes to arrive because Stanford's ambulances were previously engaged transporting drunk students to the emergency room. My doctor was livid and told me to raise hell with the police department for being so slow in a life-threatening situation. The doctor said because of my recurring problem with hemoptysis, I should always live near a hospital that has a specialty called interventional radiology because that's the only way to treat the problem. Left untreated, it could be deadly.

How often do we experience pivotal moments that we know could change our future? How many of us experience those moments almost on a monthly basis? Like the boy who cried wolf, my lungs bleed so often I almost forget how eerie, how dangerous, how unnatural it is to cough blood. Eventually I have had no choice but to get used to it. I try to find the humor in it. I get some good stories out of it. It's why Stanford Hospital is my second home.

Monday, October 15, 2012 (20 years old)

Forgot to write that I got hired to be a PHE!!! Turns out it's kind of like being an RA (resident adviser) but with a health focus. I'm the point person for mental health, sexual assault, eating disorders, relationship issues—any kind of adjustment needs the freshmen have. Stanford is not a dry school, so they don't make me police drinking unless it's causing a problem. I have a friend who is an RA at a dry college, and she has to be a narc—to give citations to people who are drinking. That is sooo not my role at all. I'm supposed to convey to the freshmen, "I'm your friend, come talk to me." It's really cool but a disturbing thing just happened. One of the freshmen that routinely drinks a lot had been at a frat party and came back even more drunk than usual. I assumed he was fine because he said he only barfed once, but a few of us went to check on him. He was sprawled on his futon retching. He started having a panic attack and hyperventilating. He kept repeating something about how he can't join a frat and how he needed us to prevent him from going to the next rush event tomorrow. It was scary to see someone so drunk.

It's now 3:00 a.m., my stomach hurts, almost everything I ate today was wrong and I should have been asleep hours ago. But at least we helped someone in trouble.

Monday, November 12, 2012

Nate came for the weekend. I just kept thinking I'm so lucky to be with him and how could I ever worry about anything when life can be this good. For once nothing in my body hurt or felt bad. We went out for a nice dinner and had the kind of real date that people dream about but rarely experience. When we got home, we had intense, beautiful, mind-blowing sex. It surprises me sometimes how amazing it can be and how good and in love I feel afterward. Nate told me his life is so much better with me in it and he couldn't imagine not being with me. It made me start thinking about how any person that's going to be with me for a long time is going to have to sacrifice "living" in a sense. And I kept thinking about that more and more, and he could tell something was wrong, so finally I told him, "I feel like being with me ultimately would prevent the other person from really being able to live," and I started to cry, because what if he doesn't actually know what he's getting into, or what if he thinks he does. That's likely what happened with my Hawaii swim coach. He was happily married and then his wife got cancer. He loved her so much and told her he would stay with her until the very end but when she got really sick and mean, and he couldn't do anything to help her, he left her. He's got a new woman now and it's clear his life is so much better.

Nate told me he'd thought about it a lot and he knows what could happen and how much things could change, and he has no idea how long I'll live or how hard things will be for me, but he always wants to be there. It was the first time we ever really talked about the future and what that might look like. It got me thinking about lung transplant and marriage and babies and whether I could see all of that happening with him. I felt in that moment—talking about the future—that I may just be playing make-believe, playing in college fantasy land, and pretending that my life is like everyone else's, entertaining the silly notions that I'll be able to work and live wherever I want, and actually have a career, and that anything actually matters even though everything I try to do gets in the way of my health.

I just kind of kept pushing Nate. "Can you really see yourself with me when I'm so sick that I can't go on hikes with you or go swimming or work or do anything besides treatment, even if you have to clean and cook and do everything for me?" and he just kept saying, "Yes, yes, yes." It was such an intense conversation, we were both crying and just cuddling and talking, and I told him I was really grateful to him for being in my life and being so caring and making me learn how to open up to someone and trust someone and forcing me to think about the possibility that something might actually last—instead of the person just abandoning me.

Thursday, December 6, 2012

This week has been rough. Earlier tonight, I got into bed and literally could not breathe for an hour because I had such sharp pains stabbing me in the back and my lower right lung. I didn't really think it was a chest pain from the lungs, I figured I pulled a muscle from coughing because it just happened spontaneously after treatment, but I was lying there wincing, unable to focus on anything else but the pain, and unable to breathe deeply so I was basically panting, and no position made it better.

I'm writing this in the emergency room. After hours of agony, I decided it was time to come in. Turns out my imagined pulled muscle wasn't a pulled muscle. It was another pulmonary embolism. The first one was really scary because I always thought you die from it. Funny how it didn't even occur to me that it was another blood clot stuck in my lungs that could break off and kill me. In retrospect the whole situation seems like a sick joke: "Hey, instead of a pulled muscle let's add another life-threatening condition to your bag of goodies, drug you up with some expensive and risky medications that may make you cough up tons of blood and require you to change your entire lifestyle and sports plans and make you come in every two days for blood tests. . . . Okay, just kidding, you have it but let's ignore it!! Now go about your merry way and never bring this up again."

Wednesday, December 12, 2012

Still in the hospital, bored beyond belief. I've finished all my shows and I'm too tired to read. Looking at photos and wishing I had taken the time to write more in this journal because details about so many things are starting to blur in my memory. I wish I had captured overall feelings and important memories so that I won't forget when I'm older. I want to be able to look at my whole life on paper and remember it. There's a photo of my brother and me taken at his bar mitzvah that makes me wish I'd written more about Micah, so I'm going to do it now.

Lots of my friends wanted fancy parties for their bat mitzvahs but Micah said he only wanted three things: the money my mom would spend on invitations to go to ocelot preservation, sports, and a moon bounce at the party—no dancing. And he didn't want my mom to cry or get (his words) "mushy" during the ceremony. He was always into animals as a kid. In second grade, he wrote a letter to the president of China, urging him to take steps to save the giant panda from extinction. And it was wild because a big magazine in China printed the letter and sent him a copy in Chinese—with the only English word in the piece being *Micah*. He used to collect newspapers and blankets for animal shelters and sell doughnuts to raise money for the Long Beach aquarium and the LA Zoo, giving them all of the proceeds, not just the profits. He used his allowance to buy a python, a scorpion, and a praying mantis for science lab at school. And when a hummingbird got trapped in our entryway at home and died, he wanted to put it in the freezer and bring it to school the next day. He's always been obsessed with French fries, his favorite book is *The Essential Calvin and Hobbes,* and his happy place is Disneyland. No roller coaster has ever been too big or too scary for him. The ONLY thing that's ever scared him was seeing a vegetable on his plate (caveat: *I'm talking about when he was seven!*) and the look on my mom's face that always said, "Just one bite." One of the best stories my dad tells about Micah is from when he was three years old. My dad took him to a freshman calculus class at UCLA. They sat in the back of the lecture hall with Micah sitting quietly for forty-five minutes, while the professor solved a complicated problem, filling blackboard panel after blackboard panel with equations. When he reached his conclusion, he wrote the answer on the board and put his chalk down with great pride. The entire class burst out into spontaneous applause, and when it died down, Micah said in a loud voice, "Do it again!"

Friday, December 28, 2012

I've been out of the hospital for five days and I can't get my brain to focus, and everything feels far away. I'll be talking and then lose my train of thought mid-sentence. I didn't get any sleep in the hospital because they kept waking me up every six hours to take my blood for six days straight. And the IV kept beeping when it needed to be changed. And the nurse kept coming in and out and then random people came in for useless purposes like taking my trash before 7:00 in the morning when they had kept me up until well after midnight doing treatment. All this upset me, but it made my mom wild. She would block the door and tell them not to wake me. She started calling herself the bad cop.

Monday, January 14, 2013

Need to write about Christmas break. Worrying that my friends didn't feel neglected because of my relationship with Nate, and worrying that Nate didn't feel like he was secondary to my friends, took a really big toll on me.

When we're together it's amazing but the truth is I haven't been able to find that proper balance yet, and maybe I never will. If I am in a long-distance relationship and only see Nate once a month, then when I do get to spend time with him of course he's gonna want to spend it alone with me. I totally understand why he would be frustrated with my mom scheduling a million dinners and plans for us, and me having to do three treatments a day and sleep so much, and me wanting to spend so much time with so many friends. He told me on Friday, when we were hanging out alone at his house, that he was stressed out by being around so many people for so long. Gahhhh! I wish spending time with my friends and my boyfriend could just be simple. Instead, it's so friggin' complicated, it gives me anxiety.

Long-distance is hard and that's why I thought I would never do it, and there have been times that I've definitely questioned whether

120

it's worth it. I sort of had an emotional breakdown one night, I think it might've been the Thursday night before I went back to school, when I was waiting for Nate to come back and I was eating and talking with my mom. She started asking me how I felt emotionally and whether I was doing better, and I kind of broke down and started crying and told her how stressed out I was, about volleyball, about the coming winter quarter, about not wanting to go back but not wanting to stay home, about my friends, about Nate, about everything. She was sad that I was so sad, but she jumped into gear and started helping me think about internships, to try to start tackling one of the problems. While I was in her office, crying and drinking tea and searching for internships, Nate showed up and we lay down and I told him some of the things I was really stressed about. It was calming and helpful.

Tuesday, January 15, 2013

Just got home from volleyball, and I can tell that I'm happier overall because I enjoy going to practice and seeing everyone, whereas before, I was just depressed to be there, dreaded going, thought I sucked, had no energy, and didn't really talk to anyone. It's going to be a really hard decision whether or not to quit, and I thought this weekend would be the deciding factor (first tournament in San Jose), but because I haven't had hypertonic saline to help thin my mucus for A WEEK NOW, I kind of feel crappy. I couldn't stop coughing the entire practice, like every other breath was a cough, and I was definitely more short of breath today at practice and yesterday in yoga. I went to Pilates with Marian (my teacher) this weekend. It was the first time I'd done it since the spring, and I honestly could not believe how hard it was. My breathing was super fast the whole time, I was sweating, my muscles were burning so intensely, and I couldn't even do all of what he told me to do properly. I honestly think that I'm in worse shape than I was in spring quarter when I was working with him, at least in terms of core, arms, and leg strength.

That's the one thing I thought I would be much better in because of doing yoga so much all summer, but the two to three weeks I took off makes me feel like I essentially lost everything. Kind of a bummer to feel like I have to start from ground zero again. And my lack of strength affects me a lot in volleyball, because I think I could always get by with difficulty breathing because my strong muscles would compensate. But now my breathing is the worst ever because my lung function is the worst ever, AND my muscles are so weak that I just feel incompetent. The wild thing is I still look strong despite being so weak, which is great that I look healthy but also kind of sucks because it means the extent of my bad health is completely hidden and people still expect sooo much of me.

Tuesday, January 22, 2013

It's now Tuesday, so I've been sick for a week. The last time I wrote was a week ago, when I was starting to feel really bad from my weeklong hiatus from hypertonic saline. Wednesday night (last week) I had to go to the ER, even though I went to clinic earlier in the day and they said nothing was wrong because my lung function was the same, 53 percent. Right after I left clinic, when I went to the pharmacy to try to get hypertonic saline (and failed), I got stabbing chest pain, had to go home and sleep, and woke up with fevers and chest pain. I went to the ER that night, and got released at around 1:00 a.m., but my mom flew in because she was already supposed to be coming for the San Jose tournament, so I just asked her to come early. They didn't really figure out what was wrong with me, but the whole time I was in there my chest hurt, I felt sick and tired, and I was sick to my stomach (nausea and reflux even though I hadn't really eaten). I went home that morning and all day Thursday just lounged around, slept until around 2:00 p.m. and when I got up, I didn't feel any better.

Friday I woke up assuming I'd be better, so I went to get a massage because I had pulled a muscle in my neck on Tuesday at volleyball, but after the massage I took my temp and it was 102.6, so I had to go back to the ER. Actually, I tried to go be seen at the clinic, but they wouldn't see me, which exposed some operational issues with the clinic that are really upsetting. The coordinator was extremely rude about the whole situation and showed no compassion whatsoever for the fact that I felt terribly sick, was in pain, and had a high fever. She told me to go to the ER; they admitted me and started me on IV antibiotics and then they did an abdominal X-ray in addition to the chest one, and discovered I was completely backed up with DIOS (distal intestinal obstruction syndrome). It was unfortunate, but I knew that they would say that, because I could feel it. I had just thought I could treat it myself at home by eating less for a few days and taking more laxatives, but it did not work at all.

They admitted me into the B1 unit, which is for GI stuff, instead of the usual C3, where pulmonary patients go, and it was just one of those totally embarrassing stays where everyone is talking about your shit (literally) the entire time. It's dehumanizing. I tried taking Maxitrate on Friday night plus two doses of Glycolax, and that made me feel really sick and nauseous all night but worked a bit in the morning. Then the NP Laura wanted to try a CF enema, so I did that; it was an extremely amazing coincidence that my nurse that day happened to be Heather, who I love and who is the one who did my cleanout the last time I had to do it.

Heather is so sweet and gentle but it was really painful and actually didn't do anything at all. My X-ray showed that the problem was 40 percent fixed but I still had 60 percent more to go, so I drank over a gallon of Golytely (Such a feat! That drink is disgusting, and the quantity is unfathomable) throughout the rest of the day (Saturday), and it worked the rest of that day and night. By morning, I took another X-ray, and they said I was fine, so they discharged me! They say they fixed the DIOS, but since I got discharged, I've still been feeling overly full, nauseous, like I can't eat normally. It's getting a little bit better now, but my GI problems are really interfering with my life, and nothing is happening quickly enough! I've been dealing with these problems for years, so it's hard when people just ignore them and try the same old approaches to fixing it (adding more laxatives to the bowel regimen) instead of realizing that something else is wrong (like Dr. Nguyen is now doing). I started two new drugs that Dr. Nguyen prescribed; one is gabapentin, which is apparently a nerve drug that's supposed to relax the nerves in my stomach, so I don't feel full after one bite. The other is misoprostol, which is normally used to induce labor or cause abortion, but I'm using it because it moves things through the intestines. Both seem like really powerful drugs, and it appears that I'm using both of them for off-label reasons, so they make me nervous, but I'm so desperate I'm willing to try anything.

Dr. Nguyen is not hopeful that these are going to fully solve my issues. She said they should help with my gastroparesis (partial paralysis of the stomach) and with intestinal motility, but they're not going to deal with my weak sphincter and reflux issue, which she thinks is the biggest issue because it could be harming my lungs. I think it's definitely harming my lungs; if not directly causing me to aspirate, it definitely prevents me from doing treatments and exercising sometimes. She has one more medication that she will try for me if these ones don't help significantly, I don't remember what it is or what it does. But she thinks I will definitely need to have a fundoplication surgery, which is where they tie part of the stomach around the esophageal sphincter (I think), basically closing it so that no reflux can go up. The downside is that it prevents you from being able to throw up or burp, so if you have gas it has to pass the other way, and if you need to throw up, you're screwed. And the results are irreversible, and last about ten years, so it's a huge long-term issue if I don't like the results. But it would be nice to not feel like I'm throwing up my food after every meal; I just worry that I'll be bloated all the time.

Anyway, I got discharged from the hospital on Sunday and came back to chill at Lissa's and went for a walk with Dr. Weill's dog with Sarah and Lissa, which was nice. But I was wiped out when I got back and checked my temp again and had a fever of 102.6 again. But after taking Advil the fever went away and I began to feel a little better, so I stopped by the volleyball party at French House. It was nice to chill with everyone for an hour or so, and I didn't drink at all, I just got to hang out. I even had fun with the drinking games because I asked a guy beforehand if he'd drink for me and then stood next to him. (Once was Alec, once was José.)

Thursday, January 24, 2013

I went to practice tonight just to watch, I wasn't feeling up to playing yet. But Steve was really nice, he asked how I was feeling, and we talked about what he does at the hospital, and he told me he wants to go back to school to be a physician's assistant because his research job is boring and unfulfilling.

I feel bad because I didn't really talk to Nate the entire time I was sick. We Skyped on Sunday night (maybe it was Monday?) for about an hour, which was good, but before that I hadn't talked to him (other than texting) in over a week. He was pretty understanding, though. I was upset last Wednesday because I was just so pissed in general about what was going on with the clinic and how I felt and the barriers to getting saline, and then when I told him how upset I was he didn't really have a reaction or express sympathy or ask what was going on. I got extremely mad and when I was at the pharmacy, I just had an emotional breakdown because I was so angry, and I started crying when I was finishing up with them, so I stormed out and left to walk back to my car. Because of all the construction redirecting people and getting rid of the shortcuts, I had to go all the way around and take what felt like a twenty-minute walk back to my car, but before I did that I just sat down on the floor in a secluded area and blasted music and bawled. It was really a low point. But I felt much better after crying so hard for such a long time, and then I took the long walk back to my car, in beautiful weather, and then I sat in the sun and waited for the car from valet, so by the time I got in the car to go home I had calmed down a bit. Going to bed now. So behind on homework, but I can't complain because I'm only in two classes now! My workload won't be reflected by my units, though, because I'll be doing seven hours a week for Green Grid Radio. It's a lot of work but it's so cool to be part of an environmental storytelling radio show and podcast.

Wednesday, January 30, 2013

Things have actually been going really well the past week. I think the two new medications I'm on (gabapentin and misoprostol) have made a small difference in how I feel with regards to GI, and maybe also the fact that I'm being very conscious of how much I eat, what I eat, and how fast I eat it. I'm eating slower, trying to do smaller quantities more often, and I'm eating meat now. That is a HUGE development for me, a huge sacrifice, and a really significant sign that I became absolutely desperate. For me to have to be in the hospital for three days and feel sick for a week potentially all due to an intestinal blockage was just too much for me to handle. I've gotten much more used to the procedure you have to go through when that happens, the embarrassment, the discomfort, etc., but I just can't get used to the idea that this will keep happening forever and ever and there's nothing I can do about it. It just seems so silly, so preventable, it's something people literally laugh about on a daily basis (constipation), I just cannot and will not accept that it's something I'm condemned to for the rest of my life. Also I think that the severity of the issue is incomprehensible to me, because I have no idea what "normal" is supposed to feel like; I can be feeling totally fine, or just a little bit in need of going to the bathroom, and then get an X-ray and find out that I have a severe blockage. And of course—it affects me in every way, because when your body isn't excreting toxins, they build up, they make you tired, they steal energy away from other functions, it makes you feel physically sick (full and nauseous and bloated), it means I'm not absorbing nutrients, which further saps energy, it makes it hard to exercise, it causes reflux, which also affects the lungs, and the list just goes on and on and on. I really really think that one of the main reasons my lung function has declined so much in the last few years is because of all these GI issues, and this hospitalization was just the straw that broke the camel's back. It's what made me say, "Enough is enough; I'm sick of dealing with this!" So I began to consider the idea that my vegetarianism, which I started in high school for a variety of reasons, could have been a culprit in worsening GI issues and overall health, and the logic makes sense:

When you are a vegetarian, you eat a lot of high-fiber beans, legumes, vegetables, etc., or high-fat things like cheese and hummus. It's hard to get enough protein, so you have to eat more higher-fiber foods in order to get the protein necessary to feel full and have energy.

I don't digest things like beans and whole wheat products and vegetables very well at all, so I can't tolerate large quantities of them. Eating them for every meal, every day, would probably cause me to get backed up, because I can't break down that fiber, so everything gets stuck. And anything that just stays in the stomach doesn't get digested so I don't get any nutritional benefit from it. Nutritional deficiencies set in (like Coenzyme Q10, iron, calcium, etc.).

I'd get backed up, and then in addition to not getting nutrients from what was stuck, I wouldn't get any nutrients from food that I would continue to eat and not absorb, which always leaves you feeling hungrier because vegetarian food doesn't fill you up as much.

All of these issues would lead to me having worse energy (because of malnutrition, but also because of the GI symptoms, and the negative impact of all of it on my lungs), feeling hungrier all the time but at the same time always feeling like my belly is full/distended. To make things worse, all of this would make it harder to exercise, because you can't work out when you have all those GI symptoms and constantly feel full, and when you have no energy and no ability to build muscle or endurance; AND it would make it harder to do treatment (and sleep) because of the symptoms.

Sooo, eating meat solves the problems in a few ways (or at least helps a bit):

> I can eat smaller quantities to get the same amount of protein.

> I can eat a low-fiber diet without resorting to eating a diet of solely refined carbs.

> I can still enjoy vegetarian foods, but in smaller quantities.

> I won't get backed up as much because I can eat less quantity of lower-fiber foods.

> I will absorb more of the nutrients I eat if I'm not getting backed up.

I will have more energy because I'm being nourished, avoiding blockages, and reducing GI symptoms that interfere with my health.

Thursday, January 31, 2013

I haven't talked to Nate now in about a week, so overall in the past three weeks we've Skyped twice (if that). It does feel really weird . . . but our schedules have just been completely opposite for the past week. He's been working every single day, and he's at work by 7:00 a.m. every morning, and in bed by like 9:00 or 10:00 p.m., and I can never talk until the afternoon (when he's at work) or later at night (when he's asleep). The only good thing about it is that this time it's not me that's preventing us from talking, so I don't feel guilty about it. And I'm not worried about not talking to him for a few days, I know nothing will change, I just don't like it when I'm the one causing it because other people can get upset. He never seems to get upset, but I don't want him to start getting upset if I don't make enough time for him. I know I will talk to him tomorrow probably, and we will catch up. I do miss him a lot.

Friday, February 1, 2013

So now I've been eating meat for about a week, and I think I can already tell the difference. First of all, it's just easier to be able to eat healthy things, because if I'm eating out or on the go, I don't have to just pick the one vegetarian option they have, which is good because often those options are cheesy, high in fiber, or just not very filling and protein-rich. Second, I actually can eat less and still feel full. Today I ate:

—Breakfast: Luna power bar, dried cherries.
—Snack: Greek yogurt with granola and fruit and coffee.
—Lunch: beets, tofu, jasmine rice, some other stuff I threw on there, piece of toast with a little butter, a cookie with a little peanut butter.

—Dinner: PB&J on gluten-free bread; watermelon; two pieces of chicken; two chocolate-covered marshmallows.

—Post-volleyball snack: chicken soup; Brie and crackers; piece of dark chocolate with three dried apricots.

Anyway, I didn't feel perfect today with my stomach; I think I ate dinner too close to volleyball (I ate at 6:00; usually I eat just after 5:00 on days with volleyball), so I was having some reflux and felt too full, but overall it wasn't too bad.

AND I had sooo much more energy at volleyball. I felt like a different person. It's going to take me a while to get back into the groove of playing middle, but I'm finally able to hit the ball and actually put some power behind it, run across the court to shag a ball without feeling faint and feeling my entire body burn, do the blocking warm-up without needing to pass out after. We even scrimmaged for an hour of practice, and I did fine! On longer rallies I was really exhausted, and the pace was a little slower than it often is when we scrimmage, but still, I usually can barely last five minutes in a scrimmage. So I was really happy, and I do think it's diet related. Plus all the other factors of getting enough sleep, being happier, doing three treatments a day, etc.

Tuesday, February 12, 2013

Today I was really happy! When I woke up at 9:00 I was still exhausted, so I decided to go back to sleep until 11:00 and skip my 11:00 class (World Food Econ). I woke up, got ready and did treatment in a leisurely fashion, got some work done that I've been putting off, and then met Sabrina at Tri Delta for lunch. It was beautiful out, and my stomach felt better than it has in like a week. We sat outside and ate good food in the sunshine and caught up. Then I went for a walk with Nicole because she was at Tri Delta and asked if I would want to, so we went into the faculty housing community area and walked for like a half hour. It is such a cute area, so woodsy and it seems like it would be an amazing place to grow up.

It's right here on Stanford's campus and I've never even really known about it! Then I went to Dr. Nguyen, and got some updates about my GI care, and finally feel hopeful for the first time in years. The gabapentin and misoprostol are helping but things aren't perfect, so the next step is we're going to try Botox on the stomach to keep the valve open so the contents of my stomach will empty faster. She thinks this will help my reflux, and she thinks my reflux is tied to my coughing and worsening lungs. Which I never really thought could be possible, but now I do; she said that in the results of my pH probe test, every time I clicked the button for a cough, I was having reflux. And tonight, at practice I felt like I was having reflux and I could NOT stop coughing. I'm excited for the results of the Botox. If that doesn't work, I think there's another medication she will try, and if that doesn't work, I will probably have to do the fundoplication surgery, but at this point I want to get better. And I also have hope for the first time in years that not only will I feel better in GI and have more energy, but that my lung function could maybe go up, too. I had completely given up hope on that and was just hoping to keep it stable at 50 percent without it continuing to drop further and fast. Things are looking up!

Sunday, February 17, 2013

Volleyball . . . or just team sports in general . . . brings you back to the basics. You are with people; you want to win. It's a ritual we're all so familiar with, it means something so different yet so similar to all of us, the whole thing, the waking up early, the long drives, the girls piled into one car blasting music, the random hotel rooms in random towns, the big gyms filled with players from all over, the refs, the same old warm-up, the pregame jitters, the highs and lows of a match, the sheer ecstasy of an amazing win, the sideline cheering, the shit-talking, the parents bringing snacks, the putting off your homework and focusing purely on one thing, the long days, the team dinners, the happy fatigue, and the long drive home. All of these things reminded me of my entire adolescence, with water polo tournaments and swim meets and obviously volleyball tournaments and matches. All the sports are different, the details of the ritual vary, but the essence, the feeling, the camaraderie, are the same and the memories blend together. When I look back at these times, I don't remember the nausea I'd feel from waking up so early, or the times when I didn't play, or when we lost, or when a coach yelled at me, or when my back hurt; I remember everything I just described, all with fondness. So while some of the things can feel mundane at times (like the long drive to the UC Davis tournament when I was tired and fighting with my mom on Friday night, the nausea of Saturday night after our dinner at the Spaghetti Factory, etc.), the weekend kind of oddly made me feel alive again and jolted me out of this insane schedule of constant busyness, allowed me to focus on one something and zone out the endless mind clutter, and to feel connected to the team in a real way for the first time in a long time.

Tuesday, February 19, 2013
I meant to do this on Valentine's Day, but I didn't, so I'm doing it now. It's a letter of gratitude/appreciation/respect to myself.

Dear Self,

I love you. Most of the time. I should love you (me) all the time, but I get distracted by all the negative things I think about myself. You're amazingly capable and have overcome incredibly challenging circumstances, managing to have friends and be kind and care about others and work hard in spite of everything. Obviously there are times when you dwell on reasons why you're unlucky (having CF, resistant bacteria, finding it hard to breathe, feeling tired all the time, stomach issues all the time, having to be dependent on parents, not being able to travel really, etc.), but in each of these categories you've managed to figure out how to live well in spite of these inconveniences.

Now, things I want/need to work on:

— Following through on commitments, not
  overcommitting.
— Making a habit of calling friends to say hi, even if only
  quickly.
— Scheduling treatments in advance, and actually doing
  them.
— Not obsessing about my weight/figure.
— Finding time for myself . . . to do yoga, read, watch a
  TV episode, go to the gym, go for a walk/hike/swim.
— Finding the joy/gratitude in every day, even if it's
  mundane, even if I'm tired.
— Not eating such huge meals, so I can feel better.

    Love, Mal

Monday, March 11, 2013

So my busiest week ever at Stanford took its toll, and I've been an inpatient in the hospital since Friday (it's now Monday). Last week was a whirlwind . . . when I look back at my calendar there are no spaces between the numerous events that filled my entire days. I was up until around 2:00 or later every single night, working or being at meetings for the econ group project. Finally, on Wednesday night last week I decided not to go to my meeting for econ (I had already gone to my STS class, an interview with Eli Zigas, a PHE meeting, staff interviews, and Green Grid Radio meeting, so I was just done for the day). I went home and went to bed early, and slept in (ish) but had to go to an econ meeting the next morning, then prepare for my interviews, then go to my live show that was airing the Garry George interview (he's a bigwig at Audubon) and Chase Mendenhall (ecologist and evolutionary biologist from Stanford) was coming as a panelist, then I had to go to volleyball, then to an econ meeting right after. This particular econ meeting, being the night before our presentation was happening and paper was due, went until 5:00 in the morning. We were at Old Union until 2:00, at which point the boys left because they basically had done the entire project for us the whole quarter. The four girls kept going but proceeded to work really slowly and be pretty unproductive (pretty much me and Cassie doing work while the other two tried to help, but they couldn't because the work was really a one-person job). Finally I got home at 5:00, went to bed and woke up at 6:30 to do treatment before our presentation at 8:15. I felt like a dead person when I woke up, and during the presentation it was just so hard to stand up. But the presentation went fine, everyone did their parts and it looked very professional (thanks to the boys and Cassie and Katya). When Roz and Wally asked us questions after, I was able to step in and answer some of them.

Tuesday, March 12, 2013

Continuing what I didn't finish last time. After Pilates on Friday, I went back to do TOBI. I don't know how I had any energy to do anything, but I did it. Next a stop at Philz, which felt much deserved, then I went to lunch at French House with Sabrina and Adrian, which was amazing. It was a really gorgeous day, and after my Philz I finally felt less like a zombie, and we had a good lunch out on the porch in the sunshine. We laughed a lot and caught up. Then I went to the hospital for clinic, and lung function was 42 percent at the highest (the other two were 40 and 42). It definitely rattled me a little how low it was. I felt so helpless this whole quarter; my life had been out of control and had taken me to this place of such extreme busyness and insanity, and in the midst of people who didn't know my situation who were depending on me to pull through and not be flaky. It made me feel like I HAD to do a bunch things that were important for school so focusing on my health wasn't an option. Ironically, though, with a lung function at 42 percent I was still higher functioning than when it was 55 percent last quarter; I had energy (other than the nights when I didn't sleep at all), I played volleyball and was doing relatively decent, I was getting work done, going to all my meetings, etc. I thought my lung function would probably be affected but I wasn't entirely sure; part of me thought it might even be better. I think what I tend to do is just mentally prepare myself for whatever the results are going to be, so I play out a scenario in my head of it being better, it being the same, or it being worse. This time was definitely worse. Kelly, the NP, came in fairly certain I was getting admitted. Dr. Mohabir, the head of the adult center at Stanford, was, too, although he almost let me wait two days to come in so I could play in league championships, but then thought the better of it because my lung function was so down.

It's just wild to me to think how freshman year my lung function was like 70 or 75 percent.

So I left clinic that day, and I had been kind of numb from being tired, and on top of that, I felt fragile. I wasn't sad necessarily; I should have seen it coming. In retrospect, it felt like I was on a train headed toward a collision but I couldn't get off. I was more scared at how low it had gotten, and what that meant, and nervous about whether it would ever go back up again.

I didn't get a bed until Friday night, so before that I went to Uncle Danny's to take a nice shower and then went to LYFE Kitchen with Danny and Hannah then to the Creamery for milkshakes. I got to the hospital around 9:00. I'm in a really nice room on the E-wing. My mom got in a little later that night.

It's been a pretty pleasant stay so far. I don't feel absolutely horrible, I'm fitting in all my treatments, I've had good visitors. Michelle and Becca came on Saturday, which was sooo fun, we snuck out and walked to the mall and had lunch with my mom and Danny and Hannah, and we hung out all day, and at night Sabrina and Adrian came and we all went to Whole Foods for dinner. I had the best time.

Friday, March 15, 2013
Out of the hospital! It's Friday, so I was there one week. My lung function went from 42 to 50 percent in that week, which is pretty bomb! That never happens, it usually gets worse the first week and then slowly, slowly, gets better over weeks and weeks. I'm happy to be out, but I was in a bad mood in the afternoon and was getting irritated with my parents when I shouldn't have been.

And I get to go to Hawaii on Tuesday! There was first the drama that I didn't think I could go because I thought I'd be on IVs, then I thought Nate couldn't go because he needs to go to Florida because his grandma is dying so his mom told him to be on standby for two weeks for the funeral. But somehow it all worked out, and I'm so happy, so excited! I packed today, and can't stop thinking about the ocean, the sunshine, swimming in Kihei, Sunday swims with Rich, good food, driving to Hana, going upcountry, seeing waterfalls, taking pictures . . . so many awesome things.

The last night in the hospital was really rough, though. I hadn't had a visitor in a couple of days, had been cooped up in the room a lot, and my IV was starting to get so painful that my arm swelled up like Popeye. I was just really frustrated about it but refused to get a new IV for one day, so I suffered through the pain, but it became unbearable last night and I just had to take it out after my nighttime IVs at 1:30 in the morning, and I refused my last two doses of antibiotics that were coming up in the morning. I don't think it's a big deal, but yeah. It was just killing me because I was trying to do homework but I couldn't type because of it and I couldn't focus on anything because the pain was too immediate. I was also lonely and tired and cranky, and not happy that I got moved to a small room in C3 and hadn't gotten enough sleep (I still haven't). But now I'm out (woo hoo), and all I have to do is study for my final, write my paper, play in the state championship finals, and then I get to go to Hawaii and relaxxxx. Going right now to study with Ali and Julia and Julia's boyfriend at Mirrielees House, so this is short, but overall I just feel relieved, like I dodged a bullet. I'm tired but hopeful.

Saturday, March 16, 2013
Went to state championships today, and we won! We are number one in California, which is pretty funny because we only had to beat Santa Clara and San Jose because all the SoCal teams had dropped out. Gabby sprained her ankle, so I thought I would play all day, and then I was really mad/insulted when I didn't play and he put others in instead of me. The first game, I was okay with it, because I was exhausted during the warm-ups, but after the first game I brought up a lot of mucus and my second warm-up went better and we lost the

first game of the second match so embarrassingly, it was like 25–12 or something versus Santa Clara. Then in the second game, he put me in and we won like 25–13, and then won the third game, which brought us into the finals against San Jose (and gave us a chance to redeem ourselves from losing to them the first game of the day). I was mad in the second match when we were doing so poorly and I knew my presence on the court would help. And things went much better when I went in! We won all the rest of the games of the day, so I was really happy.

So excited for Hawaii. The only thing I'm nervous about I guess is the tight quarters. Reason 1 is I'm nervous about the noise coming from our room that my parents could (and probably will) hear . . . definitely makes me uncomfortable but if they ever do hear it they seem to ignore it. Reason 2 is because of the bathroom situation. . . . I'm hoping my stomach will be okay while we're there because of the adjustments to medications Dr. Nguyen is recommending, but now that it's been so horrible this week, I'm not sure. It's so frustrating that it's so unpredictable, and sometimes so awful. And it's a pain to just disappear every morning when we're sleeping in the same place, to use the bathroom in a separate part of the condo we're staying in, and then try to think of some excuse of where I am . . . and I can't even use the shower excuse because I shower at night there and have to go to the bathroom in the morning. I'm sure I'll figure it out, I always do, but it's just such unnecessary anxiety that is so silly and mundane when I think about it from a broad perspective, but it's just not something I'm comfortable talking to Nate about or having him know about.

Finally get to go to bed!! About to keel over from exhaustion/nausea.

Saturday, March 23, 2013

In Hawaii now! It's Saturday and we got here on Tuesday. . . . I can't believe we've been here so long, it feels like we just got here/like we haven't even really done that much! Not sure how that's possible because we have: we've gone to the beach, been stand-up paddling, eaten at the fancy Four Seasons, gone to the goat dairy farm, went to a reggae concert at Stella Blues . . . so we have done a bunch of things but time just flies. The trip has been really restful and relaxing, but there have definitely been some moments of tension because of the close quarters. When we were in the house in Kailua last summer, because it was two stories, there was a lot of space and a lot of privacy. But here, even when we're in our room, the wall that separates our room from the living room and the kitchen isn't even a wall, it's like a sliding door with shutters on it so you hear everyone on the inside from outside, and everything on the outside from the inside. So that means there's no privacy and we haven't had much time alone, other than when we're in the ocean together, or when we went to yoga at Powerhouse Gym one night, or the day we went to the dairy goat farm (which was INCREDIBLE by the way, probably one of my favorite highlights of the trip for sure). It's really nice to be able to spend time with Nate alone when we can, but it's not very often, and I also enjoy spending time with my parents a lot, I just don't think he really does, so that can make it awkward. He's generally very quiet whenever we're with my parents, which is almost all the time. I'm sure it's frustrating for him because we would even have more alone time if we hadn't come to Hawaii and had just gone to LA, but yeah. I'm sure it's very frustrating, too, that he doesn't get to spend time alone with me because we're long-distance, and then when we are together in Maui in one of the most romantic places ever, my parents are here. Tomorrow we're moving to an even smaller condo, where we'll be sleeping on a pullout couch in the kitchen, which sounds much worse but is actually kind of the same thing.

I've loved being able to go in the ocean, but it's not the same kind of emotional feeling of returning to my home that I used to have when I come to Hawaii. I'm not sure if I feel less connected to it because I'm with my parents and we're full-on tourists, or if this place just reminds me too much of being a kid and it's weird to then come with a boyfriend and parents (mixing the family trip with the romantic trip), or if it's because the weather has been super cloudy and overcast and that makes the beach less beautiful. Or another option is that the Wellbutrin makes my emotions so stable that I never feel extreme happiness or excitement. Even when I think about spring quarter, which I should be super excited about, I don't feel excited at all. I'm not dreading it; I just feel completely indifferent. If spring break lasted three months, I wouldn't miss Stanford. I might like the place wherever I was less than Stanford, but I just don't feel this yearning excitement to go back at all, and I don't feel a lot of happiness when I'm there. But I'm not depressed, I'm just . . . flat. It's so funny how there have been multiple times where a doctor/therapist or someone asks if I have a psychological symptom and I say no, but then I mull it over and it hits me that I do. That happened when Dr. Sher, the psychiatrist Dr. Mohabir recommended I see, asked me if the Wellbutrin was giving me anxiety (because apparently it can for some), and I said absolutely not. Then when Dr. Nguyen put me on gabapentin for my stomach, I felt like I kind of had very little anxiety/stress. I have worries sometimes, but they're not really things that rack my mind all the time or make me feel physically tense like real stress does. But the other thing is I didn't do yoga at all this quarter, and that really helps with stress reduction, so the fact that I was doing so much and didn't feel completely stressed out means that the gabapentin was probably helping. But now I feel like the same thing has happened; Meg the social worker asked me in the hospital if I felt like the Wellbutrin was making me unable to feel any extreme emotion, good or bad, if I felt, essentially, flat. And I said definitely not. But I do now think that was definitely the case. Everything just seems dull. Even when I have something exciting coming up, I don't get excited for it, and I don't think I'm very fun anymore. I saw friends approximately never this entire quarter, and when I did see them, I felt sort of indifferent. So as I was going through this winter quarter, I felt like things were a lot better: I had friends on campus that I saw sometimes, I didn't feel so physically sick all the time, my health was getting stable, I wasn't crying every day and extremely depressed, I was keeping busy and for the most part able to sort of keep up with all the commitments I was juggling. But I still don't think I was happy. I would have been perfectly fine leaving at any point, as long as it didn't mean I would have stress for schoolwork later on. But I guess I'm just trying to figure out what gives me joy at this point, and I know some of the things that do: having close relationships with friends that I can rely on and have fun with and who understand me, having purpose and meaning by having goals and accomplishing them, feeling physically healthy, and not having guilt/stress/anxiety. The having-goals thing I felt pretty good about this quarter, since I was doing the PHE thing, volleyball, and Green Grid Radio, but all of those things did make my guilt/stress worse because I never felt like what I was doing was enough. Feeling physically healthy this quarter, other than when I was in the hospital with DIOS in the beginning and when I was in the hospital in the end. It was the close relationships with friends that I felt were slipping away, and I really don't understand why I'm not forming close relationships within a community at Stanford. I just don't get it; I've never had problems making friends anywhere. I really feel like having a chronic condition is getting in the way of my social life so much more now, at least indirectly, for so many reasons:

— because I feel like shit when I drink, I've completely written off the entire Greek scene at Stanford (and because I don't feel comfortable there, don't like the values or the events, and don't know anyone in it except for a few people).

— it's hard to have non-close friendships, acquaintances, and just see people once in a while, if they don't understand my life and why things are hard and why I have to be more careful.

— I'm so busy and distracted by my health all the time that I don't have the time and don't remember to try to keep in touch with people I used to be friends with.

— the friends I do have aren't exactly very close with one another, so we're not a "friend group" in the real sense like I'm used to with my friends at home.

    — my mom being in town every freaking weekend to
        help me means that I sleep off campus a ton, and just
        generally ignore the nightlife on campus.

I'm not sure whether I should go back to Dr. Sher or not. I don't know that I've necessarily opened up to her like I might with another therapist. I'm wondering if I should try someone else, but I don't want to make her feel bad. But I kind of feel like I should stick with her because she's a psychiatrist, not a psychologist, so she can continue refilling my Wellbutrin prescription or changing the dose or choice of medicine if it starts not working for me. But I don't really feel any strong desire to go back to her or talk to her right now. I feel more honest with my computer than I do with her, and that's kind of a problem. But would I feel any better with a different shrink?

SO, I was really excited to come home, but now it's weird and making me sad to be here. I haven't seen one friend yet (it's Friday, and I got here Wednesday night). It's just a reminder to me of how much things have changed, and I'm constantly remembering what it was like when I left for college, with my friends at my house the night before and the morning of, up until the very last minute, and how when I would come home, I would step off the plane and immediately text a bunch of people and see my friends immediately. Now I come home, I have no one to text that I'm back, I made plans with Natasha for two days later, Jason's so busy, Michelle is with family, Mich went to USC, and Talia's in Paris (the time change makes it too hard to talk!), Gaby is traveling, and Marissa's gone. I just feel like I have no one to see. Being so disconnected from my friends at home is really upsetting to me because it used to be that when I was feeling disconnected from my friends at school I would compare them to how close I was with my friends at home, and now I feel like I can no longer make that comparison.

When I visualize my future, I have no idea where I'll want to be, since I don't feel like I'll have a really strong core group of friends anywhere, and it scares me. I'm starting to get a little nervous about being in LA this summer, if I'm going to feel the way I've felt the past two days the whole time.

Tuesday, April 2, 2013

I feel like one of those marionette dolls. And I feel like the puppeteer is yanking my neck back and forth, back and forth, just for kicks. The past few weeks have had such wild highs and lows. Even the few days in LA there were a lot of highs and lows. I was kind of depressed for a bunch of it, as I wrote in the previous entry, but then Friday night and Saturday morning caught me by surprise and were refreshing and real and great. I had been pissed at Nate on Friday evening when he left my house because he woke up from his nap, and I was upstairs on the treadmill, and he came upstairs and looked irritated that I was on the treadmill and started telling me we should leave in ten to fifteen minutes. This despite the fact that I had just gotten on the treadmill and still needed to shower and there was still like an hour and twenty minutes before we were supposed to meet his parents for dinner. And it was just so frustrating to me that he was so nonchalant about timing when we were at the beach, and unrealistically thought we'd have time to swim. It was important to me that we exercise not just for nationals but for the health of my lungs, and he clearly didn't think it was a priority.

But anyway, I thought I wasn't going to have a good night because of that, and then I got off the treadmill and was kind of fuming. After a super-hot shower I cooled off (figuratively). Then I drove over to meet them at the restaurant (Nate left awhile before so he could go home and shower), and I got there right on time, and dinner was really fun! His parents are so nice to me. They're really easy to talk to and not intimidating, and they're down-to-earth and the food was good. After dinner we went back to his house and I did TOBI (I brought the nebulizer with me so I could sleep over), and then we went out for a long walk in his neighborhood. It was really dark but still not too cold, a very beautiful night, and we walked and talked for a long time and had fun then sat down on a curb in front of some random house under a pretty weeping willow and sat there for a long time. We ended up having a pretty serious conversation about CF and resistant bacteria and the seriousness of it and transplants and he asked me a lot of questions he hadn't asked before. I was happy that he was asking, because it's important to know how it's on my mind every minute of every day, how it's changing me every single day as it changes itself, and how it's going to affect him as half of our relationship. When we got home, we went to bed, and he asked if I minded him asking all those questions; I reassured him that I didn't, that I want him to ask those questions and that I'm completely happy to talk to him about it and that I tend to under-share because I don't want to burden people with difficult information they don't want to hear. He said he hadn't known how serious things were before our talk that night and wanted to make sure I knew that he'd always be there for me.

Even if some people know a few random tidbits or a little bit about my daily regimen, they have no freaking clue what it feels like to have your life gradually slip away from you as you have less and less control, what it feels like to wake up in the morning not able to breathe, to have to make every single decision with the knowledge that it could directly impact lung function and longevity irreversibly. People don't understand, they can't fathom that mortality is something that's on my mind all the time and that when I am so anal about sleep and when I'm skeptical about going on trips or doing fun things like that it's because I know from experience that they'll make me sicker and I probably won't get better. So I kind of figured that Nate knew about it from being with me, but I realize from his questions that there's so much he doesn't know, but I like that he wants to know more.

This morning was when things went south. I set my alarm for 7:00 a.m. to meet the PHEs at Vaden Health Services for the rollout breakfast (was not going to get up an hour earlier just to run around and bang on people's doors). I felt awful when I woke up. Could not stop coughing, felt super cold, exhausted, and short of breath. It was so hard to get myself there, but somehow, I did (and without a bike, too—I had to drop it off for a million repairs the day before). The breakfast was nice but I still felt awful, and despite coffee never felt more awake. When I got home to do treatment, I was running late (didn't get home until 8:00 because the PHEs didn't all even show up until 7:20, when I was supposed to be home at 7:30), still felt completely exhausted, and had to walk to HumBio, so I was not at all on time. There were no seats left, and not even really any standing room left in the back, so I was standing up, and squished, and my back was killing me along with my neck, and I was still short of breath. I felt feverish and just bad, and I kept changing my position—from standing up, to sitting down on the step, to lying down in the way back, to sitting up. I couldn't see the projector at all, couldn't take notes, was in pain, felt like shit, and was about to fall asleep in the back, so I figured I might as well fall asleep in my bed and at least be comfortable if I was gonna nap involuntarily. The walk across campus was difficult . . . it felt like crossing the country . . . it just extended forever. When I got home, I crawled into bed and checked my temp, and it was 101.1. So I called the coordinator and she told me to go to the ER (I also told her I had been coughing more and short of breath and tired). I don't even want to go into detail about the ER because I just want to go to sleep, but I was there from about 10:30 a.m. until 3:00 p.m. I didn't see Dr. Mohabir until like 2:45. Before that I saw two other doctors, did chest X-rays and abdominal X-rays, and two sets of labs. I didn't read at all and didn't watch TV. . . . I don't even know how I passed the time. . . . I was checking emails on my phone, going in and out of sleeping, listening to music on my phone, texting, etc. My fever came down pretty quickly once I got there, which is weird. I don't know why it always spikes really high and then drops back down quickly. I'm not sure what my body's doing. My white blood cell count was 18,000 . . . which is pretty high . . . so they decided to start me on oral Bactrim. We know how that one goes from the two rounds I did in summer, I'm not too optimistic about it. Nitay came to visit and brought me a bunch of food, which was good, it helped tide me over. My chest X-ray looked pretty much the same as the last one, so no pneumonia or pneumothorax. My gut was a bit backed up/obstructed, but literally what else is new; I have

NEVER, not even one time, had an abdominal X-ray where they haven't said that. They said we're going to need to get more aggressive with my bowel regimen but there's literally no more room to add anything; I'm already taking misoprostol four times a day, Amitiza, Colace, senna, and MiraLAX four times a day. It's too much!! I don't know what to do but I'm ready to pull my hair out about it, because that is NEVER going to get better and it's so frustrating and I'm forced to think about it every single time I pick up my fork to eat, every time I take my pills, when I go to bed at night and wake up in the morning and many moments in between.

Camille said Dr. Mohabir recommended I not go to nationals. She made it seem really certain; she said flying on a plane would be really bad because it would dry me up even further than the fever already is, and that if I was there, no doctors would be able to help if something went wrong, and that exercising when you're getting sick will make it worse. She definitely has valid points, it's just weird because they don't think I'm sick enough to admit me clearly. I wish they had done a PFT to see where I am, that would give me more peace of mind about not going if I knew my PFTs were way down. I just don't want to not go and then feel better tomorrow night. Alternatively, I don't want to go and then be horribly sick the entire time and go into the hospital right when I get back. I don't know if it's worth it to go if I'm not feeling well, because it is pretty intense and you don't get enough sleep and it's a lot of time indoors on the court with a ton of people. I didn't realize how worried they are about me flying when sick. When Dr. Mohabir came in he made it seem like it was more my decision, asking me how I feel, etc. etc. I don't know what to do. But I'm just sad and exhausted and drained and sick of being sick. I'm sick of what *B. cepacia* is doing to me. It just doesn't want to cut me a break. I'm also sick of working and I'm on day two of the quarter, so that worries me. I'm starting to wonder again if I should take the quarter off, but I just don't know. I'm just plagued with inertia because I don't want to make any rash decisions, but I also don't want to just sit on my ass and let life go on without me even thinking about what I'm doing. Ahhhhhhhhhhhhhhhhhhhhh

Soooo frustrated!
Soooo tired!
Soooo headachy!
Soooo much chest tightness!
Soooo annoyed!

Sunday, April 21, 2013

We (Nate and I) ended up staying up really late last night. Things got pretty intense. We lay in bed for a really long time cuddling and talked about a lot of stuff. I don't remember what conversations we had leading up to this conversation but at one point he said, "I'm just down to live" (literally no idea how that came up at all), and I said "DTL!" I think recently in one of our conversations he had said that his life is so much better with me in it and that he loves me so much and couldn't imagine not being with me or something. We were both quiet for a minute, and then he said he's realized at different points along the way and from some of our past conversations that it won't be easy. But he knows he wants to be with me, and he'll take whatever comes along the way. It was really powerful and made me realize how serious he feels about our relationship and how invested he is and how much he's willing to sacrifice for it.

Friday, April 26, 2013

I'm frustrated, pissed, stressed. . . . I want to punch a wall or just hug someone but also just be alone and wallow and watch TV and sleep and get a massage and stretch so I'm not a ball of tension with all this pain anymore. Had another bad night—ended up taking four Advil and asking Liane to put Bengay on my back. When I knocked on her door she didn't answer, and a minute later Christian came out, and I went in, and she was crying. I feel so bad that she's having a rough quarter. Or maybe it's just a bad week. She really is one of my favorite people, who I think is most like me on campus at this point.

Anyway, all that pain messed up my sleep, and then I thought it was a fluke but every night since then I've had stomach issues and haven't been able to sleep. And the less sleep I get, the more my stomach gets messed up. I keep telling myself I'm only going to do liquids for a day until I get cleared out and stop having these issues, but then I don't have enough of the right liquids to maintain my energy to do my work, and I get hungry, and food is there and I end up eating and then I feel sick again. Literally every time I've had a meal this week, I've felt very sick. I think it's time to seriously consider that surgery. But WTF, I don't want to have a surgery and then have three weeks of recovery! Especially since I got a sinus CT scan the other day, and I have a sinking feeling (based on how bad my sinuses are) that they're going to recommend a sinus surgery. Praying that I'm wrong, though, and that my sinuses are great and that I just need to continue sinus rinses.

Good news for Kari Karr, the friend with CF who's been having it super rough the last year. She got approved for transplant! Whenever I think my situation is tough, I think about hers and realize it could be much worse and I should be so grateful for the opportunities I've been able to have despite having CF and being colonized by *cepacia*. It's a matter of your expectations; when my expectations are set as a normal person's, I'm always disappointed with myself and with reality. When my expectations are set as a "patient" and I expect that things will be hard and I won't be able to do much, there are so many great surprises! Maybe that's the ticket to happiness, stop pretending to be a Stanford student and start spending more time on health. Nah that wouldn't work as long as I'm a student. Just nervous that by the time I'm done with school and ready to start living with my health first, I'll be so so sick. I'm really scared of that.

Miss Nate! I felt the void a lot more when he left this time for some reason. I also miss volleyball actually! I miss seeing all the girls and having a structured time to play. Sad that I probably won't be able to go to the grass intramural game this weekend because I'll probably be at Danny and Lissa's studying for my HumBio 4A midterm, which I'm going to fail anyway. Joy!

AAARRRRGGGG I LITERALLY CANNOT DO THIS WORK I JUST WANT TO SLEEP BUT I HAVE TO FINISH THIS SCRIPT AND I CAN'T FRIGGIN DO IT BECAUSE

EVERY TIME I HAVE A THOUGHT IT'S INTERRUPTED BY ACIDIC FOOD SHOOTING UP MY ESOPHAGUS AND MAKING ME BURP LIKE A BEER-BELLIED MAN. JUST GET ME AWAY FROM EITHER THIS PAIN/DISCOMFORT OR THIS STRESS/WORK, I CAN'T HANDLE BOTH RIGHT NOW. Sitting here with my heating pad and it's not helping. NOT AT ALL.

Saturday, April 27, 2013

Well, at least I'm predictable. After this shit-show of a tsunami of a week hit me (or while it was in the process of flooding me with work and me feeling like shit), I am now in the emergency room. Turns out I have another pulmonary embolism. Literally déjà vu in the worst possible way. I was in the ER exactly the same(ish) time as last year.

Thursday, May 9, 2013

I've been out of the hospital for about five days now. While I was in the hospital, I literally did zero work, and now I'm paying the price. I didn't write at all, either—just watched Netflix—so I'll catch up here: I got out on Saturday afternoon and had to study for my HumBio midterm. On Sunday I couldn't study because I had to deal with the draw, and then had a staff meeting and then had to do a HumBio PSET (on material that wouldn't help me prepare for the midterm). So I essentially had a few hours on Monday to study, and I didn't even take full advantage of them because my brain got too tired. I kind of feel like my brain is out of shape in a way. . . . I can't get it to focus on anything, and I feel like I can't think critically. My memory feels off and I'll be talking and then literally lose my train of thought mid-sentence and then just get silent. I also slept pretty terribly while I was in the hospital, because they were doing blood draws every six hours for six days straight.

The basic plan while I was there was pain control and bridging me over to a therapeutic level of blood thinners, so Coumadin pills and a heparin drip 24/7. I wasn't allowed to be disconnected from the heparin drip the entire time I was there, not even to take a shower. So from Saturday morning until the next Saturday afternoon I was connected to the pole. That meant I didn't shower for the first five days, then finally I got so desperate that I just had my mom and the nurse's assistant wash my hair while I was still connected to the pole and just dangling my head into the shower.

I had a lot of friends visit, though, which was nice! Michelle came twice, which was sooo nice, and one time she brought Chris. Sabrina came, too, and Maya, Makiko, Tyler, Kennedy, Uy Han, Ali and Julia, and Karen. I saw more friends that week than I would have if I were out of the hospital!

Something happened that made me really angry the morning I got admitted from the ER. I wrote this in an email to the family as an update, when I was sitting on a gurney in the hallway in B2, totally abandoned by the ER nurse:

"Got wheeled from the ER to B2 by the ER nurse. Arrived in B2 outside my room to discover that it's a shared room (the same thing that happened in the ER eight hours ago). Told my nurse that I cannot be in that room, he asked why, I told him because I have *B. cepacia* that endangers other patients, and he apologized and said that no one told them in the ER (to which I'm thinking, no shit that's because it's written in the charts). Then he proceeded to leave while I'm still on a gurney in the hall outside the room. The B2 nurses came over to help me into my new room a couple of minutes later, and still had no idea that I couldn't be in that room, so I had to explain it all over again. No one seems to believe me when I say I need contact precautions, they seem to think I'm just whining about something because I want my own room. Meanwhile, I lost my room in the ER, there are no rooms in B2, and I have no idea how long it will be until a room opens up, and have nowhere to wait in the meantime other than a hallway."

I'm not sure how I felt about the fact that Nate didn't attempt to come visit while I was in the hospital . . . still figuring out my mental state on that one. It's complicated. I didn't want him to come (because of my insecurity of how gross/vulnerable/cranky I am when I'm in the hospital) but I did want him to WANT to come anyway.

Mallory was always especially close to Diane—her cheerleader, her chef, sometimes even her wingmom, and always, of course, her mother.

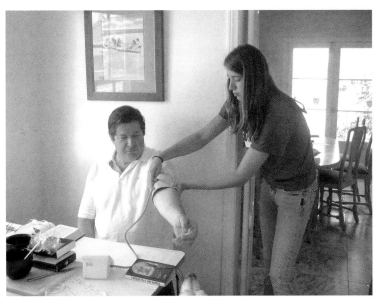

Good health was a family affair. Here's Mallory checking her father's blood pressure.

Even as a five-year-old, Mallory spent an average of an hour each day on percussion vest treatment and nebulizer. Treatment would take a lot longer as she got older, but it never got in the way of her life . . .

. . . even while playing with Kona . . .

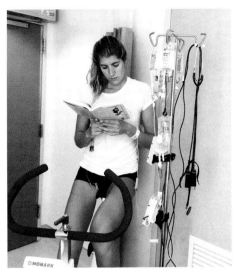

. . . or while exercising.

Mallory and her brother, Micah, were always close.

MRIs and other diagnostic tools were a regular part of Mallory's life.

Mallory was able to write a book titled *The Gottlieb Native Garden* for the National Wildlife Federation.

The almost imperceptible oxygen tube that Mallory wore with ease kept her alive and mobile even when she was ailing.

No pity party. Mallory and her mom always found a way to enjoy their time together, even during Mallory's many hospitalizations.

And nothing was more fun for Mallory than spending time with her pup, Kona!

Mallory lived happy—but was also very conscientious about her health and treatments.

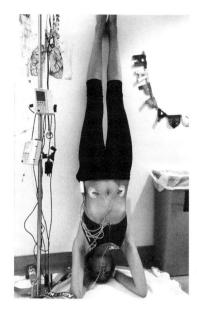

One of the best ways for Mallory to unwind: yoga. It was a lifetime respite for her.

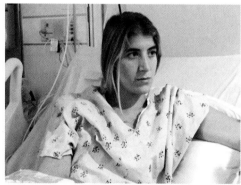

Here, Mallory listens to doctors as they give her news of an additional health complication.

The closeness of Mallory's family helped her in the toughest times. Here she is with her mom, Diane . . .

. . . and here with her brother, Micah, and her beloved Pittsburgh rescue dog, Cooper.

Mallory and Jack had no idea that this would be their last time in Hawaii together.

Mallory's version of swimming while she was tethered to oxygen in Pittsburgh. This would be her last time in a pool.

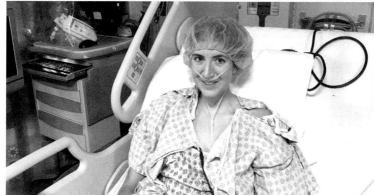

Hopeful and terrified, Mallory was still able to smile before being wheeled in for what everyone hoped would be a lifesaving lung transplant.

It was appropriate that Mallory's soul be laid to rest in Maui, her happiest place, and especially here, off the beach she most loved. Six months after Mallory died, her brother, Micah—along with her parents and friends—participated in a paddle-out ceremony to celebrate her life.

I've been trying to analyze how I feel about that whole thing but I just need to stop thinking about it because I know he loves me . . . he just doesn't fully understand how affected I am by everything that's going on right now health-wise. It's casting a black shadow that I can't get out from under.

Saturday, June 1, 2013

I literally have not talked to Nate in so long. And when I did talk to him it was so unenthusiastic. I really don't know how I feel about us at this point. I'm so hot and cold about it. It's just hard to remember why I'm even in this relationship when we hardly speak. He has no idea that my dad was even here this weekend, or what I did today . . . because he didn't ask. I couldn't tell him about what I was doing today, because I don't feel comfortable doing that. Last night I asked him to text me if he had any time to Skype this weekend, and he had a day off today and didn't even tell me until 4:00 p.m. when he was watching some stupid TV show and was going filming later and did not even ask if I wanted to Skype. I just don't know what's in it for him at this point to stay in the relationship; he doesn't seem excited whatsoever when I talk to him, he just seems to not give a rat's ass about anything at all at this point. And now that I've thought about it for a few days—about the last time I actually talked to him for real, I think that's what's bothering me the most at this point. I feel like I have to try hard to extract information from him, or extract any kind of emotion, other than platitudes like "I miss you so much," which is hard to take sincerely when you hear it every single day but he never does anything about it, like try to actually talk to me or come see me. I'm torn between these two facts: (1) it seems like I find fault with any relationship that I'm in after it's been a while and figure out some reason why I want something different. And (2) it seems like I might be staying in this relationship for the wrong reasons, like that it's convenient to have a boyfriend, and it makes me feel more secure about myself to know that someone thinks I'm cool enough to actually date, and that when I go home I have sex waiting for me, and that I'm not going to find a boyfriend at Stanford so I might as well hold on to the one I do have, and that another one probably won't roll around for a very long time.

I'm not sure if how I'm feeling right now is just me being pessimistic about the relationship, and I don't know if I am being too hard on him for working. But even before he was working, there were certain things that made me angry that I never brought up to him . . . and now it seems too late, because when you bring something up a long time after it's an issue, then they know you've been hiding feelings and I don't want him to think that, even though it is the case. I didn't realize how much his response bothered me last time I was in the hospital. I didn't think it bothered me that he didn't want to come, because I didn't want him to come. But then I realized, the fact that he did NOT have a job meant that he was essentially doing absolutely nothing the ENTIRE time I was there, and my mom had to ask him if he wanted to fly up. She even offered to pay for it, but he didn't accept, and when I talked to him on the phone about it, he actually said, "I have my own life down here." And that pissed me off so much it made me cringe when I heard him say it on the phone, because I was like no you don't even have a life right now, every day that I've talked to you you've been lazing around the house watching reality TV and eating. We've had conversations about how he's all here for me but . . . he's never actually there when the real shit is going down. He hears about it after, and he expresses his condolences or whatever. ("I'm so sorry that you had to deal with that, I wish I could've been there," etc.) But when I'm in the hospital, when I'm acutely struggling, he is not here. And I know he doesn't live here and I don't always fill him in when that's happening, but I don't have any assurance that I should do that when I don't think he's responded in the best way when faced with small issues. What assurance do I have that he's going to stick around when he does see it? I'm not always a pleasant person, as exemplified by this rant and many other things. I'm not the most pleasant when I'm in the hospital, and in that setting I'm not beautiful, I'm not caring, I'm not ambitious, I'm not active/athletic, I'm not motivated, I turn into something else entirely. I feel like this is not the first time I've had this rant, and this is just sitting in the back of my brain unresolved because I haven't brought it up. I should text him, but I don't want to say something stupid because I'm drunk, or just say something over text at all really. Too bad I'm such a coward when face-to-face with someone. And too bad we're never face-to-face. I am so scared to send something and I hate that I'm so scared about it, but I also hate that when I think about going home, I think about the fact that we're not even going to hang out really and that he is the reason why I'm going home. I also have no idea what's going on in his brain, he can't think this is normal especially after his last girlfriend wanted to talk to him every single day . . . is this a welcome break for him? Does he actually miss me? If he did, wouldn't he try to talk to me more? Or does he want to talk more and has just simply given up because I'm too busy?

I have these general sorts of thoughts about college, that I like my life, but things could have been sooo much better if my own outlook on life were better at this point. I don't want my future self to be confused when reading this later on: it's not that I don't feel super fortunate about my circumstances. I feel like I'm a victim of my own emotions. I have all the pieces in place to make an amazing life, an amazing community of people around me, and I hold myself back, I hold myself at a distance and think of myself as separate from college life, and feel too mature for it, and am too scared to do anything fun because I stay healthier when I'm in a health routine/ritual that's boring and static and unchanging. GOD I JUST WANT TO ESCAPE RIGHT NOW. BUT I CAN'T BE ALONE. MY OWN MIND IS TOO TOXIC TO MYSELF. Every time I start writing, I can start out in a moderately to mildly perturbed state but still feel fine, and by the time I put all this shit on paper I start feeling like my life is in a shambles and I'm stuck in chains and need to break out. I really just want a shoulder to cry on. And so much of it is just seeing other people have lives, seeing them have each other, seeing them have inside jokes and closeness, seeing them care about each other, seeing them have spirit and genuine enthusiasm for life, and I just feel like that's all gone and I can't think of a single person, not one person in the entire universe, that I feel close to right at this very moment.

Sometimes things are so good, and then sometimes they're so dark. My outlook can shift in a matter of moments. I know I've always been thoughtful, and I've overanalyzed things, but I just feel like I have so many demons now. It's like in two different moments, I can look at the exact same set of data (my life) and get a completely different interpretation. Demons of vanity, insecurity, worry, fear, stress, so many.

Saturday, June 15, 2013

I'm HOME! I ended up going home on Thursday of the last week, instead of waiting until Friday or Saturday, because Mom and I were efficient with packing and done Thursday. I was happy to come home that one day early, because I knew nothing much would be happening Thursday night, I'd be done packing, and I'd have to sleep in a creepy empty room.

Nate and my dad picked us up from the airport. It was really good to see him. On Wednesday (the day before I came home), Nate and I kind of got into a fight over text because he told me he couldn't pick us up from the airport because he was going filming, and that he'd see me for dinner later in the night. And I was like, "Ummm, excuse me? I haven't been home in six months, you haven't seen me in two and a half months, and we've barely talked at all for the last month, and you're making plans for the day I get back?" So I got pretty pissed and told him basically that I had to reevaluate the purpose of our relationship if I was at the bottom of a long list of priorities as it seemed. And he sent me very long responses that were very in-depth assuring me that I wasn't at the bottom, that he's sorry he hasn't had more time, that he's really excited for me to come home, etc. etc. etc., and we ended up making up by the end of the night. But it was really stressful while it was happening, and it's interesting that both times recently I've gotten mad at him, it's been over text, it's been very civil, and then it's resolved. This time, though, I feel like I was more honest about my feelings and laid more out on the table because I brought up other things that had bothered me but that I had previously not mentioned (like him being so apathetic over Skype, him not telling me anything about the movie but then acting like it's so important, him canceling his trip to come for the MGMT concert after I already paid for his ticket and not offering to pay me back, and maybe some other things I don't know). And it was good that I told him, but then he thought it was about the money and I was like no, it's not about the money, and he thought it was about work and I was like no, it's not about work, I always understand that you have work, it's that you have seemed apathetic and just disinterested when we've talked lately and you've failed to keep up on my life at all. For example, when I mentioned that I was having a procedure he didn't ask what it was; I told him about that and he was really sorry. So he responded well to it, and defended himself but didn't try to make me seem like I was wild or go on the attack or anything. And by the time I went to sleep things were fine, which was good because otherwise it would've been really awkward to come home.

Thursday, Nate and I slept here at the beach apartment together, which was GREAT. I'm so happy that I have my own apartment and that I'm not living at home; I would be unspeakably bored living at home, with hardly any friends, no good activities to do in close proximity (the only things are shopping and nails and stupid stuff like that), too much contact with my parents and not enough independence, etc. This is a perfect balance because I have my own space, and some time alone, but at the same time I still get to see my family a lot. I have a feeling I'm not going to get to see Maria as much as I imagined, though, which is really sad. I'm going to have to make a really conscious effort about that. But also, it would've been really bad to be living at home and having Nate sleep over all the time, first of all because I don't think we sleep well in that bed together (I can just never sleep), and second of all because if we ever had sex the entire household would hear, which I'm just not down for. Living here we have privacy and don't have to worry about that, and he can come and go, and it's close to his work, and for me it's close to the beach, to restaurants, to yoga, to hiking, etc.

Saturday, August 3, 2013

I'm starting to feel (again) like I'm not seizing my life and my opportunities fully right now. And I think the reason why is that I've kind of felt vaguely sick ALL summer. It was like my stomach started acting up right when I got home and has relentlessly pestered me with nausea, vomiting, bloating, cramps, constipation, diarrhea, everything, for a month and a half now. And it makes me think of the whole willpower thing Pidge always talks about, how if you have pain or negative energy or discomfort or whatever it is, it uses up part of your mental energy every day just trying to suppress thinking about it and noticing it, which drains you of your energy to do other things. For example, if you have chronic pain, and you're trying to focus on your work, a lot of your brainpower is going to be focusing on just adapting and dealing with the pain, and that will take away from your concentration, ability to think, etc. And I think I really suffer from this problem because I'm always distracted by the fact that something is wrong with my GI tract, and if it's not bothering me at that moment, I'm afraid it will the second I eat something, and so I'd like to know what percentage of my thoughts revolve around my GI issues. And then when you add lung issues and difficulty breathing and worrying about the difficulty breathing, it doesn't leave a lot of mental energy for intellectual vitality, enthusiasm for my jobs, physical energy for surfing and volleyball and yoga, etc. I just feel kind of like my entire being is "tight." When I go to yoga and my body is tight it's painful and so doing yoga feels liberating, and I come out of a class (if it's a good one) feeling like I just came out of a cocoon, and I have a newfound energy because I'm not in pain. But I think the way I am now stretches beyond my body being physically tight, it feels like my brain is, too, and it needs calming, stabilizing, rejuvenating, so I can reclaim some of the energy and enthusiasm I used to have for life itself.

Something else I've been thinking about is what's going to happen with me and Nate at the end of the summer. I think I finally feel like I'm on the cusp of explaining my GI issues to him, because we're coming up on a year and it's something he needs to know in order to know me and understand me. He hears me complain of discomfort and pain, but he doesn't know why it happens, what the specific problems are, or that simply going to the bathroom is such a huge source of stress for me. I was low-key embarrassingly freaking out that when he took me to the ER they were going to diagnose me with DIOS and try to bombard my system with laxatives on top of laxatives, and that he was going to want to visit and I would have to explain why I'd rather he not visit. But then they found the appendicitis and I was relieved. Then the doctors here spoke to Camille at Stanford, and Camille said that she and Dr. Mohabir thought the whole thing was just constipation related and that there was nothing wrong with my appendix and that I should do a cleanout (exactly what I anticipated they would say). So then I was frustrated because I didn't want to do that. I said if I'm just going to be taking a bottle of MiraLAX, I should be able to do that at home, not here. So for hours I was really angry and frustrated and confused because no nurses were coming to tell me the plan or giving me any meds and all they had prescribed for me was one packet of MiraLAX and I was just completely out of the loop as to what was going on. Finally, Wednesday night late at night a fellow came to my room, a fellow from general surgery, and he said they definitely thought it was my appendix, that they disagreed with Stanford because they didn't see signs of blockage or abnormal amounts of stool in the CT scan. Which I was really happy about, because it pisses me off no end when Stanford just dismisses every single problem I have with my stomach as constipation and tries to give me more laxatives when I'm already taking more than should be humanly possible. But anyway, I did tell Nate Stanford's theory about me needing laxatives and that I thought it was wrong, but it was sort of misleading because I acted like that's something I would never need and that other CF patients have that problem but I don't.

Monday, August 19, 2013
When Nate and I left the hospital and were driving home, we started talking about what we're going to do in the fall.

It was a sad conversation. There were a lot of long pauses in between each of us saying things. I would say something and then it would be quiet for a few minutes, and then he would talk, etc. We got home and quietly went upstairs to bed and continued talking about it there as we fell asleep. We decided it wouldn't be realistic to stay together as long as he has this job in production. And he mentioned that maybe he should just quit his job, partly because of me and partly so he could work on his own stuff, but I said I did not want to be any part of the reason for him to quit his job, I wouldn't want him doing anything to sacrifice his own career for me, that wouldn't be right. I said even though it would be so sad to end it before going to school, it would be better to do that and leave the door open for the future instead of getting in a fight in the fall and just not communicating and then breaking up on bad terms, which he agreed with. But we did mention that we'd see how it went and if it was unbearable to be apart, we'd figure out a way to be together, or we could be together in the future. I'm not doing the conversation justice because it was a lot longer and a lot more was said than that, and it was hard for both of us, and we were both crying a lot. He said it would be easier to break up if I weren't so perfect. I said I couldn't really imagine my life without him at this point since we've been together this long, it seems so normal and natural that I can't imagine what it would be like to not be together. It's going to be so weird to go from living together and taking a trip up the coast to take me to school, to just breaking up.

Sunday, September 22, 2013

What can I even say? Are there words? People ask how I feel about it, about closing the book on the relationship, the person, the love that has consumed me for a year and a quarter. I use "closing the book" as an analogy, but I actually have the same feeling when I close the last page of a book. I try out a book, and I'm not sure about it at first. I'm not sure whether to keep going, or put it down and pick up a new one. But then slowly, without even realizing, I get more and more engrossed until there comes a point when I can't imagine not being with the characters in the book. It becomes like a side story within my own life, and once attached, putting the book down after reading the last sentence feels like a hasty goodbye, all too abrupt and never enough. I seek closure and I never feel like I get it.

And if I feel that way about a book, how could I not about a relationship, a person, a love that actually was mine, not just a fake character's life that I became overly invested in? Is there a way to shut down this feeling that the relationship came to a screeching halt? We were in the car, driving down the freeway, both of us in unspoken agreement to push the pedal to the metal, keep driving toward an end we both knew was coming but neither of us could fathom. We approached the cliff, we saw it, we knew we would fall. Would slowing down have made the fall, and the "splat" at the bottom, hurt less?

It's like being on a boat, in perpetual rocking motion, until your body becomes so accustomed to the motion that after you step off the boat you still feel like you're rocking. The ground is moving underneath you and if you close your eyes, you're still on that boat, out on the water, nothing has changed. Until you open your eyes and see that everything has.

We lived together for three months. We shared a king bed with a white comforter that was soft and too easily stainable. Two nightstands and a closet. A balcony with a peek of the ocean, where we sometimes sat and drank whiskey ginger ales and lit the big candle whose flame could never withstand that coastal breeze. A bathroom with a shower that didn't look big enough for two people, but somehow accommodated our joint baths. A kitchen that existed in a perpetual state of partial cleanliness. His Saturdays (or his Sundays, depending on the week), the one day off we would look forward to all week. Bike rides down the path to Will Rogers and random adventures like *Point Break* (the musical), and Sky High with the two four-year-old boys who bounced high into the air like popcorn kernels when we stepped across the trampolines, and free morning yoga, and friends and food on food on food. Moments of distance, of sadness, of missing each other even while living together and yearning for more time together. In other words, a life . . . not a fantasy, a life.

And then when it seemed like we couldn't accelerate any faster, we did. Last Wednesday, we piled our stuff into the Chevy and drove to Big Sur. For the first couple of hours, before we hit Santa Barbara, we listened to music, and talked and talked. Then we hit traffic, he fell asleep, I kept driving, and finally we reached Los Agaves, the Mexican restaurant in SB where we ate lunch. The rest of the way up we listened to *This American Life*. Three episodes we got through, I think—"Kid Logic," where we learned about a kid who got into a plane and asked, "So when do we get smaller?"; "Deception," where we learned that pig rectums, called bung, are cut into thin rings and sold as imitation calamari (this horrified us, and two hours later we had calamari for dinner); and "Self-Improvement," where we learned about a man who decided to walk coast to coast, NY to SF, as a "peace pilgrim," but then gave up after three days because it was cold as hell. There was no moral to the story on that one, just the pilgrim's realization that sitting in a fast-food restaurant alone, or sleeping cold on a highway (or in other ways making himself miserable when he had the means to not suffer), would not bring him closer to God or make world peace a reality. We laughed, and we gasped, and we discussed, and we whiled away the time, perfectly content to listen to Ira Glass discuss fried pig rectum while looking out over the gorgeous, winding coast just feet to our left. Perfectly content to just sit together, no one to answer to and nowhere to be.

We got to Treebones, the yurt resort in Big Sur, at dusk, and settled into our yurt. The location was just beautiful, with a 180-degree view of the vast ocean melting into the horizon and joining the sky like an ombre eternity. We had a delicious dinner in the main lodge area, with calamari (still thinking about pig rectums), flatbread, filet mignon, cheesecake and sorbet and wine. The next day we explored the area, went for a hike, and took lots of photos together. Finally took a couple of photos to put in his birthday frame, which will come just before we break up. Had an amazing day, multiple beaches, long drive on the coast toward Stanford, great lunch with more spectacular views, a hot tub and swim before dinner, sex in the yurt, and another dinner like the night before. The next day, another beach, this time less explorative and more sadness and cuddling, more driving, and then the Flight of the Conchords concert, where we threw sadness into the wind and just enjoyed the evening, lived it, and loved it.

Our goodbye tonight at Danny's house was not right. It was too short. It was too light. It was like saying goodbye to a friend I just met for coffee. Even Danny commented on how short it was. I know he was probably trying to hold himself together because he had to spend the next few hours with my brother and dad. But talk about lack of closure . . . WTF!!

Monday, September 23, 2013
Today was the "first day of classes" but I had no classes. I only have class Tuesdays and Thursdays this quarter. Stumbled upon this passage that Wyatt put a link to on Facebook:

> You'll look for love in new places. You'll reach out to friends, old and new, to hug, to laugh with, to cry with.
>
> You'll have vivid dreams about your beloved.
>
> You'll tell stories to shared friends, and you'll write things down.
>
> You'll have emotions that you're unable to put into words.
>
> You'll take the photos down off the walls and the mantel.
>
> You'll want to get on with your life.
>
> You'll feel guilty about wanting to get on with your life.
>
> The shape of your day, the way you move about your life, will change.
>
> You won't be the same.

It seems applicable to me right now.

Tuesday, September 24, 2013

I'm so pleasantly surprised. After being nervous for months about moving into 680, dealing with the living conditions and moving into my room and the bathrooms and the kitchen and school and coming back to Stanford, I am so happy right now. Obviously sadness about Nate is tempering that happiness, but yesterday we texted throughout the day and when he had big news about work, he called me and we talked for around ten minutes. It was nice to hear his voice. Things felt the same except that at the end I didn't know whether to say "I love you." I said, "I miss you," he said, "I love you," so I said it back. Like nothing has changed. When I told him about our special dinners and how I didn't want to take anyone but him, he said I should tell him when they are and take him . . . which is confusing. We're broken up. But yet we're talking, I would absolutely not feel right about hooking up with someone else, and he's saying he wants to visit and be my date to something happening in over a month? I really feel the need to clarify whether he thinks we should see other people or not. It's a matter of whether we're actually letting go or if that's just something we're pretending to do. I don't like the idea of him hooking up with other people, obviously, and especially dating someone else, because I don't feel like the book was ever fully closed. And I don't know if I should be trying to move on, or if he would be upset about that. Understanding how he feels about that would also help me clarify how he thinks we'll act when I come home (i.e., whether we'll meet for coffee as friends, or whether he'll sleep over and we'll act like we're back together), and how "over" he thinks we really are.

Wednesday, September 25, 2013

I went on my first "run" today of my new resolution to start running, a resolution that began yesterday. I would run thirty seconds, then walk two minutes, and I did that for sixteen minutes and then walked for four minutes. Surprisingly, it got my heart rate up A LOT—more than it should have—which did also show me that my lungs are worse than I thought they were. I was being really optimistic and thinking that I was just imagining that they were worse, and that they were actually improving since I got back to school, but then I went to clinic today and doing PFTs was hard, which is never a good sign. And they were lower by around 10 percent, two were 42 percent and one was 44 percent. So Dr. Mohabir decided to admit me, but he's letting me come in tomorrow. He wanted to let me go to the class I had tonight and the one I have tomorrow morning, which I thought was very thoughtful. I initially didn't agree that I should go, and I wanted to do blood work or a CT scan to confirm that something is really wrong, but he said it wouldn't change his opinion because he now likes to go based on symptoms and what the patient says. So I'll be there Thursday to (hopefully) only Monday night, and then I'll come home with IVs for a little bit (hopefully not too long). Definitely puts a damper on my fitness plans; I was excited to keep swimming, and go back to yoga, and start to run, and play sand volleyball while the weather is still this beautiful. I hope I don't miss all the nice weather.

It was comforting, though, to notice that I wasn't too upset by his decision. Maybe it's because I saw it coming. I predicted before I came to school that I would go to the hospital at some point before my birthday. Or maybe it's because I'm in a happier place. I kept finding myself wanting to talk to Nate, though, about it . . . and I will tell him, obviously. But I think it will be fine in there, I'll have work to stay on top of and classes I'm excited about, and I can get started thinking about the coffee episode I'll be producing for Green Grid Radio and making plans for that. And hopefully people will visit. And I want to force myself to walk and walk the hospital halls, and stairs when I can, since I don't feel too horrible. The bummer is that when I get out, I won't be able to swim while it's warm, but hopefully I'll continue with my very minor running regimen, and I'll walk. I'll get exercise walking to class instead of biking. The other bummer is that I decided to continue with no classes MWF so that I could take one day a week and go surf in Santa Cruz . . . but I obviously can't surf with a PICC line. And I definitely will lose the window of nice weather they have, if they have any right now.

Sunday, September 29, 2013

As usually happens, I've been unable to accomplish anything since I've been here in the hole. I have my reading for anthro (which is my only real homework) and I told myself to work on the coffee episode while I was here, but I just haven't been able to find the energy. Being here is just draining emotionally, and physically. But none of this is new . . . every time I'm in, I feel this lethargy, this apathy, this desire to just sit in bed even though sitting in bed makes my breathing horrible, my back curved, my legs tight, my neck tense. All the things that combine to make me feel awful while I'm here, every time, without fail.

Friday I still felt all right, I guess; I snuck out and went for a long walk with my mom and it felt okay. Cindy offered to fly Jesse up to come visit, which was great. She came to the hospital yesterday morning (Saturday) really early and stayed all day. After all my morning treatments and IVs, we snuck out of the hospital to walk to the Town and Country mall pretty close to the hospital and did a little shopping. But then I started to not feel well and got really woozy, so we came back to the hospital. They turn a blind eye to me taking long walks, but one nurse raised an eyebrow and smirked when she saw me carrying a bag from Town and Country. After the next round of treatments we started watching the show *Everwood,* which I became addicted to even though it's pretty corny. Jesse came again early today, and she just left. (It's Sunday evening.) Today I snuck out again and walked with my mom over to Stanford Park Hotel, where Jesse stayed last night, and we had breakfast with Pidge and Jesse.

Then last night I had a mild fever, and a headache and a persistent sore throat, and then I was coughing before I fell asleep and started throwing up. So today I woke up not feeling great and had really no appetite. My appetite has been really spotty. Sometimes I just don't even want to look at or think about food, the idea of it and the smell of it nauseate me. And then sometimes I'm ravenous and could eat a mule. It's really weird and I'm not sure what it's related to.

But what I do know is that I feel worse now than when I got here, and I'm not sure whether being admitted was a good idea, but

Dr. Mohabir wanted it to happen and so it happened. The problem is that I just don't bring any mucus up here. I think for people with bacteria whose mucus isn't as thick and viscous and green as mine, they come here and do four treatments a day and they bring up more mucus than they ever would at home. But for me, the chest-percussion vest I use without doing anything else just doesn't cut it. And I could vest all day long, and it wouldn't replace even thirty minutes of exercise outside of here. When I'm out of here, I lie down at night and the mucus just flows freely out of me, and I assist the process by coughing hard but it's not so hard that it makes me throw up (usually). It just comes out like a flood if I've exercised and done treatments. But here in the hospital, it just doesn't happen.

Nate shared the Big Sur pictures with me on Google Drive, so I could see them. They're really cute, the ones he put up. He didn't put them all up. There's only one picture of us together that's good. There are a lot of solo pictures, and while they're cute, they aren't really what I wanted to have. I wanted a good one of us together on a real camera, not an iPhone. And we got one. But more would have been nice.

Tuesday, November 26, 2013 (21 years old)
I'm home for Thanksgiving and thinking about what I am afraid of . . .

> Death
>
> Aging
>
> Being alone
>
> Being forgotten
>
> Forgetting my life, memories
>
> Not ending up with the person who will make me the happiest
>
> Not having a family
>
> Not having a fulfilling career

Close family dying

Losing my relationship with Micah

Looking back on life with regrets

That moment when I realize I don't have my "entire" life ahead of me anymore, that it's actually winding down

Never fully accepting myself and being proud of myself

Never being able to let anyone in

Forgetting is terrifying. One day, you have a vivid memory of an experience, what happened, what it looked like, how it made you feel. And you take that memory for granted, and then one day you wake up and something makes you recall it and you realize it's only half there, or even less. You start to question whether it happened in the first place, who was there, all the details that make it significant to you. Waking up and forgetting your dream is the same thing, just in a sped-up time-lapse kind of way. You have a dream and it's so real, it's happening to you, and then you wake up and the feeling of the dream stays with you and you still think you remember it. But the second you try to recall a detail, to write it down, to make it concrete, to make sense of what it meant, all the very details that will help you do that slip away, like water you try to hold in your hand, that will never be permanent.

What happens when everything that's happening to me now becomes like the water, trickling out of my reach until this whole year, decade, life, seems so distant it's no longer my own? How can our experiences shape us so deeply if we can't even remember them a year down the line? What determines those memories, which randomly stick with us forever, like my memory of swinging on a broomstick I hung from the decrepit basketball hoop in my backyard with Micah, trying to imitate Quidditch?

Friday, November 29, 2013

It's so confusing with Nate. We hung out on Monday night but I felt really ambivalent. I was super confused at the fact that I didn't feel happy really to be with him even though I had been missing him so much. I just felt weird in a way that's hard to describe. We talked on the couch for a long time about a lot of things, and it was really clear to me that the past few months have been worse for him than for me. He doesn't seem happy that we are apart but I'm not sure if it's "us" that he's missing or just that he's not happy in his life.

Sunday, December 1, 2013

Back at school and want to continue writing from where I left off last time. After I hung out with Nate on Monday I went upstairs and talked with my mom because I couldn't sleep. She and my grandma both think that I need to tell Nate how I feel, how I'm ready to move on, but as the week has gone on and I've thought about it, I realize my feelings aren't that simple. I definitely don't want to be in a relationship with him right now, but I don't want to rule anything out for the future. His current situation with life—his schedule and his location—makes us incompatible for now, but who's to say how I would feel if I were to move back to SoCal and he changed jobs and was fulfilled and happy and had the ability to be a better boyfriend? I would probably fall back in love with him then and want to be with him. So I just think it's not worth it to hurt his feelings, it's pointless in fact, because my feelings could change and the main thing he needs to know is that we're not getting back together right now and I don't want to act like we're together or lead him on when I'm home. And he knows that, because on Tuesday he asked if he could sleep over that night so he could bike into work the next day, and I texted back to tell him I wasn't comfortable with that and didn't think it would be a good idea because it would make things more difficult emotionally for me. Which isn't exactly the truth, the truth is more that I spent the whole quarter trying to move on and I can't just hit the pause button and live without him for months and then hit play when I'm home like nothing has changed. I had to get used to not being with him and now I can't just flip back and forth. So he asked if we could talk about it, so later in the day he called me and we talked about it. He told me that Monday had been extremely difficult for him and that he was on the brink of tears the entire time he was with me. He said he's having such a hard time already that sleeping over wouldn't make it worse, it would just allow him to spend as much time with me as possible, which is what he wants to do when I'm back. He just wants to forget about his life for a while and be with me. But I was firm in saying that for me it would definitely make it harder to do that so he didn't press the point anymore. But the talk was hard. It was sad. We talked about whether he would come to Thanksgiving, because he was questioning whether he could do it; he said it might be really uncomfortable, and he didn't want to have to field a million questions about work in small talk with people and have to make up shit about how it's great. And I told him that was fine, that's his choice if he doesn't want to come, but that it would break my heart if he was alone on Thanksgiving, and I told him that it seems like he's hiding if he chooses not to come. He ended up deciding to come.

Two days ago (Friday) I went with my mom to the Burton store on Melrose to buy a wet suit, and I went in the dressing room with a ST 4/3 suit, which I've been wanting for so long, and I was in the dressing room by myself tugging the suit over my left ankle. All of a sudden, I coughed and felt the pooling of blood in my lungs that always means hemoptysis is coming. And sure enough, it was. There was nowhere to spit it out, so I'm just standing there wearing a thong and a bra, alone in the dressing room with no paper towels or cup or trash can to spit into, so I have nothing else to do but spit blood into my hands. So I'm cupping both my hands and collecting a pool of blood, and of course it's getting on my face because I have to use the backs of my hands to wipe my hair out of my face, and meanwhile I'm still naked and can't put anything on because I'm covered in blood and have a wet suit dangling off my foot that I can't get on or off. I poke my head out and start calling for my mom, yelling her name and "Mom!" over and over again, but she doesn't hear me, she's somewhere far away in the store. Finally, I just try to make eye contact with an employee, and I find one guy and I'm like please help and he seems to be able to tell that something is wrong. So I'm still hiding behind the door and the guy that was helping me find the wet suit comes over to see what's up, and he can only see my head and my hands, and I try to say, "Please find my mom," but right after "please" I cough again and spit more blood into my hands. He looks freaked out and says, "Oh my God," but he leaves to go find her. She comes back and slams the door wide open and I'm just sitting on the bench trying to cover myself up, still covered in blood and still with the wet suit hanging off my foot, and she tells the guy to come in but when he opens the door to come in I start telling him not to come in, so he doesn't know what to do, and my mom sends him to get paper towels and cups. And she keeps running in and out and I keep telling her to shut the door and meanwhile there are other people in the store who walk by, and there's just blood all over my face and hands (starting to coagulate in my hands, which made me want to throw up) and the floor by this point . . . it looks like a murder scene. Finally, the guy brings towels and I start trying to clean up, but I can't take the wet suit off myself without using my bloody hands, so a female employee comes in and she pulls it off for me. I'm bracing myself and holding on to the bench, and she's pulling and pulling but it won't come off my foot and I'm still all bloody. It was quite a sight, hilarious in a really brutal and creepy kind of way. Finally, she gets the wet suit off, they bring me some wet wipes, and I wipe the blood off me. But then I realized I came all this way to get a wet suit so I didn't want to leave without even trying it on, so after all that, I ended up starting over and putting it on but trying to use as little exertion as possible. We ended up buying the wet suit, and I met one of the employees who teaches surfing and is from Hawaii and is super nice so I might hit him up for lessons when I'm back in the winter. After that incident I had twenty-four hours where I couldn't exercise or do any treatment, which really freed up my whole afternoon and I wanted to do something fun, but it was ugly at the beach and I had no one to go with so I ended up going home and eating with Micah and Margot, then going to visit Talia at her house. That night we went to dinner at Tamara's house.

Yesterday I went to the beach with Talia and we were going to go to yoga but my stomach was so awful right when we got there; I was so nauseous and in so much pain that I could barely walk or talk, so we sat on the beach for a while then went to Shutters and drank tea, then met Tamara and her friend at Café Gratitude. By then I was feeling better but we already missed yoga. I haven't exercised all week even though I've wanted to go to yoga every single day; it just keeps not working out. But yesterday I went on the elliptical and watched *Parenthood* with my mom and it was hard, but it felt really good to move.

Thursday, December 5, 2013

I'm in the hospital again. I'm not that bummed about it because it's actually kind of a good time. I'm not missing volleyball tournaments, classes or finals, or a trip. It's never fun, but I've decided I want to try to write 1,000 words a day. Doesn't matter about what; doesn't matter if it's just rambling about my day in this journal form, or if it's an outline of an essay or a radio show or my Senior Reflection podcast, or if it's just musings on whatever. But one problem that I have with keeping myself to a regimen of writing is that sometimes I just don't know what topic to write about. And it's like I know if I had a topic to write about, or a story I was working on, then I would be fine and I could write endlessly. It's the idea part that leaves me sort of dry. So one thing I was thinking of the other day when I was bored in class is that I should think of random combinations of words (either song titles, or just words I find interesting, or phrases I've heard, things I see in a news story, whatever), and then use that as a starting point and build a piece from that. For example, I was singing a song that the band Roots of Creation sang when I went with Nate to see them live in Maui at Stella Blues, and I realized okay, I could write something entitled "Roots of Creation" that would have nothing to do with that concert. Just to get myself into the habit. As I'm thinking about jobs more and more, I realize that finding joy in writing and having an easy habit of being disciplined to do it is what will make or break my career. I know I'm not going to be able to be the scientist in the field doing experiments on tropical rain forest biodiversity or coral reef ecology; I'm not going to be the CEO of a business; I don't want to be a lawyer or a doctor or an administrator. It seems like what I really need to do is go back to the basics of what do I care about, and then how do I make a difference in that arena.

Things I care about that I think I could make a meaningful difference in are the environment, human rights, public health. I would love to work for an NGO that works on global social justice issues like healthcare access, sustainable development, food justice, human rights, poverty reduction, sustainability, etc. And I could do anything for an organization like that, and then maybe I could go back to grad school and get a more advanced degree in something (either journalism or communications if I realize that's my calling, or something science based like an environmental program at the Bren School, or a marine science program at UCSD, or something else entirely, like the master's in nonprofit leadership at USD). There are a lot of options for more advanced degrees and certificates. Getting a certificate or degree in environmental communication would be good, but if not, maybe creative writing, maybe marine science, I don't know. I think by then I would probably want to just be a writer (hopefully established enough at that point to be on my own and have the upper hand, have people wanting me to write things for them, or writing my own books), or maybe I'll go into education of some kind (teaching outdoor environmental programs for kids) or working with kids or animals in a more casual way (that would be sort of sacrificing the academic route in favor of something that's more personally meaningful).

It seems like I keep coming back to writing as the main way that I can make a difference. So I just have to keep myself on it, get myself to do it.

Saturday, December 14, 2013
I got a really sweet message from Melissa on Facebook that gave me a little bit of clarity, shifted things into focus. Melissa is the girl with

CF who lives in Monterey and surfs with the Mauli Ola Foundation, who founded the Living Breath Foundation. She's so awesome, I really like talking to her, and I feel like we are so similar. Like I am who she was six years ago when she was my age . . . she's twenty-eight or something now. Anyway, I feel like my daily life and my general routine make things get a little out of focus—I lose perspective, lose clarity, get confused about what I want, what my priorities are, sometimes feel unhappy. And then every once in a while (or hopefully, often!), something will happen that brings things back into focus. Her message, for example, was talking about the quality of life she's managed to maintain even though her baseline FEV1 has only been hovering in the low forties now since graduating college. She's basically on a very similar trajectory to mine. I remember when I spoke to her dad, I think she had just graduated college a couple of years before. And that was when my FEV1 was around 60, and her dad said that Melissa's had been there a few years before but that now she was in the forties. He said the main difference in her life was that she was more tired and didn't have as much energy to do things. But since then it seems like she's managed to stay stable, which makes me hopeful, because when all you do is decline year after year, what is there to make you believe it will ever stop? When everything seems completely out of my control, there's no comfort, no relief. It's scary and it makes you see your goals dissolve right in front of you as you think of the years that will be shaved off. But hearing from another patient who is really similar to me (similar progression at a similar age, but she's a few years ahead . . . beyond that, similar interests, loves the ocean, very outgoing and lots of friends, good family support, wants to grab life by the horns, etc.), who is doing fine in her late twenties and is not looking at transplant and is happy and has a good quality of life—that's comforting. That's what gives me the most hope.

She said she quit working after about two years, because she realized just how much work it really is to stay on top of treatments, sleep, exercise, eating, dealing with doctors and hospitalizations and pharmacies and insurance, plus doing anything for personal enjoyment/social life. I get that. I know how time-consuming everything is. But I'm not ready to give up on the idea just yet of contributing something to the world. I'm scared that I'm losing myself to this disease—not my physical body, but my values, world view, beliefs, sense of hope, life goals. I always envisioned myself making positive change in the world. Being compassionate. Helping other people as a career. Gleaning happiness from helping other people. Not caring about money, materialistic aspirations, or possessions. Finding love with a man who shared these goals, who could also support me in the goal of keeping me alive and building a beautiful, close, supportive, smart, outdoorsy/athletic/spontaneous/fun family. For some reason, I feel like I'm losing some of those things. Especially my focus on money—recently, I've been craving things more that are expensive, and not finding as much happiness in costless things as I used to. For example, I crave massages all the time, and love the idea of a really nice meal at an expensive restaurant, and when I pass by an expensive store, I'm tempted to go in and shop, when in the past, I would rather go for a hike or go in the ocean than get a massage, and I'd rather eat random things from the grocery store than go for a nice meal, and I hated shopping. Those are just some examples. I just don't want to become a person I never used to be just because my disease is limiting my spirit or my sense of adventure and spontaneity. But I do know it is limiting those things. I need to figure out how not to lose that, because I consider that a core part of who I am. And I remember when I was "losing" my athleticism (losing the prowess at least), and I was freakin' terrified because I didn't know who to be. Now I think I have a much more solid sense of who I am, but it scares me to think about all the things I used to want to do that honestly at this point just seem tiresome and too much of a hassle. For example, I have wanted to move to Australia for as long as I can remember. It was the number one thing on the bucket list I created for my entire life. Now, when I think about it, I feel a combination of fear and a "let's just not and say we did" mentality. Why do I feel that way? Why don't I want to go out and tackle that goal and just try it??? It should be completely feasible. I'm graduating college on time (which I should be happy about!). I have the financial means to do it. I could find a part-time job doing anything . . . it could be something meaningful or just something to help pay some bills and meet people, like working at a coffee shop or a bookstore or whatever. I should trust that I'll meet people. But that's where the fear kicks in. I'm afraid I'll make up this whole elaborate scheme, that I'll chase this dream that I thought was mine but that was always just half-baked, and that I'll get there (wherever there is in whichever dream I'm talking about; doesn't have to be Australia, could be Hawaii, could be Denver, could be any of the other places/things I've talked about) and come to the realization that I always thought I wanted it but never knew what it was I wanted. That it's not what I thought it would be, and that I'm not going to be happy there. That I shouldn't have come, that it was a stupid idea, that I made the worst mistake of my life and I'm going to waste years of my life. My happiness is so fickle. That's part of what scares me, that there are so many things that can knock me off the happy train, that can make me doubt myself, doubt my instincts and my talents and my plans. I'm actually terrified and it is sooo silly. But it's not death that really scares me right now, it's not failing to be successful, it's not being unable to find a job. What seems to be scaring me is that I don't know myself well enough to figure out what will make me happy and DO THAT.

I'm also afraid that whatever decision I make, whatever I decide to do, will come back and bite me in the ass by making me sick and accelerating my progression and potentially sending me to an early grave. I'm worried that I'll spend years chasing experiences instead of chasing people, and that I'll chase experiences halfway around the world before I realize that I'm losing my health and I lost time with loved ones that I can never get back.

But then, when I think about the alternative, when I think about staying put and planning my life around other people and playing the safe route of familiarity, that's even more terrifying. Terrifying for me to consider the opportunities I could miss out on, the mind-and-soul-expanding experiences that I so desperately need to satisfy this lifelong wanderlust desire to move and put myself in other people's shoes and get out of this bubble. I'm scared of having a future of regret, where I look back and realize that I could have done amazing things but didn't because I was too scared. I'm scared of being scared and then looking back and realizing that I was scared. Fear is a healthy emotion; it protects us from dangerous things. But unwarranted fear shelters us from growth, and I think my unwarranted fear (SO MUCH FEAR) is preventing me from reaching my full potential as a human being. I think I'm changing because there's a shell that I was supposed to grow into but I can't. So instead I have to retreat back into something else, into being a person that I was trying to escape being. I'm being swathed in the qualities I needed so badly to escape and to rid myself of.

I need to find compassion again. I need to find perspective. I need to fulfill my goals and I need someone to understand what my goals are and support them. Not my long-term goals of family, etc. My short-term goals of acting instead of sitting, moving instead of being still.

What else am I afraid of? I always make lists about this but now I want to expand on things.

> I'm afraid of being alone and I'm afraid that I will leave Stanford with no lasting friendships to speak of except for maybe two friends who will never live in the same place as me again.

> I'm afraid that I've thrown away beautiful relationships and closed myself off to potential new ones.

> I'm afraid that I'll continue to do that because I don't know what the signs/symptoms are when I am doing it.

> I'm afraid that I'll FORGET what I wanted in the first place, so I won't be able to make positive change toward my goals.

I'm afraid I'll grow complacent.

I'm afraid that trying to keep myself alive will be such a valiant effort that everything else I want falls to the wayside, taking my spirit with it.

I'm afraid that I'll never be able to let anyone in truly, never be able to love someone completely, including their imperfections.

I'm afraid that I'll drive people away or just lose them with time and distance and disease and misunderstanding.

I'm afraid that I will waste precious time not being happy.

I'm afraid that I might be doing that right now, might have been doing that for most of college.

I'm afraid that I'll begin to resent the experiences/achievements of others since I've sacrificed so many of my own.

I'm afraid that I'll never accept myself completely, that I'll always be self-critical.

I'm afraid of the day that staying inside and sitting on the couch sounds more fun than being outside having an experience because breathing is so hard. (There are days when that's already the case, but thankfully not every day.)

I'm afraid that my GI problems will never improve and that they will continue to be my Achilles' heel, the main thing that leads me to pass up many opportunities, preoccupies my mind and pulls it away from more important/interesting things, steals many experiences.

I'm afraid of being overwhelmed by fear and of letting that stifle me.

I'm afraid of forgetting, and of being forgotten.

Wednesday, January 8, 2014
It requires so much brainpower to just organize my medical life that I feel like I have nothing left to give to my personal life. I'm always tired, in the sleepy tired sense because I don't sleep well but also in the physically tired sense (because I have "anemia from chronic disease" according to Elika, which there's no treatment for), and finally in the mentally tired sense, probably because of the exhaustion of using all of my brainpower toward dealing with insurance and pharmacies and medicine refills and not getting sick and when I do get sick, getting better and contacting doctors, and staying out of the hospital and when I'm in the hospital, getting out of the hospital, and it's just so overwhelming sometimes it makes me wonder if my entire future will be dominated by CF. It used to confuse me so much when patients always seemed to talk about CF or didn't have anything else going on in their lives and their lives revolved around CF, but now that's me.

Friday, January 17, 2014
The main thing that worries me these days is that I know my mental state is highly volatile, and sometimes, the higher I am for a little bit, the lower I sink when things turn even a little bit sour. So I hope this is not just a temporary high because I've been feeling generally good and have been having fun times with friends and I'm intellectually stimulated by what I'm doing at school, and I hope that I won't sink into a deep despair the next time I'm sick because everything has been stolen away. That seems to be what happens sometimes, so it's less worrisome when my mood is just level, and I'm not super happy but not super anxious/sad. But why can't I live in a state of serenity and happiness that's stable, not ephemeral, and dependent on

outside circumstances?? That's what I need to work toward. That's the goal.

Monday, January 27, 2014

Things were really wild last week and this weekend (it's Monday now). At the beginning of the week (post last weekend's tournament), I was on the verge of quitting volleyball, I got super sick last Monday and had a fever, I went to the GI doctor, and she told me I have to get the awful disgusting dehumanizing procedure called a Gastrografin study. You're in the operating room and they give you an enema but there's contrast in it and they X-ray your abdomen as it's going through to make sure they're directing it to the right spot. Last time I got one (I've only done it once before), I literally felt like I was getting wheeled to my death, or that I was onstage naked and being asked to dance, or something equally traumatizing, and then afterward I felt like I had just been assaulted. And the person who performed it was a really really nice old man, so that made it better . . . but what if some time in the future it's a young man? Or just anyone close to my age? The idea of it just makes me want to put a bullet in my head.

Anyway, I was really confused after my appointment with her. I was frustrated. I feel like she doesn't have answers anymore, so whenever I go, I just update her on how things have been, and then we'll do some temporary short-term solution (like the Gastrografin study) or she'll add a new medication (which I need to stop doing because I'm running out of options). So it's frustrating to feel like they've kind of given up on hoping that the situation will ever change. And I need it to change, because it actually prevents me from living my life to such a huge extent. When I think about future living situations, travel options, programs to participate in, even just the course of my days now that I'm living in 680, bowel issues are at the forefront of my mind in making decisions. Even for example this past Saturday, I was hooking up with a guy on Saturday night and I literally needed to kick him out because I hadn't gone to the bathroom that day and I felt like my stomach was going to get backed up if I didn't get to leave in the morning right when I woke up and go to Uncle Danny's to use the bathroom. It's honestly such a shit-show (literally) and it affects me so much I have such a hard time accepting it. I literally can't go to the bathroom in my own house, I have to leave. Which worsens the situation because if I have to go to the bathroom at a time when I can't leave (for example, if I'm in the middle of treatment), I'll ignore it and wait, which is really bad for the situation.

But enough of those complaints. It's always the same. I have to just figure out how to be okay with it, because I'm never going to accept my health and my body and my person as long as I think it's so disgusting and frustrating. I actually can't love myself because of it, because (a) I find my whole GI situation to be so disgusting and (b) I get mad at myself and ashamed of being so ashamed, so it just builds and becomes this heightened emotional angst that's so ridiculous. And I don't talk about it to anyone, literally anyone. I especially can't imagine ever talking about it to a romantic interest, so how can I ever be with someone and let them in if I'm constantly trying to hide such a big part of my life, something that I have to think about and deal with so often? I don't think I should date anyone until I resolve this issue with myself, because until I can just be open about it with a boyfriend, I can't have a relationship that will last. I know it sounds dramatic, but it's the truth. I can't live with a boyfriend until I deal with this, because the thought of sharing a bathroom with girls is bad enough, sharing a bathroom with boys I'm not interested in is out of the question, so sharing a bathroom with someone I AM romantically involved with just seems impossible at this point. So I picture myself at fifty, alone, never becoming serious with anyone because I can't travel with them or live with them or let them stay at my house for more than one day. God, it's so messed up!

Tuesday night, I went to practice and could not even do the butterfly drill. When I would raise my arm up to down-ball the ball over the net, it made my arms feel like lead, and then I would jog around to the other side, and I'd have to bend over and catch my breath from the twenty-foot slow jog. It was bad. Thankfully it was not a very intense practice and after we did butterfly and plyos and the easy warm-up, we watched this defense video for a while, then we came back to get into partners to hit and pass. Kennedy was my partner and it was not going well for me, I was getting tired just hitting down-balls at her, and then when it was my turn to pass, I was doing okay in the regular passing but I was short of breath. But then when it was time to do tips, I was doing run-throughs and I felt like my airways were starting to constrict and I couldn't really breathe and then all of a sudden I had a full-on asthma attack, I'm talking down on the floor crying because I could not breathe at all and felt like all my airways and throat had closed and I was breathing through a bent straw. And I was down on the floor tearing up trying to calm myself down so my anxiety wouldn't make it worse, and Steve came over and Kennedy went to look for my inhaler but I didn't have it so I borrowed Steve's, thankfully he had it, so I took Xopenex even though I had just taken it right before practice. Then I decided that was probably enough for me and I left, called my mom and asked her to call first thing in the morning while I'd still be sleeping and try to get me into clinic the next day.

In clinic Wednesday, I had a low-grade fever, poor O_2 sats, and FEV1 was like 1.7 something, 41 percent at its best, so they decided to admit me, even though my mom over text was trying to convince me to go to Hawaii instead (even though we know from experience that that doesn't have lasting results and just delays IVs). I asked Dr. Dhillon about that, and he said that doing "half-ass" treatments to try to delay IVs when the infection is flaring probably just makes resistance worse and makes it harder to treat, which is the opposite of my parents' opinion, that my bacteria is so resistant to everything that we should do whatever we can to increase the length of time between IVs.

So when Cami said, "You know you're being admitted, right?" as if it were a no-brainer, in the first instant I reacted strongly against it internally and was like, "No! I don't know yet! We need to check the white blood cell count, we need to see if the infection is actually worse!" What it was, I realize now, is that I didn't trust my own impression of my symptoms. I still have this idea that somehow, I might feel short of breath, think I'm sick, not functioning at the full capacity of my ability, and have lower lung function, but still not be sick. It's like I don't trust my instincts and I have this idea that even though I was sick enough to beg them to see me in clinic, it's just a mistake on my part and the tests will show that I'm actually fine and can go home. But it's silly, because it's very obvious that my body speaks to me in a clear language of symptoms that spell out when I need to come in. I can feel my lung function go up and down, I can tell by my breathing, my exercise capacity, my sleeping, my energy level, my appetite.

And it's interesting and random that I was supposed to come in that Friday for a Gastrografin study that was supposedly going to be "diagnostic" instead of therapeutic, according to Dr. Nguyen when she ordered the test weeks after I had had my last blockage episode. She said she wanted to see if there was some kind of mechanical obstruction in my intestines, like strictures or something. But then when I got admitted, they were planning on ordering the same procedure but as a therapeutic, not as a diagnostic (for therapeutic you eat beforehand and they clean you out, for diagnostic you're supposed to be cleaned out like for a colonoscopy before you go in so that when they X-ray you, they can actually see the intestines and not just the shit). It's all just so disgusting that I can't talk about it to anyone. I can barely even admit to myself that it's something I might have to deal with again. When I was scheduling it with the lady on the phone weeks ago, I asked her to check who would be performing the procedure, and then I looked up that radiologist online to make sure it wasn't a young(ish) man. It was an older man, and I was not happy that it was a man at all, but I knew that if it were a young(ish) man I would probably have a panic attack in the operating room.

Anyway, when I came in I didn't feel that I was having any GI problems, so we talked it over and got to the bottom of the therapeutic vs. diagnostic confusion, and I told them that I really didn't need any kind of enema for therapeutic purposes because I wasn't having an obstruction episode, and they realized that if I did have some kind of mechanical obstruction, I would be throwing up and not keeping food down, so there was no point in putting me through that horrific experience if we knew there was no mechanical obstruction. So thankfully I didn't have to do it.

We also had the discussion of port vs. PICC line for this admission. I thought maybe it would be a good time to get a port, because it's implanted under the skin and just has to get reaccessed each time. The PICC line needs a whole procedure each time you need IVs. But if I got the port, I wouldn't have been able to finish the volleyball season, because the interventional radiologist said they weren't comfortable with me playing with a port. But I do think that when the season is over, I will get one. It will just make my life so much easier. HOWEVER, I want to travel this coming year, and I know the port requires maintenance even when you're not on IVs, so I need to make sure that that's something that can be done wherever I decide to go—maybe Costa Rica, South Africa, New Zealand, wherever. I'm always feeling the travel itch and I know that if I don't scratch it now, I'll never get to. I need to push myself.

So the third day in I got a PICC line. Within the first few days they also did a CT of my sinuses and lungs. The sinus CT showed significant worsening since last year, and the ENT surgeon said that all eight sinuses were either completely opaque (meaning completely filled with mucus) or filled with splotchy fuzzy-looking white patches, which signals fungal infection. So I'm being treated with the IV antibiotics tobramycin and Ceptaz, the oral antibiotic minocycline, and the oral antifungal posaconazole. They chose this one because voriconazole damaged my liver when I was on it for months and gave me stones in my liver, and I'm going to be on the antifungals for a few months. I also need sinus surgery while I'm here, which is just really complicated. I need to do it now because they said it's pretty urgent and shouldn't wait a few months, and if I don't do it within the next week, I probably won't get to go to Cabo or nationals, both of which are really important to me.

So I'm waiting to hear when I'll be getting sinus surgery still, and when I'll be getting GI Botox endoscopy in my pyloric sphincter, and I've been here for a week and still there's no date set for either. But interestingly, I'm not itching to get out. It's weird, I don't know why. Part of it I think is that my life has just gotten so complicated that I don't miss it and the respite is sort of nice. It's a different setting where my only focus is getting healthy, that's it, nothing else. I do treatments, I sleep, I talk to people, I take my meds, I eat, I walk, I work with the personal trainer. And I get into a little routine here that is actually pretty pleasant because the weather is nice. They're running the IV Ceptaz over three hours three times a day instead of thirty minutes three times a day, because the infectious disease people that were consulted for my case this time said that it's more effective that way. And since in the petri dish my sputum cultures are resistant to all eight antibiotics they tested against it, they said anything to make the IVs more effective should be utilized. And I think it's working, since my PFTs went back up to 47 percent in the first week here! I feel so much better already than when I got here.

My routine is nice, I wake up around 9:30, have my coffee, and do respiratory therapy. I eat breakfast and the nurse brings pills and stuff and then I go to the bathroom. NPs and doctors come through between 10:30 and 11:30(ish). Then I get disconnected from the IV (at that hour they are finishing the IV iron, which I need because I'm also pretty anemic) and go for a walk, usually to the mall, until around 1:00. At 1:30 I do respiratory again and start IVs again, which run until around 5:30. Then I go for a little walk (and in the interim when the IVs are running, I'll work with the personal trainer lightly outside by the fountain for an hour), and then I have respiratory and more pills at 5:30. At 6:30 I'm free again until 9:00, so usually I've had visitors come at that time and we either go to Special Patient Services and have dinner or we sneak out to get dinner somewhere. Then back at 9:00 for more IVs, all nighttime pills, and the final respiratory treatment.

I will admit it's been great having my mom here because if she weren't here, I wouldn't be able to leave the hospital for my walks, wouldn't be able to get my hair washed, would be much more dependent on the staff, I wouldn't have food to feed my friends when they come, I wouldn't have someone to talk to and chat with in the room all day, someone to help me and push me to keep active, etc.

Monday, February 24, 2014

Grandma had a transient ischemic attack, or mini-stroke, the Sunday that my mom came up here. It was really scary, and I wanted my mom to go home and be with her. I wanted to go home to be with her, because I don't really know anything about strokes, and I thought she was going to die. But my mom refused to leave, and that stressed me out that my nonurgent health issues were taking precedence over my grandma's urgent ones, when I'm completely independent in the hospital and don't actually need someone to babysit me.

Tuesday, February 25, 2014

I've been talking a lot to Melissa. We talk on Facebook chat when I'm doing treatment at night, or we text a little throughout the day, and she's been sending me Snapchats but I only just received them all tonight because I didn't know you had to accept a friend on Snapchat. Learn something new every day! It's so cool to know someone with CF where I talk to them in real conversations, not just brief how are you, hope you're feeling well comments on their pictures and stuff. It makes it more like a real, living, breathing friendship. I just wish we could hang out in person, surf together, do things like that. She told me tonight that she makes these cases for surfboards out of fabric, kind of like socks, and she makes them herself, and I told her that could be an amazing business or fundraising venture. To have those board bags handmade by her (and/or other people with CF maybe) and sold with some of the proceeds donated to CF or sold through Mauli Ola with the proceeds going to them. It just seems like something that needs to exist. I could picture a line of these really cool beautiful artistic board bags that say "Surf to Breathe, Surf to Live" or something like that on them with amazing designs. I still want to get in touch with Andrew about making a CF bracelet with the company that he works for, Bead Relief; they make different bracelets for different causes and portions of the proceeds go toward those foundations. So I want to work with them to make a specific CF one.

I've been surprisingly happy. I keep wondering if they've accidentally increased my Wellbutrin levels, because I feel like normally I'd be going stir-crazy in here, having horrible FOMO, being angsty that my friends weren't visiting enough, being pissed that I don't know when the surgery is going to happen, etc. But the fact that I feel well definitely helps now, and that I'm sort of back on track with my work and stuff. I think maybe part of it is the book I read, called *How to Be Sick,* by Toni Bernhard. It's one of the fifty books for 2014 that I will read (except this one I've already finished). It was basically a guide to living with chronic illness inspired by the beliefs and practices of Buddhism. One of the ones that resonated with me was the idea of *dukkha,* or universal suffering. And the distinction between physical/objective hardship, which everyone experiences, and mental/emotional suffering, which is within our control. And through the acceptance of the fact of *dukkha,* or the universality and constancy of illness, hardship, etc., you can come to accept that life is a series of ups and downs and you have to just roll with the waves with equanimity, acceptance, and hope.

Another one that resonated with me, I don't remember what the Buddhist word for it is, is the practice of compassion aimed at yourself. I definitely lack that sometimes, and often blame myself for when I get sick, and I try to figure out why things happened (get a little bit of that from my mom!), and I'm just a curious person and I sometimes feel like everything that happens has a cause that I'll be able to discern. Part of what I need to do to achieve greater inner peace is to just let go of the notion that I have total control over this disease. And a lot of what's in the book at first glance might strike you as telling you to just give up, that nothing you do is going to change your trajectory because everything will just happen the way it happens and you have to accept whatever happens. But it's not saying you have to give up your efforts to improve your health, it's just saying that you should work toward greater health while still cultivating compassion toward yourself, keeping the idea in mind that when you do get sick it's not your fault, but that you can still work to make it better. I'm rambling, but I've been thinking about that while I've been here. My infection is resistant to every single antibiotic that exists, and somehow my initial reaction to hearing that news from the infectious disease people was thinking that it was somehow my fault, like I had these twinges of regret, but I wasn't even sure what I was regretting. Like regretting bad choices in general that could have caused this, regretting every time I let myself get sick and go on IVs when I could have prevented it, etc. And that's just not healthy. It's not my fault. I'm doing the best that I can and, whatever happens, it doesn't define my existence, it doesn't define my character, and I know that I can maintain peace and happiness even as I get sicker. It's just something I have to work at. The chant/song that really stuck with me that I now sing to myself (it's really just a poem, but I set it to the tune of *Mi Shebeirach* so that I could remember it) goes like this:

> *Rest in natural great peace, this exhausted mind.*
>
> *Beaten helpless, by causes and conditions, like the relentless fury, of the pounding waves, in the infinite . . . ocean . . . of samsara.*

And that really relaxes me when I'm feeling anxious or stressed or I can't fall asleep, both because of the words and because the *Mi Shebeirach* has always resonated with me a lot.

On a positive note, George Lavender from Making Contact Radio sent me his comments on the second draft of my script for Green Grid Radio. It's essentially done, I just have a few more tweaks to make. And the release date of the episode has been pushed back because he's still waiting for pitches from producers for the other two segments!

Can't believe I totally forgot to mention another thing that I think has been keeping my spirits up and preventing boredom: TIN-DER. It's so absurd, I never ever ever thought I would get it, I was so morally opposed to it, but Becca and Michelle both use it and say it's hilarious and that they have such funny conversations through it even if they never meet the people. So I was like, "What the hell, the worst that can happen is I'll hate it and delete it five minutes after I get it." But it's such a great way to kill time when I have like five minutes to spare and don't want to start reading or don't have time to do anything really. And I've matched with all these really cute guys and one I feel like could actually turn into something, like we chatted in Tinder messaging for a while and he was writing me these long paragraphs and I was writing long paragraphs back and he seemed really smart and genuinely interested in getting to know me. And then he texted me his number and asked if I wanted to go to this place called upcider in SF sometime, so I texted him to tell him that I was currently in the hospital but that I would love to go sometime after that. He's pretty slow to respond usually, like there's always a few hours in between our texts, and there was an entire day between my last text to him and his response, but when he does respond he's so interested, responds to everything I say, asks questions. . . . And as an added bonus, he's 6'5", from Australia, lanky and blond. So essentially, he seems perfect and I actually really want to meet him. I'm fairly certain he's a real person (haha!) but still if I did meet him, I would see if he could bring a friend and I could bring a friend or something.

Wednesday, February 26, 2014

For the chronically ill, the never-enough mantra doesn't work. Exercise is vitally important for people with many types of chronic illness, but for those of us fighting for our health every day, we can't compare ourselves to the perfectly healthy people pumping iron next to us at the gym. We don't want to be told to push past pain in a CrossFit studio when that pain is a very real, very important signal that something in the body is not right. Some of us can't hope for an endless upward trajectory of fitness; we can hope for stability; we can hope to feel well enough to get out there and move, whatever that may look like; we can hope for an exercise session that restores a sense of well-being.

As a former competitive(ish) athlete, I grew up defining success and failure in terms of the win-lose binary. If I wasn't getting better, I was failing. The only way forward was up. Stagnation was betrayal. But moving backward was inevitable when I was hospitalized multiple times a year, forced to sit on the sidelines through lengthy courses of IV drugs. This meant that beyond battling my disease within the walls of those hospitals, I also battled a belittling inner voice guiding me toward the conclusion that my athletic efforts were doomed.

This kind of thought pattern provokes a deep-seated feeling of inadequacy. Living with a progressive, life-threatening lung disease—and resistant bacteria—means that while it can be managed with medications, there is no cure. As I've gotten older, my lung function and exercise abilities have declined in parallel.

But exercise remains one of the most important ways to manage my disease, as it expands lung capacity, clears sticky mucus (preventing infections), and increases cardiovascular fitness (which helps improve oxygen saturation and delivery).

There was a period of time, when my identity transitioned from "athletic person" to "sick person," when exercise was no longer enjoyable. And that's when I knew something had gone wrong. I felt astray and turned to Pilates. It's been so healing and helpful.

Friday, February 28, 2014
Today is my sixteenth day in the hospital, I think (it's Friday and I got here two Wednesdays ago). This is my longest stay in a while, I think in total it will be eighteen days. I've gotten into a bit of a groove here, though, like I'm used to being here. And at this point because I had my sinus surgery yesterday, I don't even want to go home today because still I'm tethered to the oxygen. Plus, I can't sleep lying down, my nose is bleeding all over the place, I'm coughing up blood, I can't do full respiratory yet, and I'm still taking IV pain meds.

Last night was so rough. When I woke up from the surgery, I was in a recovery room with a male nurse who I couldn't see very well because I didn't have my glasses.

The male nurse was mean (as far as I can remember) and I was suffering extreme pain and it wasn't controlled. And I was so thirsty I could hardly breathe and he had no sense of urgency, I was asking him for ice chips and he was like, "Oh sure, in a minute, I'm charting something." No compassion. And I asked for my parents to come and he wouldn't let them come back. I don't remember much of what happened then.

I was wheeled back to my room and all I know is that I was in such pain that I demanded to have the pain medications at exactly the right time, every four hours so that I wouldn't have that pain again. But then I had my next dose of pain medication and it made me so nauseated that I had the bowl ready to throw up into but nothing in my stomach to throw up. So I took an oral Tigan, and that didn't work at all so then I took IV Zofran. Throughout the night I was wearing the oxygen, too, because my O_2 sats were only about 88 to 89 on room air. So I had the oxygen mask on, and I had burns on my face from where they put tape over my eyes and my cheeks. They looked like chemical burns, huge red marks across my cheeks. And my entire nose was bloody so every time I moved or coughed it would start pouring blood out again. I had a blue sling on my face that held gauze under my nose so the blood could just drip on it.

I'm just soooo angry. I've had the worst forty-eight hours of my life. Maybe that's an exaggeration. But pain, nausea, weakness, oxygen deprivation, the inability to pee leading to the need for a Foley catheter, more oxygen deprivation, nose pouring blood all over the place, coughing up blood, respiratory therapy every four hours, blood all over my sheets and gown, the burns burning my face, inability to eat, antinausea medication, all of that last night, and now today, blood and fully congested nose, oxygen deprivation, fatigue, and constipation requiring yet another enema and Mucomyst blast.

Friday, March 7, 2014

I am so happy to be out of the hospital finally! I got discharged yesterday after exactly three weeks. It was six days post-surgery before I left, which everyone was surprised about, but I felt so sick that I did not feel at all ready to leave until Wednesday. And the week post-surgery was so so rough. It was like there were multiple phases of this hospitalization. The first was me feeling really ill, with Pidge there, sleeping with oxygen, not doing much walking, being hooked up to the IV all the time, having a million tests done, and having consults with infectious disease, CF, GI, and ENT. Then Pidge left, my mom came, I started to feel better, and by the middle of the week I felt basically back to my baseline. I was sneaking out a lot to the mall, to my dorm, etc., had many friends visiting, started working with two personal trainers (we would go out to the front of the hospital by the fountain and do foam rolling, stretching, exercising, etc., and we got so many stares it was funny). Michelle came and stayed with me the last two phases of that and it literally felt like I was in a dorm, not a hospital. My PFTs went back up to 47 percent after the first week, and after the second week they were 48 percent. Then I went into surgery and was just catapulted miles backward. It was just completely awful. But I think in the long term it will help.

One fun thing. I'm making plans to meet the guy from Australia at a place called the Sutro Baths in Golden Gate Park in SF! And for some nice distraction at the hospital, one of the ENT surgery residents that sort of followed my case (but wasn't there for my surgery) was so so so attractive. Like two to three days post-surgery, I woke up one morning in the deepest sleep I've probably ever been in to a tall super-handsome guy shaking my foot to wake me up. It was kind of clear he'd been trying to wake me up for a while and I just wouldn't. And apparently, we had a whole ten-minute conversation, of which I remember nothing. Then the day before I got discharged, he and Dr. Hwang came to my room to talk to me and I was so unprepared. They came because my mom had basically been sort of mouthing off in a disgruntled fashion that nobody had given me any information about the recovery, examined me, talked to me, etc. etc. So they came to answer questions and stuff and it reaffirmed how attractive he was. Too bad there's no way I'll ever see him, except perhaps outside Dr. Hwang's office!

Off to bed now. So much more to write.

Thursday, March 13, 2014

It's now two weeks post-surgery and I'm feeling SO much better. Worked out yesterday and the day before with Kelley, and the first day we went for a run and I was basically at the same ability level as I was before the hospital! Which means I didn't lose too much over that month, which is great. I could run for a minute and a half and then walk two and a half minutes. We went around the lake and it was absolutely beautiful.

Tuesday, March 25, 2014

What is my life?! Sometimes my life is so awful it's surreal.

I was feeling really good for the past few weeks, but I couldn't sleep. There was that period of like seven days in a row where I woke up at 8:30 a.m. or earlier, even when I was exhausted, even when I took melatonin, no matter when I went to bed. So I wasn't getting enough sleep, and then one night in SF (the Saturday before last where I drank and only slept two hours) set me back and I never really got to catch up from that because I had to turn in my script, study for finals, etc. Wednesday was the breaking point, though. I was studying that day, having a normal day, then had to go to my three-week post-op sinus appointment to get suctioned, and I thought that would be no big deal and I'd continue working afterward. So I took a Percocet, and an extra gabapentin, and walked over to the hospital in the beautiful weather so I wouldn't have to drive on those meds, and the meds started to hit me as I walked over there. I was walking with the guy from Green Grid Radio, one of the news guys, whose name is Derek, I think. (I should absolutely know it but now it's too late to ask so I have to go back to the emails and then check Facebook to make sure.) Anyway, I got to the appointment feeling fine but then it was the most horrifically painful experience I've maybe ever had, despite all the pain medications. The nurse-practitioner couldn't even do it like she normally does for everyone, she had to get the head surgeon, Dr. Hwang, in. And he basically had to use a wrench and scissor-type devices to carve these two massive fist-sized balls of crusted blood out of each of my cheek sinuses. It was so so painful, I was crying and we had to take multiple breaks to numb it more, and he was being so nice and compassionate about it but I was just at a breaking point and so tired and was already stressed that I just couldn't keep my composure. After the appointment I walked out into the waiting room, after over an hour of that torture, and Makiko was there waiting for me since she was picking me up, and when I saw her, I just broke down and started crying again and we sat there while I just sobbed. It was insane. We sat there for at least ten minutes and then we went home and I just wanted to curl up in bed for the rest of the day but I had to meet with Christy to go over my script, and we ended up talking from 6:30 to 9:30 p.m. because we were talking about other stuff, too, and then I had told Perri that I would study for HumBio with her but by the time that came around I could barely think and it didn't really work out. I went to bed at around midnight, hadn't studied for the final, was exhausted and still drained from the appointment, and the next day I was going to have a waxing appointment, Pilates, a final, and then pack for Cabo and peace out early the next morning on my flight. So I was stressing pretty hard but not even consciously.

When I was sleeping, I had this vivid dream, that I still pretty much remember, of being on the beach and being completely overheated and checking my temp and seeing that it was 103. And right after that I woke up in real life and felt absolutely awful. Head was pounding, my body felt like a dead weight that was falling into the bed, and I was so hot and sweaty. I took my temp and it was 102.2, so I got really worried.

I spent the next four hours on the phone or email: canceling waxing, canceling Pilates, emailing prof about the final, talking to parents about what to do, calling CF clinic, talking on phone to infectious disease and ENT people, trying to figure out who to believe, deciding whether to go to the ER. Finally I went to Danny's to take a shower and nap and decided I wasn't going to the ER, because my fever was down to 99.5 with Tylenol so I thought I should take the final, so at 3:20 p.m. I almost drove right back to campus to take it at 3:30. But then I was talking on the phone to Sarah at CF clinic again, and she really really encouraged me to go to the ER, so I decided it would be irresponsible to ignore a fever that high and go to Cabo the next day, even if the fever was almost gone by that point. So I went to the ER thinking they were going to ask things like, "Why are you here?" and send me home, or just admit me for no reason for "observation," but then they drew blood and my white count was 29,000, which is insanely high. I don't know if it has ever been that high another time in the past. So at that point it was a "slam dunk" that I was getting admitted, as the nice ER doctor said.

That was Thursday. I got released Monday. I was supposed to have to stay till Wednesday for a week of IVs, as per Dr. Patel's order (he was on the whole time I was there until Monday), but then on Monday, Dr. Mohabir came back (he hadn't been there the whole previous month when I was in with the sinus surgery and everything), and he decided to release me that day!! And I asked if I was okay to go to Cabo, and he said, "Yes! Live your life; you should go." So then I got discharged and we quickly remade my flight reservations and figured out my plans.

Packing up now to get ready for my flight. Have to repack all the meds I packed last night (because I'm at Danny's), but at least I'm not packing for the first time now. I have a backpack of clothes, that's for both Cabo and LA, but I don't need anything more, really, and it makes it easier because I have two wheelie medical bags. I'm a little nervous to see what the dynamic is down there in Cabo, because I heard from Sabrina that the scene isn't exactly her scene . . . lots of day drinking, drunk people, etc. I'm definitely not into that, either. I want to hang out in the ocean, enjoy the sun, be with friends (Maya is there, too!), and go out like one night. Just crossing my fingers I don't get sick again.

Thursday, April 17, 2014

Jesus, it's 2 a.m.!!!!! I don't know what's wrong with me—I need to sleep but can't with so much on my mind. I drank a little too much caffeine today, so tomorrow I won't have as much and maybe I'll take a melatonin or even take a nap. The other night I stayed up until 2:30 a.m. working on an outline for my senior reflection. I've been working on it for months (the prep) but now I'm stressing about the fact that I have to actually write my script. In the script and a podcast I'll be comparing the degradation of my lungs by the colonization of a superbug to the degradation of native Hawaii by the colonization of foreigners. Sue McConnell and Andrew Todhunter are among the top five coolest professors on the entire campus.

Thursday, May 1, 2014

Haven't written in a month! A lot has been going on, a lot of really amazing fun exciting things. I feel so much more engaged here socially than I have probably since freshman or sophomore year (the beginning of soph year at least), and something inside me just feels different about my present and my future. I feel hopeful, I feel optimistic, I feel like things will unfold that will be happy and fresh and provide meaning and community. I feel like I have a better sense of what I want and need out of life (friendship, community, lots of sleep, good health, access to the outdoors, engaging work, adventure, etc. etc.).

But that's all really vague. I've been exercising a lot, which made me feel good for a while. I'm also starting to think about graduation. It's coming so quickly!!!! I'm gonna "walk" but stay for one extra quarter, which turns out to be a good thing since I'm not ready to leave!!

Monday, May 5, 2014

What a difference a day makes. Well, a few actually. Today I'm having a lot of self-loathing and body hatred going on, which I can't stand, and I don't know how to stop it, but every time I look at myself, I criticize what I see and I hate the manliness of my upper body and the distended pregnant-looking nature of my stomach and the increasing strength of my legs and calves, and I just feel large now when I used to feel lean and slight. And I know I should be proud of that, my lung function is improving, my ability to move and participate in life is improving, I'm happier, but for some reason I just can't shake this awful horrible body image that I have. I really think I should see someone, because I get so anxious about food and eating, and most of it is related to the fact that my GI issues (mainly constipation/slow gut at this point, not so much the reflux anymore) plague me constantly, every single day, and are always on my mind, and I can never do anything right. When I eat, it's bad, when I don't eat, it's also bad, when I eat high fiber it's bad, when I eat low fiber it's bad, when I try to do a cleanout, it doesn't work anymore because I've had so much of all these meds that my body doesn't even respond to them anymore. Even coffee has zero effect on my system now. It's like what we're learning about in Human Behavioral Biology, how your body adjusts and autoregulates, so if you're constantly throwing more and more laxatives at it, it's going to stop having peristaltic contractions in the intestines on its own, and that, combined with the mucus in the gut and the inability to digest food properly, makes for an ugly situation that's ever-present and that I have no idea what to do about. It's literally the number one source of anxiety in my life still. And it leads to feelings of hatred toward my entire body, shame, embarrassment, disgust . . . and it makes me know that until I deal with my insecurity and shame around this issue, I'll never be able to be with anyone and have it become serious, because I push people away and keep them at a distance so that they never know about this stuff so that they won't stop being attracted to me and start thinking I'm disgusting.

But back to the good things. I've been exercising a lot, I was swimming once or twice a week at the beginning of the quarter, but now I'm doing more yoga, sand volleyball, working out with the trainer (Kelley, not Paul). I haven't been working with Paul or doing private Pilates with Grace, because I don't have a lot of time and our schedules are not aligning this quarter. I also started climbing and got belay certified, so every Monday I go with Makiko and Kevin, and either Brett or Neli, to climb. Last Monday or maybe the one before it, Neli and I went to the pool afterward and played pool water polo/basketball with Adrian and a bunch of French House people, which was so fun, and unplanned, because we just ran into them. I've been very distracted by my extraordinarily hot bio TA, whose name is Ryan. He's a bio PhD and he is just so supremely attractive, and he is obviously extremely intelligent, and he seems so sweet. Creepily, I Facebook-stalked him and discovered that he's engaged . . . but it's so funny how I'm motivated to look good when I go to bio class. It's ridiculous because there are about four hundred people in the lecture hall so why would he even see me, and even if he did see me, he's engaged anyway, and even if he weren't engaged, what makes me think he would be attracted to a student, and if he were the kind of guy to pursue students, what makes me think he would be attracted to me? The whole thing is just so absurd but I just think it's fun to see someone where you realize that if the circumstances were right, they would be exactly your type and you would definitely pursue it. . . . I mean like if I met him in a class and we were both students, or some similarly normal situation. But regardless, it's been a nice distraction, and it was funny I saw him at the climbing wall actually when I was with Brett, Kevin, and Kiko, and my heart jumped actually! I'm such a twelve-year-old child sometimes it's so funny.

Speaking of men, I don't know if I'm into Dylan (the tall guy from Tinder) anymore. My interest seems to have waned. I wanted to be considerate a week ago when I realized that I wasn't going to be able to hang out with him for like three weekends in a row and that I couldn't go during the week, so I called him up and left a voicemail saying that I was sorry but was just really busy but that I did want to see him when I wasn't so busy in a couple of weeks. And he called back and was super nice about it, and was like don't even worry, it's all good, I'll see you soon, etc. I'd like to see him this Saturday (right now it's Thursday), because it's Senior Formal on Friday and I'm going to be staying in the city that night and then doing brunch and whatnot. I'm wondering if I should give Liane, Catherine, and Sabrina my car to go home that day with all my stuff, and then stay and hang out with him for the rest of the day and just Caltrain home? Because I feel like we're just in this limbo where I don't know if I want to keep seeing him, I don't know if it's worth it, and we just need to have a fun date together just the two of us for me to decide how much I actually like him. It's been like an out-of-sight-out-of-mind situation, so it's really hard for me to gauge how I feel about it. It's been fun, it was a really nice distraction when I was in the hospital and recovering from surgery, but now there are so many fun things happening on campus that I don't know if I want to keep running to SF just for a relationship thing that I know isn't going anywhere past June. The thing is that on Saturday I wanted to go to Charlotte's birthday party at her house (aka the "nudist colony"), and there's Blackfest and other things happening on campus, so I think it might just be easier to go home. I don't know, it's hard to weigh what I want to do (I know it's a good problem to have, though, to have too many good options to choose between).

Saturday, May 24, 2014

This has literally been the most action-packed quarter I've ever had at Stanford, and the most fun. I appreciate Stanford so much right now and am so grateful for the four years I've had here, even though at times things were very bumpy. It makes me realize that whenever I was not happy, it was a result of special circumstances, not the place itself being flawed. Looking back, there are things I could have done differently in order to make my experience better throughout the entire thing . . . but I think I learned and grew from the period of time where I was really unhappy. And it makes me all the more grateful for how happy and healthy I've been this quarter. For the past year, whenever I have had a chance to wish, on birthday candles, under a tunnel, at 11:11 when I remember, whatever, I have wished to be healthy and happy. I feel like I can finally say that things have fallen into place, and I've achieved both of those things. It would have been nice if I could have achieved both of those things earlier in college, so that I wouldn't have wasted time here being unhappy, but I just need to accept with equanimity that the suffering and pain I went through probably made me a stronger person and will somehow serve me in the long run. Not that it was "meant to be," or anything like that, but there's just no point ruminating on what could have been.

POST-COLLEGE LIFE

When I was an awkward high school freshman trying everything I could to fit in, I got invited to join a group of friends seeing *Star Wars: Episode III* at midnight on opening day. My parents struck down the idea immediately, as they were very strict about our sleep habits. I was devastated, to say the least, but Mallory was there for me, with a Hail Mary solution that just might work: "You should write them a persuasive essay."

Sure, it sounded wild, but this was my only hope. Not only did Mallory have a constructive suggestion for me when all seemed hopeless, but she also stayed up to help me brainstorm and outline my arguments. She said good night and wished me luck before climbing into bed, and I finished the essay around 2:00, leaving it on my mom's desk. Mallory woke me up at 7:00 and said, "It worked, you're going to see the movie."

In that moment, and through her empathy and generosity, my sister taught me about the art of persuasion—a lesson I won't soon forget. This is just one of countless stories I can recall of Mallory brightening the lives of the people around her.

—Micah

Sunday, June 15, 2014

Today I graduated college. It was a beautiful day. Beautiful ceremony. For Wacky Walk I was a tree and so was Maya. It's this wild tradition where you dress up that's both silly and irreverent. Gia and Danny were tree-huggers. I thought I would be too exhausted to enjoy the day, but it was too big of a day with too much adrenaline not to enjoy. The ceremony was not boring; Bill and Melinda Gates spoke, and their speech was great.

I'm feeling too many things right now and I'm a little bit drunk so it's difficult to type. Currently doing treatment and listening to the Giving Tree Band. I was really happy all throughout the first ceremony, in the Stanford stadium. Just thinking about how much I've accomplished and how lucky I am to have the family support that I have, and to be in such a beautiful place with such amazing intellectual and social vitality. And to be healthy enough to enjoy the day (the entire last quarter at Stanford without a hospitalization, first time since freshman year!). I'm so incredibly grateful, and happy, and blessed with the experiences I've had and people I've known.

I've met such incredible people in my time here that one of my biggest worries going forward is that I won't be able to replicate that kind of community (on both an intellectual and just a normal friendship level). I've met some amazing people in my last quarter here, too, that I've had a lot of fun with, or gotten closer with people I already knew.

Wednesday, June 25, 2014

Thinking about why I spend so much time writing in this journal. There are two really important reasons why I write about my life that I need to openly acknowledge to myself. The first is that I use the journal as a way of chronicling my life so that future me can look back at a time period and put myself in younger me's shoes. The second is that I have this feeling that when I die someone will eventually find this and my life won't be forgotten, even though when I really think about that and what that would mean, it makes me horrifically uncomfortable. Just to think about the things I've written in the thousands of pages I've probably written, and the bad things I've said about people, and the deeply personal stuff that's revealed, and mostly all the descriptions of having sex that I would never want my family to read or think about (haha!).

Tuesday, July 15, 2014

So happy to be spending the summer in Hawaii. Becca and Ari didn't come when I did so in the beginning my mom stayed with me and then Jesse, Gaby, Ali, and Stacy visited!

Fourth of July here was wild. They have this annual event called Floatilla!!!! A tangle of hippies, drunks, military folks, surfers, tourists—hanging out in the water on a formation of floats! Loud music coming through speakers, phones submerged in plastic cases, alcohol being passed around freely like it was water. Fireball bottles floating in the water. Recycling bins on paddleboards, Good Samaritans collecting beer bottles. Pacific Drunk-People-on-Rafts Patch is the new Pacific Garbage Patch. You have to Jet Ski to get out there; it can barely be seen from shore. I went with Gaby and Stacy but we got separated in the crowd. So much fun but ended up with fever so had to cut it short. A kindhearted man paddled me back. In a wild turn of events, Stacy ended up dating him.

What an incredible summer in Hawaii! After the Fourth, it was so busy, so fun, I didn't need to write. But thinking back I marvel at the prowess of my body and how incredible those three months were. Documenting to remember:

6:00 a.m. surf sessions in glassy conditions. Paddling for hours, never getting cold, never getting tired. Pop-up after pop-up, wave after wave. Infatuation with Shawn, the lifeguard I had a fling with. My friend . . . my surf guru . . . my what-even-are-you?

Confusion, mixed signals, so much laughter.

One day, coughing up blood before a surf date, I considered canceling and decided against it, too excited to see him, too worried that if I canceled, I'd never surf with him again. As unpredictable as he was at the beginning of the summer, just out of my grasp, is how consistent he later became, dependable, loving, and always-there.

Papayas and frozen waffles, açaí bowls and coffee. Sustenance that fueled my surf habit. The daily drive along that road from Kahala to Waikiki, from the suburbs to the surf in our sturdy Toyota 4Runner rental. Boards hanging out the hatchback, "Take Me to Church" by Hozier blaring from the speakers.

Sandy feet on my yoga mat, the sweet teacher we'd see after class at Whole Foods. Our bodies would sweat salt onto the salt already on our skin from the surf beforehand.

Surfing with DJ one day in front of the Kaimana cottage. Disorganized surf spot with shifty surf, lots of reef. Trying to escape the crowds, we paddled way out to a break where only very advanced surfers were lining up. We planned to stay on the inside and catch the smaller ones, staying out of the way of the others. My arms got tired on my seven-foot, six-inch sippy noserider so I switched boards with him, taking his eleven-foot log, heavy as lead.

A six-footer rolled through and I noticed too late to paddle over it; the wave tossed me off the board and the massive fin sliced half the circumference of my thigh just above the knee, then down the back of the leg to the mid-calf. Didn't break skin, thank God, but caused a hematoma the size of a softball. The pain it caused left me immobile for weeks.

Tandem surfing competition with Shawn in Duke's Oceanfest. Learning how to do lifts with Bear, the World Tandem Surfing Champion. Shawn's magnetic smile, his mind-boggling ability to surf while holding me in the air.

Pali Highway, surrounded by towering heights of green, like the set of *Jurassic Park*. That time it rained down on us when we were in an open Jeep, when it went from sunny skies to pouring buckets in an instant.

Windy days on those beautiful east side beaches, Kailua, Lanikai. The Whole Foods in Kailua where they jacked up the price of water when Hurricanes Julio and Iselle were coming. The hurricanes were supposed to devastate the island; we prepared to be indoors for days, bought hundreds of dollars of water. Safeway stores all over the island were out of water. We hunkered down; the Big Island was ravaged.

My roommates, my partners in crime, my incredible friends. Becca and Ari, BFFs for life. Other friendships forged. And Shawn. Always Shawn. One day I found out my unrequited feelings turned out not to be unrequited. Double-date night on Taco Tuesday, alcohol and greasy tortilla chips and then, sadly, fevers.

Mom flying in to help me move home. The very last night, massive hemoptysis and hospitalization the next day. Shawn showing up with fresh-picked avocados from the mountain, sunflowers, and dominoes. Yoga and sneaking out to secret patios. Dr. Mohabir saying I couldn't fly home. Ten days in the hospital followed by a ten-day hotel stay since our lease was up.

Those three weeks of sickness when everything changed, with us, and with my health.

That summer of 2014 was freedom. It was fantasy. My life was a movie that I didn't want to end. No perception of my body being limited in any way until my very last night on the island. Every day, I did what I wanted and my body obliged. It supported my purest passions and athletic endeavors.

That summer we did the ledge. I stood on the highest tower,

seeing the most beautiful world in every direction. And then hemoptysis. I plunged, free-fall. The fabric of my perfect life unraveled.

Now I see no rock holds or crevices to help me climb. There is no climbing back up. When you're falling, there's only one direction you can go.

Wednesday, October 15, 2014 (22 years old)

I made a big decision yesterday! I talked with my professor Andrew Todhunter for about an hour. Told him about my options for work post-Stanford and how I was feeling lost and confused about what I should do. He advised me to avoid a real job (important to hear from an adult who's not one of my parents). I know they want me to avoid a real job for health reasons, and Andrew has the perspective of a healthy person who avoided a real job for different reasons.

Andrew encouraged me to become a writer and to take on a book project (to write about Susan Gottlieb, an important environmentalist, and her renowned native garden). Reasons:

- I care deeply about the environment.
- Will make money.
- Great on my résumé.
- Give me confidence to do a book-length project.
- Experience will translate when I'm ready to write my own book.

I talked to Andrew about what's important to me, and how to go about being a writer. What the days are like, how to keep yourself on track/disciplined, how to network to get work. Lots of philosophical talk, but also lots of practical talk. He's so helpful. Later met with James Campbell (another one of my professors), who is so inspiring.

Thursday, October 16, 2014

When I was young, I learned about the selfish gene.

Lying in bed at night, cuddled beneath the covers, my dad's voice would soothe me to sleep with talk about the complexity of the human genome, the spiral shape of a DNA helix, the way forces of natural selection would make harmful mutations die out with their host, but allow random beneficial mutations to proliferate and spread through a population, causing such changes within a species that one common ancestor could play grandfather to a bonobo, a rhesus monkey, and a human, or a Brussels sprout, mustard seed, and stalk of broccoli.

Every night, as he'd wax poetic about the marvels of evolutionary biology, only taking a break to throw in some astrophysics and history, I'd fall asleep to the letters *A, T, C,* and *G,* amazed at this world we live in, developing this *profound love* for the theory of evolution, for the belief that random chance and probability could shape a planet composed of rock, water, and protozoa into the beautifully varied community of life that exists today, from the highest peaks of the Himalayas to the lush richness of the Amazon to the eerie black depths of the dark ocean floor.

We worshipped Dawkins and Dennett, the unusual versions of childhood heroes my brother and I clung to, and they illuminated if not the why, then at least the how of human existence. Evolution seemed like a religion, but it wasn't one because it does not require faith, it encourages you to question, to dig, literally, to understand the origin of our species and the complex history of the genetic matter that existed, mutated, and evolved to construct this current world of ours. This community of species we share the planet with, a community that has lost members like the dodo, the Kauai o'o bird, the Caribbean monk seal, the Baiji white dolphin.

We read *God's Debris* and *The God Delusion,* debunked the logical proof of God's existence put forth by Aquinas, read the Bible as literature, and occasionally laughed at the more outlandish elements of certain stories . . . Lot's wife turning to a pillar of salt for looking over her shoulder, Joseph's brothers' inability to recognize him when he became pharaoh of Egypt, Noah's Ark and the idea that two of every species alive today could fit into one boat without all eating each other, the blood in the river and the frogs and the leeches; but we learned some lessons anyway, in Sunday school and in discussions at the dinner table, what my parents called the "point" of their atheist version of Judaism.

But one day, I realized that evolution, the almighty natural force that I revered with the core of my being . . . *evolution isn't acting on me.*

I'm exempt.

If natural selection were happening unhindered, I would be dead. There would be no Mallory Smith, age twenty-two, Stanford graduate living and breathing, making friends and reflecting on the origins of the universe. There would just be some ashes scattered in the Pacific Ocean, or however my family would choose to honor a life that had no chance to ripen.

I was born with two defective copies of the CFTR gene, one mutated copy from each parent. You have one copy of the gene, and you get a heterozygote advantage, an increased fitness because of a lower likelihood of dying of cholera. But with two copies of the gene, you're salty. The old adage goes, "The child will soon die whose brow tastes salty when kissed."

At this point, keeping myself alive is a full-fledged mission, enlisting all of my energy and hours every day. I need to fight the chronic deadly resistant bacteria eating away at my fragile, scarred lungs. Fight the billions of bacteria overtaking my lungs and clear out the mucus so I don't feel like I'm breathing through a straw with a boulder weighing on my chest. Staying alive, for someone with CF, requires active and constant effort *against* natural selection, requires a grand *fuck you* to that force which, left to its own devices, would have us suffocated from respiratory failure before adolescence.

What does my survival come down to, what is responsible for my ability to trump natural selection? Medicine. Medicine gives me the gift of life. Medicine exempts me from the forces that paved the way for humanity to emerge, that shaped life on Earth for millions of years, since the very first cell sprang to life in the primordial soup.

How is that fair? Why do we, today, get to override evolution? What will that do for the future of our species? More important, what does that mean for the millions of other species on this planet who don't have that unfair advantage, who still exist at evolution's mercy?

I want to live and I want people the world over affected with illness, ridden with deadly diseases, to live, to survive, to *thrive,* and to reproduce, creating imperfect little perfects. I want us to be viewed as worthy enough to pass on our genes, even if we'd be outcompeted by those whose genome is "better" in a world where natural selection still reigned supreme.

My life is a miracle. Life in general is a miracle. Our existence is the result of stars exploding, solar systems forming, our Earth having an environment hospitable to life, and then, finally, millions of highly improbable events accumulating over millions of years to bring us, a capable and conscious bag of stardust, to the here and now.

Sunday, February 1, 2015

The last time I wrote was a few days after my birthday. That shouldn't bug me. I was happy, I was busy, I didn't write, who cares? I actually do care. Because there were a lot of times I felt like I needed to write to clarify things in my life, and I didn't, because I hadn't written recently and I wasn't in a mood at that particular moment to catch my own journal up on my own life. Deep regrets.

Today I had an interview with Beth Pratt of National Wildlife Federation, who was so interesting and will be a great resource for the book. Tomorrow I will interview Lili Singer from Theodore Payne Foundation for Wild Flowers and Native Plants. Also talking to Garry George from Audubon, Lisa Fimiani from Friends of Ballona Wetlands, and Carl Richards (landscape photographer). Also going to look at an apartment in Manhattan Beach with Lauren! It looks like a gorgeous place.

Tuesday, February 17, 2015

I think I'm more vulnerable than I used to be to the idea of death. I don't know if that's just right now, this very week, because I'm sick, or if it's just a sensitivity that's increasing over time. Two things spurred this: First, the *Parenthood* finale. The death of Zeek, the grandfather, left me bawling, and not just tears but the entire body shaking kind of bawling. I think it's where my mind wandered that makes me feel unsettled.

When Camille walked in and saw Zeek lying on his chair, and she called to him and he didn't respond, it triggered the thought that one day my own parents might have that experience with me, and I thought about how they would feel in that moment and how they would react. It physically pains me to think of it, but I can't not think of it when I see death in any form. And then when they're scattering his ashes, I think about the fact that my own grandpa will die, maybe soon. The emphasis on family is so strong, it makes me realize I don't always express how important my family is to me.

In the show they have flash-forwards to where all the characters are in a few years, new babies, new relationships, family still strong, lives going forward in the most predictable, wonderful way, and I think that that will never be the way my life goes and that makes me sad. Sad for me and for all the people that will be affected. When I get sick, my parents stop their lives. If I were sick to the point that Caleigh is sick, I would feel terrible. It's enough to be scared myself, but to know that my own situation might be taking away happiness from others is devastating.

I was thinking about how good I have it right now! I'm healthy enough that even when I'm sick, I can move my body and do some exercise. I can get through a hot power yoga class alongside healthy people. I live close to the ocean and can surf. I have incredible friends who I love and have fun with. I have a degree from Stanford. I have incredible family support. I have a new puppy who loves me. The word I've used the most in this paragraph is love; my life is filled with love, with fun experiences, with happiness. And I should have the attitude that I'm so so lucky, and most of the time I do.

But there are moments when it strikes me that all of the things I love will be lost. Breathing will get harder, and at some point I'll have to live at home so my parents can help me full-time. A time when I'll get disability money from the government because I can't work.

I may or may not find someone who can hang with my disease, who can support me in the way I need to be supported. Sometimes I'm hopeful about that, but oftentimes I'm not, because even if there were people who would be good enough to do it, I might not let them in; even though I seem open about some things, ultimately I'm private, and have never let anyone in. I should not have envy, I recognize that it's a dangerous emotion, but I do for people who have freedom, who can travel, who can see other parts of the world and make their own decisions and do things without worrying that it will drive them to the hospital in the future.

All this thinking led me to the moment where I realized that this might be as good as it gets. It might only get worse from here. When things are going well, I often think something bad is about to come, because I've learned things can only go so well for a limited amount of time. I hate the impending sense of doom, that this goodness I'm living right now cannot last, will not last, that it will be stripped away. The higher you fly, the farther you fall. The healthier I am, the more I start to feel sturdy and strong and capable and normal, the more the slap of reality stings when it knocks me down, shows me my fragility, reminds me that my innards are working against me, not for me.

I thought, if this is as good as it gets, and I died right now, would that be so bad? It's the quit-while-you're-ahead mentality. Obviously I would never act on that. I'm not depressed, I've actually been quite happy and filled with gratitude lately. But I was thinking, if I died right now, it would be like ripping off the Band-Aid. My family and the others who care about me would be devastated. And it would be a huge thing, the thing that happens when people commit suicide where people say, "How could they do this to me? How could they do this to their mother?" etc. I've always been shocked when people say that, because suicide is not about anyone else. It's a last resort for a person who feels they have no other option. That's not how I feel right now.

If I do die soon (from CF) and someone reads this, they might think I was suicidal. But I'm not. I was just thinking about how my death would cause a lot of pain initially, but then my parents and friends could live their lives without having to worry about me, without having to take care of me. It kills me how much pain I might cause others if I die.

Tuesday, March 17, 2015

Well, I've emerged from the hellhole of RSV (respiratory syncytial virus, what it turned out I had) and a new chapter is beginning to unfold. I've started moving my stuff into my new Manhattan Beach apartment, which I LOVE. It's two blocks from the beach and I can tell it will be an awesome active lifestyle there. I booked a trip to Hawaii, which is where I am now. This trip is such a trip (like the mind-fuck kind of trip, not a literal trip). It feels so long since I've been here, but also like no time has passed. The weirdest thing is that the last time I saw Shawn in person we were on such a different level with our friendship, relationship, whatever you want to call it. It's kind of a guessing game as to how to act around him, like whether we're just friends or something more, and I don't know what he wants, whether he still likes me (although I think he still does). I think he's conflicted, I'm conflicted.

Hawaii has been amazing so far. Yesterday, the day we arrived, we gained time so it was a long day but we packed a lot of fun into it!

Today I woke up at 5:00 a.m. naturally—thank you, jet lag! We were in the water from 6:15 to 6:45(ish), and it was stunning. Incredible. It was dark when we got in the water, the sun hadn't risen yet, so we watched it rise from the canoe in the water. Plus surfing the waves on the canoe was awesome. The water was a gorgeous shade of blue and early-morning surfing has a calmness to it that afternoon surfing does not.

I'm super happy to be here and already feeling so much better in my lungs. Which makes my head feel better. The magical combo of sun and salt makes me recover a lot faster and surfing the warm water in Oahu is the best medicine.

Tuesday, April 7, 2015

Sometimes I feel like my life is a novel with someone writing it, and making sure there are enough high points and low points, drama and emotion, conflict and resolution. That's why whenever there's a long period of good times, I have the sinking feeling that something bad is to come, that the good, contented stability can't last. Because contented stability doesn't make for a good read.

It also has such distinct chapters, with seemingly abrupt transitions between chapters. One month I'm sick with RSV, living in Beverly Hills, and spending time with my puppy, Kona. Then, boom, in Stanford, nervous breakdown about work and life. Then back home, moving stuff to Manhattan Beach apartment, then an unplanned trip to Hawaii.

In Hawaii an abrupt turnaround and I'm feeling better, thrown back into fun with Shawn, as if no time had passed, surfing and paddleboarding, canoeing and volleyball. Then in Maui with Ali and our moms on a mother-daughter getaway, crashing from how much I pushed myself in Oahu, thinking I'll need to be admitted and hoping I can put it off until after a road trip with Shawn. Then back to LA, living at the beach officially, spending my first night there having so much fun. Then Shawn in town, which was a mind-twister. My two completely separate worlds colliding, then spending time with his family in Santa Ana, going to Club 33 and a day at Disneyland with them and spending the night in his family home.

I need to reflect on how strange and unusual my life is and how booklike it seems and not beat myself up for not journaling more often (even though I want to remember every minute of it).

Wednesday, April 8, 2015

I woke up feeling bad (physically and emotionally) and figured I should tell the doctor so I called the clinic to talk to Ronnie to tell them about my symptoms and my voice was breaking the whole time on the phone. I can't keep it together and it's pathetic. I was sitting outside in the sunshine and feeling sorry for myself, which makes me feel worse because I know it's absurd. And when I hung up the phone after leaving a message, I put my head between my knees and couldn't stop crying. I think these inexplicable tears are more frustrated tears, self-directed, scornful tears, because I think I brought this sickness on myself and now can't deal with it.

My mom saw how stressed I was and mentioned that she could find someone to replace me on Susan's book. The job is an opportunity of a lifetime . . . to be paid to write about the environment and work for the most awesome woman who is so incredibly understanding about everything in my life and so flexible on deadlines. I can't bear not to finish.

But if I can't even finish one writing job, my first writing job out of college, what hope is there for me to ever not only get another job but have the confidence to look for one? I'm just hemorrhaging my parents' money and my guilt about that makes me sick because they work so hard every day and will work way after they could have retired so that I can have a good life, when I can't even suck it up and work a few hours a day, sick OR healthy.

Thursday, April 23, 2015

"We've come to think of healing in mechanical terms, as repairing something broken, like fixing a flat tire. But for most of human history healing has meant more than repairing the body. Healing has meant restoring a sense of wholeness to a person—or even a relationship or community."

This is from the story I produced for my senior reflection. I titled it "Biome," but when it played yesterday on the podcast *State of the Human,* they called it "Salted Wounds." The Senior Reflection class was amazing—and the Stanford Storytelling Project does an amazing job of teaching people how to use story to create social change.

Wednesday, April 29, 2015

Jesse is writing a song for me!!! She wrote one before, but it was too "happy." CF is a mind-fuck and any song about it should reflect that. I sent her a detailed note about what living with CF is like. Can't wait to see what she does with it!

Friday, May 1, 2015

Spoke today in Margot's medical genetics class at Cal State Northridge. It really affected some of the students, hearing my story. They couldn't believe what my life is like. They couldn't reconcile how I look with my reality. Their questions were so widespread; they asked about drug development, my emotional resilience, and what dating with disease was like . . . the whole range.

I was touched that all these people who didn't know me felt like my "speech" made them think I was open enough to answer those kinds of questions honestly, which I did. It made me want to do more speaking where I'm not reading from a piece of paper, but just talking candidly in front of a group of people who actually want to listen and to learn.

I was dreading waking up early for it, driving all the way to Northridge, etc. But it was totally worth it.

Monday, July 20, 2015

Had this idea today that I wanted to write down before it leaves my mind or I stop feeling inspired or I forget it or something inside me tells me it's not possible.

I want to start an online media source (podcast? website?) that tells the stories of people who have struggled with something in their life and found hope somewhere. Anything from chronic illness to poverty to grief to depression, etc. The hope can be from anywhere, unexpected places.

Names to consider:

— re: life (about life, but also implying some kind of
   renewal/starting over)
— Project Redemption (or The Redemption Project)
— The hope-knock life (play on words *hope* and *hard-
   knock life*)

Saturday, August 29, 2015

"Breathe deeply, until sweet air extinguishes the burn of fear in your lungs and every breath is a beautiful refusal to become anything less than infinite." —D. Antoinette Foy

Kari died yesterday. She was a hospital buddy, but more than that, she held a torch that illuminated a new direction for me at a time when my health had left me in a hopeless terror. She was a friend and a fighter with a radiant goodness and fierce compassion, smiling her sweet smile no matter how sick she was. The world became a little bit darker today, when Kari lost her battle with CF. I'm stunned and sickened.

Rest in peace, Kari. So many people loved you. Breathe easy. You are infinite.

Monday, September 7, 2015

I want to get a stick-and-poke tattoo of the letters *LXV*—65 in Roman numerals. Caleigh's brother Michael got that tattooed on his inner arm and it looks sick, and I would want to do it on my inner wrist but a lot smaller, so it could be covered with bangles or a watch. I Facebook messaged him to ask how he would feel if I stole his idea and he was like it's totally fine, art isn't owned, I think it would be great if you got it!

Sunday, October 11, 2015

Melissa is in the ICU at Stanford, fighting desperately for her life. Now is when it would be good to believe in prayer. She's a mermaid, my soul sister.

Friday, October 16, 2015 (23 years old)

I clenched and unclenched, then curled and uncurled my toes as I lay in bed, my torso and neck rigid from my efforts not to cough. With shallow breaths I counted inhales, one, two, three, and exhales, four, five, six, trying to pay attention to the *TED Radio Hour* podcast I often listen to while falling asleep. On this night, though, at 10:00 p.m. on October 12, 2015, nothing could distract me from my physical pain and discomfort or my emotional anxiety. My throat was sore from the hacking cough I'd had all day, my lungs searing with the pain of pleurisy and infection. My mind was numb from the half bottle of cough syrup I'd chugged to prevent bronchospasms, but also racing with the fear of what another sleepless night would do to me.

After twenty minutes, I got out of bed and took an Ativan for anxiety. I took a Vicodin for the chest pain, sipped more cough syrup, and did another half-hour breathing treatment. When none of these things provided relief, I knew I could no longer put off going to the emergency room. Physically tense but mentally drugged and fatigued, I called the pulmonary fellow, packed my things, and prepared for another admission. It was a rote going-through-the-motions scenario.

When I was sitting in the waiting room of the ER, waiting to be triaged, the reality of the situation hit me with a staggering force: there I was, the night of my twenty-third birthday, sick, scared, and not even surprised.

Did I ever picture that this is where I would be on my twenty-third birthday? Absolutely not. In life, we often pass the time operating on a scale of minutes and hours. We wait for the bell to ring, signaling the end of a boring lecture. We watch the hours pass at work, waiting for 5:00 p.m. We monitor the timer as we run on the treadmill or the elliptical.

It's rare for us, with our microfocus on minutes and hours and days, to zoom out, to step back and ask the big questions: How did I get here? What did I envision for my life, and does my reality match that vision? Or perhaps better questions: How did I not realize, as I got older, that this is where I was destined to be? Why did I let myself envision anything else?

Real change is often made by people who are too young, too inexperienced, or too naive to know that what they're attempting would be considered impossible by others. These folks blindly pioneer and innovate, despite the limitations and restrictions perceived by others. They change the world, even if they fail to do what they set out to do initially. They change the world by challenging us to look beyond the perceived limitations that we all have, by forcing us out of the boxes we let ourselves get caged in.

In a way, I unwittingly did that for myself. I was sheltered as a child from the brutality of cystic fibrosis, from the likelihood of dying young, from the statistics and stories that say it all. But driven by my own curiosity, I eventually began to seek out stories of patients with *Burkholderia cenocepacia,* the bacteria that has colonized my lungs. They were horror stories—case reports of kids that were healthy one day and dead two weeks later from the rapid necrotizing pneumonia known as cepacia syndrome. I pored over those case reports, then compartmentalized the information, putting it away somewhere in my brain, where I didn't let it affect my decisions or actions.

I managed to remain naive about my future. It never occurred to me that I wouldn't have a career. It never occurred to me that I wouldn't graduate college. It never occurred to me that I wouldn't marry and have a family. It never occurred to me that I could die in my young adulthood. It never occurred to me that when the time came that I needed a lung transplant, I might not be able to get one.

If I had understood the likelihood of any of those things in middle school and high school, would I have dedicated myself to academics and athletics like I did? No. If I had thought I couldn't go to college, I wouldn't have struggled through the difficult concepts in calculus, stressed about AP and honors classes, or done my summer reading. If I had perceived myself as weak and "terminal," I wouldn't have believed I had the strength to play three varsity sports. If I had thought I wasn't going to be around much longer, I wouldn't have formed the lasting friendships that now make up the richest parts of my life. If I hadn't had hope that my future was bright, I would not have stayed resilient throughout months of hospitalizations every year and the inevitable health crises of a chronic illness.

Anytime I feel disappointed by my health limitations now, as an adult, I think about the very best parts of my life. In a way, the thing I question most about my upbringing—my naïveté about my illness and the disappointments it inevitably caused down the line—is the quality that made those very best parts of my life possible. It's a trade-off; I've been disappointed at times, but I have also exceeded beyond imagination since I didn't plan for early death.

I wonder sometimes, was it worth it? Should I have been made more aware of my prognosis, been less sheltered from the realities I would face as I aged and my disease progressed? Would that have made things easier or softened the blows as they came?

Most of the time, I think not. The fears I have now that my teenage self didn't have to grapple with allowed me to develop a sense of self before getting slammed with doubts, uncertainties, and anxieties that come with chronic progressive illness. My life might have had fewer surprises, but it would certainly have been less full. And some of the worst surprises in my life have often led to the greatest breakthroughs: extreme disappointments that closed one door simultaneously opened others.

Like many twenty-three-year-olds, I sometimes feel lost and confused and directionless in my career. Throughout college and in my postgrad life, door after door has been closed to me, career-wise, and more and more things I've desired have become impossible. I just have to hope that one day, after more experience in my freelance writing career, I will feel grateful that those other doors were closed to clear the way for the right one to finally open.

Monday, October 19, 2015

Monday morning, I woke up in my apartment with the pain of a thousand knives collectively stabbing my left mid-back in my left lower lobe. An 8 or 9 on the hospital pain scale—I reserve 10 for being hit by a truck.

My breaths were shallow and quick as I labored to get enough oxygen. After stumbling out of bed, I walked to the coffeemaker, panting and hunching over with my elbow on the counter. *Fuck,* I thought to myself, *I can't do this.* Whether I can get up and make coffee in the morning is a current metric to gauge whether I'm okay or not.

"Mom, I need you to drive down," I said over the phone, sprawled on the bed, searching for a position that would enable me to breathe better. "I'm in pain." I tried not to cry, but my voice cracked.

She came quickly to find me drugged up on Vicodin. My deep breaths and coughs were still excruciating. I've had blood clots in my lungs and the shocking pain of this mundane Monday morning mimicked the pain of those days spent in the ER, discovering infarctions and emboli. It occurred to me that I might have another embolism, and that another day in the ER might be in order. A few hours later, I was on my way to the UCLA hospital in Santa Monica, to find out if (medical) history was repeating itself.

Imaging tests done in the ER showed no pulmonary embolism and no collapsed lung. But the pain did have a cause: multifocal pneumonia throughout the lower lobes, with a cavitary lesion on the left side. I had finished a course of IV antibiotics just two weeks before, and there I was, even worse off than before and ready to begin anew.

When the hospitalist assigned to my case told me I was ready to go home after three days in the hospital, I knew she was wrong. In my gut, I knew that despite my outward appearance of normalcy, my lungs were still embroiled in battle. My body was still crushed with fatigue. And all going home would mean was continuing to undergo the exact same treatment and therapy as in the hospital but being responsible for all of it myself, with no help.

Three days in the hospital and two weeks of home IV care later, I returned to my life. But two weeks after that, the crippling pain was back, bringing with it the distinct understanding that someone had fucked up my treatment in a grand way. You don't recover from a pulmonary exacerbation only to develop *pneumonia* (significant, severe pneumonia, according to the doctors) just two weeks later, unless the treatment wasn't right. The fuckup, I think, was a doctor thinking she was doing right by the patient sending her home to recover, when in reality, being sent home before you're ready doesn't fix things. The second fuckup was not listening to me when I said I wasn't ready.

Now I'm back in the hospital again, far worse than I was when I was first admitted. The depth and frequency and force of my cough are frightening, as is the seemingly inexhaustible well of sticky, green, infected mucus I'm producing and expectorating.

Slowly I'm improving, getting weaned off the oxygen supplementation, beginning to get up and walk and stretch my legs, hearing promising reactions from doctors who listen to my lungs, that there's reason to be hopeful.

We can't fully blame a doctor who sends us away, who thinks we're exaggerating our symptoms, even if we end up far sicker than before as a result of treatment cut short. We have to blame the disease, the disease that tries to define us, the disease that none of us asked for, the disease that's killing us, the disease that, no matter how brutal, binds us together.

The year 2015 has been a tough one for the CF community. It's been a month since Kari passed and now it's Melissa who's gone into free fall. Other patients have said it's been an unusually brutal year as they, too, have lost friends to CF.

When someone dies, we all feel the effects, rippling through the network, upsetting the sense of calm that was always an illusion to begin with. We think about them, and how much we'll miss them, and the loved ones who survive them; but we also think about what it means for us, what we can expect, how we can grieve and cope while continuing to care for ourselves.

For months, Melissa and I talked nearly every day. I worried about how sick she was feeling and for how long, but it never once occurred to me that on my twenty-third birthday she would be on life support, and I would be in the emergency room, gasping for breath, begging for relief. It's weird to not be able to talk to her.

She will struggle, but she is mighty and will survive. New lungs will come. And I, with the help of powerful drugs, will beat back the bacteria inflaming and infecting my lungs like one would hack down forest undergrowth with a machete. I have to believe that. For her, for me. For all of us.

Saturday, October 24, 2015
Recently, I was running on the treadmill at the gym. More of a slow jog, really, broken up with a minute of walking for every couple of minutes of running. My lungs were searing, and not in a good way. Music was blasting, so I was able to ignore how much my breath was quickening, how erratically my heart was beating. As I slowed to a walk and turned the music down, I felt the spurting feeling I know all too well: like the moment a sprinkler goes off, a blood vessel burst in my lungs and the blood sprayed out, collecting in my airways and gurgling upward to be coughed out.

Staggering off the treadmill, I made my way to the trash can. I hid behind the half wall, not wanting other gym patrons to think I had tuberculosis (or any kind of contagious illness). I coughed and coughed and spit out fire-engine-red blood into the towels, which I promptly discarded. Then I gathered my water bottle and phone and left the gym, rattled in more ways than one.

Yoga is the antithesis of exercise programs that try to force insecurity on people and make them feel they are not enough. Yoga urges us to take a deep breath, to be grateful for exactly what our bodies can do on a particular day. Yoga reminds us that whatever health we do have is a miracle not to be taken for granted. Yoga restores peace, confidence, and a sense of spaciousness for those who are claustrophobic within the trap of disease. Most of all, it gives us hope.

My first attempt at yoga was a ridiculous haze of movements that felt wrong, positions that felt awkward, stretches that felt painful. I was seventeen then, just out of high school and riding the high of being named by my high school Athlete of the Year all four years of school.

Many women with cystic fibrosis experience a worsening of disease symptoms in their late teens and early twenties. In my case, one or two hospitalizations a year turned into five or six. Friends got used to me popping pills and pushing injections while in the dining room, in lecture halls, and at parties. They got used to me disappearing and did their best to keep me in the loop about life outside of my hospital-home. Acquaintances tended toward confusion at the mismatch between my healthy outward appearance and the evidence of sickness around me: the needles in my biohazard bin, the catheter in my arm, the syringes sticking out of my purse, the machines filling up my dorm room.

During that horrific period of change and doubt and fear and humility, I was still on a college club volleyball team. The girls were wonderful and the team was competitive. But I couldn't stand that my shrinking lung capacity was shrinking my options, both on and off the court.

So I found my way into a yoga studio. It was Dr. Mohabir's idea to meet me at yoga one night, and for the first time in a long time I experienced the *joy* of movement. I shed my self-loathing, because in yoga, we are on our own journey. With no expectations. We move at our pace. The "coach" guides with gentle suggestions, not commands. Child's pose is always available. And in that particular class, reared back in child's pose while my doctor pumped out *chaturangas*, I saw myself in the mirror and realized that there is beauty in rest. Endless beauty in not feeling the need to progress. There is a time and a place for progress, but there's a time and a place to yield to the idea of just simply existing.

In the years since my first yoga session, I've had months in which I'm on the mat four times a week and months when I don't practice at all. But it's a safe space, one for which I will always be grateful for showing me self-love, for showing me peace, for showing me the magic in stillness. When I'm too sick to briskly walk a block, I can still get into the studio, as yoga is not about the physical postures; if I enter the room, become present in my physical body, notice the

222

hurts and the sadness and the love and the beauty, if I control my breath in what little way I'm able to, it's a success. Yoga shattered the old parameters and built new ones that I love.

Tuesday, November 3, 2015

Back in the hospital again. It's the ultimate hamster-on-a-wheel scenario: running to stay in place, never getting ahead, time passing by, giving the perception of motion, but with no ground covered.

Friday, November 6, 2015

It's not the big, groundbreaking health events.

It's not the scariest set of test results.

It's the petty frustrations and humiliations that wear on me, overtax my patience and goodwill, and leave me drained and weakened.

It's that moment when you snap at someone because they're the sixth person to ask you if you're pregnant, even though the urine test already came back negative.

It's when they don't send a respiratory therapist for seven hours even though you can't breathe and are in distress, but you can't blame anyone in particular because it's "the system."

It's when your IV antibiotic hasn't arrived, because it wasn't ordered. Why not? The dose is weight based and they don't have your weight, even though they could've taken it at any point during the seven hours you were in the ER.

It's when circumstances are so absurd they defy logic.

It's when the pharmacist tells you that you can't keep certain medications at the bedside, medications you've kept at the bedside every hospitalization.

It's when hospital personnel don't properly gown and glove for your contact isolation status, but then tell your visitors they need to.

It's when you call to ask for hot packs because you're shivering so much it's making you cough up a storm, and twenty minutes later you ask again, and twenty minutes later you ask a third time and they tell you not to use them because you have a fever.

It's when you finally have a minute alone so you break down and cry, and right then someone walks in to take your vitals.

It's when four different people each day ask detailed questions about your bowel movements in front of your visitors.

It's when you feel like you're going to have a panic attack and ask for Ativan, and the doctor on call makes you seem like a drug-seeker and says no.

It's when you want to go to sleep at 9:00 p.m. but can't because the nurse/pharmacy is so late with meds that by the time everything is finally done you can't sleep.

Friday, November 20, 2015
Caleigh is getting new lungs today!!!

Saturday, November 28, 2015
As I'm stuck in this hospital, I ponder the ever-nagging question: When to disclose?

In my case, since I grew up in a small bubble in Los Angeles—and went to a K–8 school—my assumption was that everyone knew about my cystic fibrosis early on. They'd heard my cough, seen the high-calorie shakes I chugged in class, watched me pop pills at recess and lunch, noticed I was never in school a full day.

My family was all about disclosure. I never considered that other patients might handle the issue differently. *Mallory's 65 Roses*—a book for kids that my mom wrote about me having cystic fibrosis—guaranteed everyone around me knew, since my mom read it to my class each year.

Near the end of high school, I learned of a patient who had such a mild case of CF that she was able to hide it from everyone she knew. She never took pills in front of people, and she hid her airway clearance and nebulizer equipment from friends. I was stunned—when every minute of your day is in some way focused on the physical needs of your body, how can you hide that from the world? Wouldn't that task in and of itself exhaust you until you could no longer keep up the healthy façade?

I took for granted how easy it was when everyone around me already knew about my illness. I liked it that way.

The issue of disclosure became much more pressing for me when I left home, left my tight-knit community for college. On the first day of school, I showed up to my dorm room and began setting up my equipment. Adele and Sabrina, now highly successful medical school students, were intrigued, nonjudgmental, and curious. They had the perfect reaction to rooming with me and it set the tone for me right away that people could hear about my disease and not immediately write me off as either a hyperbolic drama queen or a sickly person that's too diseased to be fun.

Freshman year was a year of introduction frenzy, meeting others in CoHo, on Wilbur Field, in the dining hall, at a friend's pregame. The people who lived in my dorm saw me do treatment and thus knew about my condition, but people I ate with, partied with, sat in class with, roamed the campus with, didn't ask me about it so I never brought it up. I popped pills all the time, coughed a ton, missed a lot of classes (and people talk), so I assumed everyone knew. I found out later on, when I started being hospitalized all the time, that a bunch of people did not know.

Telling people that you have a life-threatening disease has a way of making people extremely uncomfortable. The rare few who respond exactly how I hope they will are usually the ones who become my closest friends. I worry people will view me differently, worry about what they say in front of me, worry what's okay to ask and what things I'd rather not talk about. My preference is for people to ask but I wonder if the burden is on me to disclose.

Saturday, December 12, 2015

It's an important day today, the two-month mark from when I got admitted to UCLA hospital for this tumultuous, challenging, soul-testing period. It's been two months since my birthday, which came and went before I had the chance to celebrate. Two months since I've lived within these hospital walls. One year since my last admission at Stanford Hospital—a place that felt like home but is now a distant memory. It's amazing how the tricks of time change things, distorting and morphing perceptions and attachments. Now UCLA feels like home.

I fondly remember the days when college friends could visit me at Stanford Hospital. Being in a huge hospital where I could walk thousands of steps, see trees and ducks and water and an extensive collection of beautiful artwork. I could sunbathe and bump into people I knew from school, all without leaving hospital grounds.

But I did leave the grounds during breaks from IVs—sneaking out with my mom daily, walking the ten to fifteen minutes it takes to get to the Stanford Shopping Center. Getting juice from Pressed, having my hair washed at Hair International, drinking piping-hot coconut ginger or masala chai tea from Teavana. Being close enough for my professors (James Campbell, Sue McConnell) to visit. Just being in college—having that sense of purpose, that identity, that attachment to a prestigious university—said enough that people knew I was smart.

I'm tearing from these memories. Not because they're bad, not because they're great, but because they're over. It feels like that period of my life ended abruptly, and not because I wanted it to. I didn't want to let go.

And I figured that when I *did* let go, it would be because I was on my next wild adventure—traveling in New Zealand or Australia, living in Hawaii or San Diego, having a job, literally doing anything besides being in LA. But the wild thing is, now that I do live in LA, I'm entrapped in comfort. Sucked into safety. And not just the emotional safety that drives people to stay close to home: I mean the literal safety of my survival. I don't feel that I'm at a stage of my life where I can afford to live far from my family. They do too much. As much as I hate to admit it, I need them too much. I sacrificed health to go to Stanford—maybe I would have declined no matter what, but I definitely declined more by being away at college. It was worth it, 100 percent worth it. I wouldn't go back and change a thing, except maybe I would delete my period of depression.

When I graduated from Stanford one year ago, I never envisioned that 2015 would pan out the way it did. I fully expected to maintain my connection to Stanford, both through close college friendships and by frequent visits to see doctors once every month or so. I figured whenever I needed to be admitted, it would be there. I did not realize that I would live in LA, and that when I got sick, I would need to be hospitalized here—that flying back would be too dangerous. I figured my care in LA was temporary and I would either stick with Stanford or switch to San Diego (if I decided to move there).

But now, more than ever before, my life is dominated by fear. No, that's too extreme. I don't feel fear in every moment. It's my decisions that are driven by fear. My decision not to get a part-time job and just freelance is driven by fear. My decision not to move to San Diego is driven by my fear of living in a new city alone, too far from my family and Kona.

I'm listening to Trevor Hall's new album right now in my hospital room, alone at UCLA (which is rare, and right now, appreciated), mourning this transition. I'm happy here (as happy as one can be spending two months in a hospital) so it's not that I'm suffering, nor do I think Stanford is the only place for me. It was just my place. My home. And when you lose a home you have to mourn it, which is something I haven't had the chance to do—mostly because before this period, the transition didn't feel complete. Now, with the entire staff of Izzy's Deli knowing me from my daily visits, and the hospital staff recognizing me from taking care of me for so long, this is my new place, and I know that it's a good place.

Being in the hospital this much does weird things to your brain. It's almost scary that it feels so normal to be here, that being out of the hospital is what feels unnatural. The idea of being at my apartment, for example. The last time I was there for any period longer than a couple of days, Micah was there! He was supposed to be there temporarily but decided to stay. I've been there when my new roommates lived there, but that doesn't feel like the norm yet. And taking care of myself, doing everything on my own plus going back to working—that feels incredibly intimidating after being taken care of in the hospital for so long. It's a big day in here if I get to take a shower and do an hour of "exercise"—how am I going to tack on all the time needed to do my treatments, take care of all my meds/sinus rinses, clean equipment, and deal with pharmacies? PLUS work, PLUS exercise, PLUS trying to have a social life? It's too much. And if that feels like too much, how the hell am I ever going to add anything into my life?

I'm going a little bit wild in here. I need to just get out and into my life and stop thinking about it.

Tuesday, December 15, 2015

I never thought I would say this, but I've come to love the feeling of being on opioids. It was never part of my treatment but as my chest pain became unbearable I needed it to breathe. With morphine and Oxy there's no pain and no sadness. I don't take pain meds when I don't need them, but my pain came back last night for a little bit, and it was not that severe but verging, so I took the smallest dose of Oxy. I'm scared of myself a little bit. A lot of the time I feel normal, but then sometimes when I think about things, I'm like, *I want to get some Oxy to have on hand just in case I have pain,* which I think is valid, but then I wonder if it were just sitting in my drawer, and if I were having a bad day . . . I don't want to put myself in any situation for possible abuse. And I never thought I was at risk before. But now I realize it can really happen to anyone and I need to be careful, and I'm happy the doctors don't want to send me home with Oxy. They say if I have pain that severe, I should come to the ER. It's a valid point.

Wednesday, December 16, 2015

Oh Happy Days, I'm getting out—we're heading home!!!

Saturday, December 19, 2015

I've started working again this week and it's nice, it's bringing my brain back from the dead. The first day was so hard . . . looking at my notes made me anxious, because I forgot where I was and couldn't figure out what next step to take. It felt overwhelming. All my information and research were scattered. I wished the interviews I did with Scott Logan and Garrison Frost were already transcribed and started beating myself up for not having transcribed them, and then beating myself up for not having done enough research, not talking to the right people, not knowing enough about plants. But slowly I just got into it, sentence by sentence, and tried to maintain patience. I reminded myself of the central message of *Bird by Bird* (by Anne Lamott). James Clear sums it up simply: "To become a better writer, you have to write more. Writing reveals the story because you have to write to figure out what you're writing about. Don't judge your initial work too harshly because every writer has terrible first drafts."

Now, it's my third day working, and I have a good flow going. I don't know that I'll finish by the self-imposed deadline of Dec. 30, but as long as I am working every single day toward that goal, I feel okay about it.

Today I had a really nice time with the Sadwick sisters and my cousin Clara. Rebecca and Ari brought their sister Kayla. We went to Fonuts and stayed for hours. It was nice to be out of the house. It was a beautiful day; we had pastries and coffee.

The whole time I was getting calls from Coram Home Health because I need a PICC line dressing change and they haven't been responsive. I called them twice yesterday, Friday, because that was the day I needed it and they promised a nurse would get in touch with me. No nurse called. I called back this morning and told my contact that it was urgent, and I needed the dressing changed today. He said he would call a nurse. A nurse did call, but she said she didn't have any supplies and that I would need to get supplies from Coram. I had her call Coram to ask. Coram called me back and asked what I needed, and I explained everything. Then another nurse called and we went through it all again. Coram called back yet again to get the exact specifics of what I did and didn't need. I asked when the supplies would arrive and they said they couldn't give an exact time (of course; they claim that every single time) but that it would be sometime tonight. I thought everything was settled. I figured the worst thing that might happen would be that I'd have to stay in tonight, waiting for supplies and the nurse.

Then at 1:45 a.m., Daniel from Coram calls back and says, we can't get this for you because you're no longer on our service. You switched to a different pharmacy so it's their responsibility; we are not involved and can't help you. I said that the other pharmacy was not an infusion pharmacy and would not have these supplies *and* that they're closed on weekends so I wouldn't be able to get anything from them for days. He said he would call his manager.

He finally called back and said the manager said no. I asked him if he heard me when I said my local pharmacy was closed on the weekends. He said, "Well, they agreed to take over, so they need to do this for you." I said, "That's inconsistent because Coram agreed to send me two weeks' worth of tubing even *after* I had switched to the local pharmacy, so it was within the manager's power to say yes." He continued to say no. I said, "What you're telling me is that you don't give a shit, you'd rather I get an infection and have it go into my blood and threaten my life than get me these goddamn supplies." He said, "It's your local pharmacy's responsibility." I repeated myself, said, "They are closed and it's your fuckup that drove me to them in the first place." He said, "There's nothing we can do, this is my manager's final decision." I told him to connect me to the manager. He said, "There's no way to contact her except on her personal cell," so I said, give me that then. I said, someone above the person answering the phone is available today and you need to connect me. He said no. I asked him to give me his full name and the full name of his manager and said my dad would call them and that I was a LOT nicer than my dad would be. He put me on hold for ten minutes before I finally hung up. I was shaking.

During this conversation I asked him if he was aware that he worked for a *healthcare* company. I told him his company was responsible for jeopardizing my health due to false promises and failure to follow through on them. It's outrageous that they didn't tell me thirty hours before, the first time I called about my dressing change, that they couldn't help me.

I started out nice. I could have started by being accusatory and demanding but I didn't. I told him his company had screwed up badly and driven me to another pharmacy, but that I was not going to take my anger out on him. But then he turned out to be just another one of those assholes. I finally paged the doctor at UCLA so that the on-call hospitalist could write new orders to Coram or another infusion pharmacy to get me supplies today. But right after I spoke to the doctor, the first nurse from the morning called back and told me she had the supplies. I was relieved, but also pissed because she could have told me that five hours earlier and saved me so much stress, anger, and time wasted on the phone, yelling at an idiot who was never going to be convinced that my life was more important than his manager's indifference and laziness.

I wish I could testify against them in court. I wish I could explain in detail every single mistake they've made and every single way they've made my life ten times more complicated than it needs to be. I wish I could just check back into the hospital (not really, but right now I do) because then I wouldn't have to fight every minute of every day for what I need. It's devastating, criminal in fact. And a reminder that they shouldn't discharge patients from the hospital until home healthcare is worked out perfectly. Staying in the hospital another day would be a small price to pay to avoid this deep distress.

Friday, December 25, 2015

No progress so far on the New Year's resolutions, or even productive reflections about this year and what went well, what went wrong. Going to try an internal dialogue, but I'm setting my expectations very low.

Why do I write New Year's resolutions?

Because I want to stop feeling aimless. I want to take control over my life and actually determine where I'm going. I want to feel consistently happy again. I need to search the deepest trenches of my soul to figure out how to get there. Maybe going back to the concept of a North Star would be more useful than New Year's resolutions since resolutions seem to emphasize achievements rather than habits and processes. Like the destination, rather than the journey . . . ?

Gonna try that. My North Stars are:

Happiness

Meaning

Productive work

Strong relationships that nourish, not deplete

Community

Routines that ground and energize me

Self-assuredness, mental health

Health (Maybe this shouldn't be a North Star, since it's not my choice whether I'm healthy or sick? Have to think about this one.)

Treatment compliance

Exercise

Nutrition

Sleep

Youth, spontaneity, and adventure (lacking in this department, must balance this with health)

Friends

Family

A better metaphor for this than North Star might be *pillars.* Pillars that would make my life good.

Saturday, January 2, 2016
I had a great New Year's Eve and a great New Year's Day. I went to a pregame party with a bunch of people I haven't seen in a long time,

then to the Snapchat party downtown. It was like a big Stanford reunion crossed with a ritzy bar mitzvah, and Foster the People played. It was nice to feel like a normal person. But it also reminded me how much of my life and myself I've lost recently, because people would ask me how I've been, what I've been up to, and I either had to lie or just be really vague so I wouldn't be a downer. One guy mentioned that he's seen on Facebook that I've been in and out of the hospital a lot and I was so awkward in my response. I was just like, "Yeah, it's been tough but it will be okay."

But it was great to hang out, doing what I should be doing at twenty-three. At the actual party I realized how much of a grandma I am (not that I didn't already know). It was nice to mingle but after a certain amount of time, the venue was too loud and too crowded, and I felt claustrophobic. I was tired and I wanted to go home. I left at 11:50. It was a great night, though.

Unfortunately, I didn't fall asleep until 4:00 a.m., so I couldn't get up at 8:00 a.m. the next morning to be ready to drive to the Rose Bowl with friends. I went later with my parents, and Linda and Steve. When we got there, we went to the alumni tailgate, so we saw a bunch of people, ate food, etc. It was fun and warm. Best part of the day!

Stanford demolished Iowa so it wasn't the most exciting game but I don't get football anyway. I was just extremely happy to be there and so grateful to be out of the hospital. It was a beautiful day and I can understand now why some people choose to live in Pasadena. Middle of winter and it was a gorgeous, clear day, and so green, with mountains on all sides.

We left with four minutes remaining on the clock. I was exhausted and slept twelve hours that night.

The next day was not good. I started coughing up blood and it was a much bigger bleed than usual (30 mL), causing me to vomit a bunch of times. I was sitting in the bathroom on the edge of the tub, alternating between coughing blood into a cup and then vomiting into the toilet. It was quite a sight. At that moment, I was filled with an overwhelming sense of hopelessness.

When I coughed another 20 to 25 mL of blood that night, we knew to go to the ER.

All things considered, it was a smooth ER trip that ended with an admission. But I was an emotional mess. I gave Kona a big hug before I left but wished he could come with me.

Tuesday, January 5, 2016

Still in the hospital. My head hurts and my body is heavy with stress. At midnight I coughed up 10 mL of blood, then 10 mL, 70 mL. They moved me to the ICU and ordered a CT scan.

Saturday, January 9, 2016

Life in the ICU is a whole different world. The commode in the middle of the room with no walls around it strips me of my dignity and, combined with my multiple meds that cause constipation, it's impossible to have a bowel movement. When I first got moved back to intermediate ICU on Thursday afternoon, I was ready to kiss the ground of my familiar room 5498. I was relieved, and it felt like the first moment in days that I could take a deep, non-agitated breath.

I can't believe Melissa spent eighty days in the ICU at Stanford. How did she suffer through that for so long? Two days or so in there changed me. Michelle commented that she could tell I was pissed at one of the nurses. I was surprised. I said, "I'm not pissed at her, what made you think that?" And she said, "You're normally so sweet to the nurses but this time I could see your irritation on your face."

It's not the nurses' fault—in fact, they're super attentive, and the ones I had were very sweet. But the ICU policies make me insane when I feel like they are hindering my health instead of helping it.

I was psyched to get back to 5498. Natalie and Liana came to visit. When I didn't have the energy to hang out anymore, I rolled over to take a nap. When I woke up I stood up to pee and wash my face. I stretched my arms overhead and it raised my heart rate a tiny bit . . . then I felt the familiar gurgling sound, and my heart just sank.

I only coughed up 10 mL of blood, but it was enough for my mom and the docs to freak out. I had been about to take a shower—they were going to change my port needle, so I'd had them pull out my extra IV, and I was more excited for that shower than I think I have been for anything in the last few months. It had been so long, I was caked in grime. I was smelly and hairy and dreadlocked. I needed the catharsis of the hot water and solitude. And I had been waiting patiently but desperately for forty-eight hours for that shower; it had been planned down to the minute, since with four IV drugs that each run for one to four hours, there hadn't been a minute when I wasn't hooked up to some IV. This was my only chance. I had a half-hour window locked and loaded but I coughed up blood right at the beginning of that window.

The doctor rounding said no shower. I started crying when he said that and so my mom nicely asked the doctor to think about the whole patient. She told him I was losing my mojo, that this shower meant more to me than he could imagine. He said he would send a colleague to check me out.

His colleague, Dr. Bierer, the ICU intensivist for the night, came by. We talked for a while. He said showering probably wasn't a good idea because of the humidity. I said I didn't have a problem with humidity and told him that I would sit down in the shower on a bench and that the care partner could be in there to watch me. I said, all my vitals are stable. He finally caved and said okay.

In the shower, I scrubbed off the grime and dead skin and anger. The washcloths were brown after scrubbing one limb! I sat on the bench and while I didn't have the total privacy and solitude I craved, I had the hot-water catharsis I needed. It's a reliable, dependable sort of healing. When I came out, I was rejuvenated and way less distraught.

They said if I had any more bleeding that night, they would move me back to the ICU. They said they thought it would be best to move forward with embolization. I fell asleep last night on NPO assuming I would start hearing about the timing for embolization in the morning.

But when Friday morning came, I couldn't drink my coffee, and no one came by. A couple of hours later I fell back asleep for three hours, and during those hours, I know my mom was harassing the nurse and the doctors, trying to get interventional radiology to come up and do a consult to figure out the procedure time. After getting nowhere, the resident under Dr. Paull told my mom that I could eat because it was Friday afternoon and the procedure probably wouldn't happen. He said they wouldn't want to do it so close to the weekend. My mom was rightly pissed. She asked my nurse to page Dr. Paull just as the IR team came for a consult, so I woke up.

Dr. Lee, the IR head guy, started talking about all the risks of the embolization procedure and how I don't meet the standard guideline of 240 mL hemoptysis all at once. He said, based on the risks and the fact that I wasn't having life-threatening, emergent hemoptysis at that time, he didn't recommend the procedure. Dr. Eshaghian was my main doctor and as the head of CF she knew more about this than anyone else.

I made Dr. Eshaghian's case for her: I've had over 240 mL hemoptysis cumulative over the course of a few days and so have had to stop all treatments. The chronic, lifelong infection will never go away; we've been aggressively treating my infections with antibiotics, but they're not really working, and I've been in and out of the hospital for months. And the longer I go without treatments, the worse the infection gets, and then the worse the bleeding gets. He heard me out, then Dr. Paull came in and explained to Dr. Lee that my doctors were recommending the procedure, and then Dr. Eshaghian got on the phone with Dr. Lee and explained her thought process and why she really thought I should get it done.

Finally, they said, "Okay, we're doing it." A few hours later, I got wheeled down to the OR. I was nervous but also excited to get it over with. Dr. Lee was very nice and said he was going to take very good care of me. A nurse named Jason told me he was going to be responsible for my anesthesia, monitoring my vitals, etc. He told me I wouldn't be fully asleep because they'd need to communicate with me during the procedure, but that he would make me comfortable.

At one point they had to pull my pants off and expose my whole lower half, naked on the table, and one of them apologized that the room was all men. The reason for removing my pants was to go through an artery in the groin to get to the lungs. At that point I felt very scared and stressed out. I was in a cold room on a skinny table (a table that felt too skinny even for me). I was alone in a room full of men, with my vagina completely exposed. People were coming in and out and getting ready, and I was just naked, getting my groin area cleaned with Betadine. I was struck by the absurdity of it. Thankfully Jason came and gave me IV Benadryl first, then they got me sort of covered up with a sterile tent thing, and then they gave me either fentanyl or Versed, I don't know which.

The whole thing took over three hours. By the end I was fully awake and had to go through the nudity thing again. The IR fellow had to close up the incision with this collagen injection thing that was pretty uncomfortable, then he had to hold pressure on it for a long time, and all while I was exposed. He talked to me throughout the time that he was applying pressure, which distracted me, and he explained what he was doing as he closed the incision.

Eventually Dr. Lee came back and checked my ability to move, making sure I wasn't paralyzed. He told me the procedure had gone well. He said that although he had been hesitant in the morning, after going in there, he was sure that it had been the right thing to do. He embolized five blood vessels, I think, more than he thought he would have to. The only complication was that a piece of wire broke off. He said it shouldn't cause any problems because it's in vessels that are now dead anyway, but he had to keep me informed and he was going to write to the company about it because pieces of wire should not be breaking off inside the body.

Then they put a dressing on my wound, got me clothed, and I said goodbye to them all. They were a good team and I would give them five stars if one reviewed surgical teams on Yelp.

Overall, I'm extremely relieved the procedure is over. Pain is a small price to pay for the certainty of knowing I won't bleed from that spot anymore or have to go back to the ICU, for now, anyway.

Tuesday, January 12, 2016

In some ways what's going on feels like déjà vu. It reminds me of my senior year of high school. The parallels are that I'm at UCLA, my docs think I might have cepacia syndrome, I've been on IVs for a long time, I keep losing weight, and we're talking about transplant.

Beyond these similarities, this feels like uncharted territory. For one thing, I now judge people for the things they say when they're just trying to be nice . . . "Don't worry, it will get better," or other similarly clueless comments. I explode at my mom for little things and am always on the verge of tears. I'm glued to Netflix for mindless time-passing; Facebook; Instagram. Yet I can't bring myself to do anything actually productive (like journaling more, or writing something publishable, or doing actual work that I could get paid for).

The truth is I'm scared. If I went back and read my journals from sophomore and junior years at Stanford, I'd probably see identical language—about loss of identity, loss of purpose, fear, depression. But thinking back to that point, I was living on campus, going to classes, getting good grades, and I was constantly surrounded by people, so even though I felt extremely lonely and scared, I was moving forward in life. Now my life is completely stagnant. I'm losing time. Not moving forward toward anything. Not getting stronger from all the things that supposedly "don't kill you but make you stronger." I feel like each individual blow is weakening me, and collectively they are causing the foundation of my being to crumble.

None of this reflection feels fresh, it's the recycled dregs, the churned-up feelings that I'm now realizing are familiar. They're the feelings I have and the words I use whenever I'm going through a period that threatens the idea of my future. When I feel the weight of my mortality crushing me, making me wonder if there's anything left in me besides the identity of "sick girl."

In micro moments I can be okay. I woke up this morning feeling fairly optimistic—my pain was not horrible, and my O_2 was good. I drank my coffee, read my book. Then I coughed up 10 mL of blood—which scared me. Another day of withholding treatments.

When Dr. Eshaghian came, we talked for a long time about

whether to resume ataluren or not, about the bleeding, about my need for a blood transfusion.

For a few days she had asked me to hold the ataluren since she wasn't sure if it was associated with the bleeding. But then when I kept bleeding after being off it a few days, she said she was okay with me going back on it.

The ataluren question still weighs on me. On the one hand, I don't want to ignore Dr. Mohabir's advice. I think his word is the word of God: when he told me not to move to Hawaii, which I had my heart set on, I changed my entire postgrad plan. I trust him with my life. If I were dying, I'd want him on the case. And he's telling me that he wants to abolish ataluren from my medical regimen. His argument is that there's not enough evidence to rule out ataluren being the cause of my hemoptysis or increased complications. The problem is I've tried it twice and both times was so much better. Dr. E is open to continue using it since I seem to do better on it.

Friday, January 29, 2016
Tomorrow marks four weeks within hospital walls with just a few days out. This unexpected and lengthy hospitalization knocked the wind out of me (double meaning intended). In the first three days of the new year, I spent hours reflecting on the previous months of sickness and anchoring myself in the belief that 2016 would be "better."

Since 2015 took the reins away from me, I was determined to get them back. I wanted to go back to living in my apartment in the South Bay, working as a freelance writer, surfing and playing volleyball in my spare time, and fighting every day for continued health. My understanding of the impermanence of circumstances was the beacon that got me through 2015.

But CF is not impermanent. This or that particular hospitalization was—the one where I could work out in the courtyard, the one where I was bedridden; the one where I had many visitors, the one where I refused company; the one where I laughed and ate and walked and did headstands, and the one where my pain and breathlessness stole my vitality. But since I'm not an idiot, and since humans have the ability to make reasonable predictions about the future based on past experiences, I know that variations of these situations will always be a part of my life. And that's the hardest fact I have to grapple with in scary times.

My fight for control over CF is a struggle I will always bear, no matter how much my experiences tell me it's a fruitless one. Each year when most people tell themselves they're going to join a gym or eat healthier or lose weight, I tell myself that I'm going to have a less tumultuous year coexisting with my illness.

Wednesday, February 3, 2016

During my lengthy hospitalization, the dark voices in my head, brokers of hopelessness, were countered by conversations with Danielle. Never a dealer in unwarranted optimism, she validated my fears and offered some much-needed perspective. We discussed advance care planning and my end-of-life preferences, as I watched CF friends reach the cusp of death while facing life-threatening complications myself. Danielle told me about Voicing My Choices, a tool for patients to express what would be important to them at the end, should they not be able to communicate themselves. I learned from her how to effectively manage pain and how to advocate for my own palliative care needs with the doctors at my hospital. We talked about grief and fear and coming to terms with a prognosis that's dire and scary. She slept on a chair in my ICU room many nights, driving after work from one hospital to stay with me in another.

The details of many of our most significant conversations during the darkest time are lost in an opioid-induced haze, but the emotional impact of having a friend who does palliative care social work will always stay with me. Danielle is able to apprehend my concerns, and challenges me to conceptualize my circumstances in new ways. One night, as we talked about death and the impact of dying on family members, she gave me an apt metaphor for a coping mechanism: compartmentalizing grief and fear into a box, with a lid, and then opening and closing that box. It's healthy to open the box sometimes and explore and sit with those feelings, but then to be able to close it so that the darkness doesn't cast a shadow over the time one does have left.

She was able to listen and offer wisdom in a way that normal friends cannot; hard as they may try, most will never understand what it means to live with an invisible fatal illness. The balance of validation and perspective that comes from someone who's seen hundreds of families going through similar struggles helped me simultaneously accept the probability of more pain in the future and feel more grateful about what health and time I have left.

Thursday, February 4, 2016

This January will be remembered as the month of ten(ish) bouts of serious hemoptysis, worsening and severe anemia, one blood transfusion, three rounds of IVIg (immunoglobulin therapy), two doses of fresh frozen plasma, two bronchial artery embolizations, a large hematoma (a complication of the embolization that left me bedridden), severe pleuritic lung pain, around-the-clock opiates and nausea medication, vomiting, an inability to eat for two weeks, two bronchoscopies, two CT scans, many X-rays, discussion of transplant, two stints in the ICU, five hospital rooms, and over a dozen caring and brilliant doctors on my case.

It's been eventful!

Throughout this medical saga, I have relied on so many capable doctors and nurses and care partners to get me through. Ashley, the nurse who washed my hair in the ICU when I couldn't get out of bed, went so above and beyond the call of duty, she should get a gold star and a raise. In this hospital I've called home for so many months, I see housekeepers and transporters and EKG techs and care partners and nurses and cafeteria workers/cashiers and families of other patients and attendings/fellows/residents that all cheer me on as I walk in my halting and slow way around the floors and courtyards. I saw a family member of another ICU patient in the elevator and she flashed a huge smile and gave an air high five at the sight of me walking, sans heart monitor, oxygen tank, walker, and emergency wheelchair.

With my discharge planned for this coming Monday, I think

about rejoining life beyond the hospital's walls and am struck by that most banal of observations: no matter who we are, our time is limited. There's no time not to enjoy every single day, because the days go by so damn fast. One-twelfth of this new year has passed, and I have eleven-twelfths left to take control over my life's narrative.

We are the writers of our own story. That our story will someday end is inevitable for all of us, but how we get there is not. The piece that's often lost on us, though, is that our level of control extends to how we react to situations, not necessarily to the situations that arise. My effort to thread that awareness into my narrative begins with this understanding and will continue with each and every moment I decide to love the present instead of pining for lost opportunities.

Instead of trying to enforce health as a New Year's resolution, I will try to enforce an unwavering embrace of the messy, impermanent, underrated present. I'm ready to rejoin my other life, but this hospital life is not the worst.

Wednesday, February 10, 2016

One of the things I worry about now is opiate dependence and the fact that pleuritic chest pain will probably be a part of my life in all my future exacerbations. Growing up, severe pain was not a problem for me. The first time I started having serious chest pain was when I had pulmonary emboli . . . so for a while after that, I was always worried about either an embolism or a pneumothorax (collapsed lung) when I got severe chest pain. But now, for the last six months, I've had chest pain as a regular part of my symptom list, usually correlating with pneumonia.

The pain that comes is so severe, I can't do anything—can't think/breathe/move/sleep because there's no way to ignore it. It makes me curl up into a hunchback, trying to take shallow breaths so that I won't feel the pain. It's horrible. And it can last for days, a week, two weeks. This past hospitalization, when I had two weeks of severe pain from the hematoma, followed by another week of severe pleuritic lung pain, I was on high doses of opiates for three weeks. We tried a bunch of different combinations, including the opiates morphine,

Dilaudid (hydromorphone hydrochloride), Norco (Vicodin), Oxy-Contin, Percocet, etc., and then other non-opiates like increased gabapentin (for nerve pain), lidocaine patches, and a muscle relaxant.

The pain management team consisted of a really sweet attending and a terrible fellow. The fellow seemed skeptical of my motives and my pain. He kept telling me that it was going to be really hard to get off the drugs and said he didn't want to increase my dose when my pain was bearable because it would threaten my eligibility for transplant. Which is an INSANE thing to say to someone who is in severe pain and who isn't even ON a list for a transplant anywhere—someone who may not be eligible for transplant at any point in the future because of resistant bacteria or too low of a BMI (body mass index).

I still can't really process what happened. The constant upheaval of getting admitted, then adapting to hospital life, then getting released is giving me whiplash. My life feels like a disorganized shit-show. I think I need a motivational life coach to help me get my affairs in order: to help me get organized, help me finish the book project, help me toward my goal of financial independence, etc. Those are lofty goals, though. For right now, I just need to stay out of the hospital for longer than a week.

But happily I'm writing this from home, having had a super-fun weekend. Natasha is in town. We went to the beach Saturday and later played games with the usual suspects (chill night), and Sunday spent all day at the beach again. Being back at my apartment felt so familiar and so foreign at the same time. Weird. It will take getting used to, for sure, but I'm so excited to be back there.

Saturday, February 20, 2016
It's been eighteen days that I've been out of the hospital. Eighteen days!! That's the longest time I've spent out of the hospital since October. Granted I'm still on round-the-clock home IVs, but I'm out living in the world.

And I'm moving to San Francisco. I went to Stanford on the ninth and saw Dr. Mohabir on the tenth, and he worked hard to convince me that I needed to be under his care again. Some of what we discussed:

> Hemoptysis—he says it's deadly, seen too many patients die from it, wants to make getting control of it a priority
>
> Ataluren—his insistence I go off it
>
> My thinking—he says not to focus on long-term lung function but instead, the possibility that I have cepacia syndrome and how to treat
>
> Scheduling—he wants me in clinic every one to two weeks for six months to get me stable and back on track
>
> LA—he says flying/driving up to see him every two weeks not workable; that I need to move back up
>
> Marinol—he's open to starting medical marijuana pills to decrease nausea/pain and increase appetite
>
> Nausea/vomiting—need to get that in check
>
> UCLA regimen—will continue for now minus ataluren

He said he would respect whatever decision I made in terms of where to live but made it clear that he's the one with the most expertise to treat me. UCLA has no other patients with *cepacia*. I'm the only one. He's impressed with Dr. Eshaghian and said the infectious disease docs are great, but they just haven't seen enough *cepacia* cases.

I was holding it together until the parking lot. My dad gave me a hug and said he would stand by my decision. I started bawling and said that I couldn't make the decision myself, I didn't know what to do. I knew that I would agonize over the decision. Moving again seemed so stressful. He said, "Okay, I'll decide for you, you're moving."

The day was really significant because my dad had been the most upset about Dr. Mohabir's dislike of ataluren and thought his position was wrong. It was good that he came to the appointment because he got to hear the argument from the doctor himself instead of hearing it indirectly through my mom. He became convinced that I should go off ataluren and move up there. We called my mom and told her. She didn't seem surprised and I came to find out she and Dr. Mohabir had discussed it all before. She had had my dad go with me (very unusual) since he's the one that understands the medicine and she wanted to make sure he agreed with the plan. She canceled her dinner plans and started looking and found me an apartment online while I was still grieving the fact I had to leave Manhattan Beach. She asked my dad to see it the next day. Within twenty-four hours I had an apartment to move to. I went online to find a roommate. Ari responded immediately!

Since then I've adjusted to the idea but am stressed about moving. Very sad to leave the beach but my vision of going back to life the way it was last summer, before I got sick, was not worth clinging to with my health so compromised.

I'm severely atrophied. Starting to gain weight and hoping to turn some of that into muscle. It's hard to build muscle if you have no excess fat, so people have told me not to start working out until I gain some fat. It's unreal, though—I went to yoga the other day, to a class that would've been so easy eight months ago, and kept up for about 5 percent of the class but spent the other 95 percent on my back, in forward fold, or in child's pose. The instructor even came over to ask if I was okay, and I said, I'm okay; I just spent a long stretch in the hospital so I'm taking it easy and I'm here for the stretching. She looked shocked and just told me to do whatever felt right. That's precisely why I like yoga. If it were another type of class, the instructor would have said I shouldn't be there.

I am excited for some independence. But also terrified. I know I'll miss my family and be homesick at first, especially for Kona! Will miss my mom popping over with food and hanging out for an hour, taking me to Costco, etc. But it will be good for me to be on my own because I know I rely on my mom and dad way too much.

Will start making a photo book to thank them for all their help.

Sunday, March 6, 2016

I moved! It's been such a whirlwind. The surprise was that leaving my apartment was less emotional than I thought it would be. It's as if my heart was already out the door and all we had left to do was remove my stuff.

Friday, March 11, 2016

It's been almost two weeks that I've been in SF and it's amazing so far. I love waking up in my apartment, opening the blinds, seeing the trees, the water, and the Golden Gate Bridge, the morning light filling the room. Then making my coffee and sitting in the kitchen or living room. Drinking my coffee and eating breakfast. Small rituals that mean so much. In just two weeks I already feel like I have more of a routine than I did in Manhattan Beach.

I've been going to the gym every day; don't remember the last time I skipped a day. It's so nice there, I can create good workouts for myself, and I'm definitely getting stronger. Curious to see what my lung function is next week. I think my weight is going up, probably as a result of working out and gaining muscle mass. At the gym yesterday I weighed 145 and supposedly had 11.2 percent body fat. My period is still not regular, though, so it might be low.

I was sad when my parents left. It was nice having them here and they did SO much for me. This whole move was only possible because of their involvement. But now it's time for me to accomplish things—starting with making a daily schedule, writing a to-do list, getting it done, going to the market, cooking for myself, cleaning for myself, scheduling my medical appointments and my drug refills/deliveries, etc. All the little things of daily life that my parents helped me do before. It made me feel incompetent, but at the same time I needed their help.

Thursday, March 24, 2016

Going on four weeks in SF now. It feels like I got to hit the reset button after the worst health period of my life. Yesterday marked seven weeks out of the hospital and I have trouble comprehending how lucky I am, after more than six months of never staying out longer than a week or two. I'm getting used to the idea of waking up each morning not wondering if I'll have to go to the ER that day.

But I'm worried about Caleigh. She's in the hospital post-transplant with a wild infection in her left lung that showed up as a huge mass on her CT scan. Hearing how hard things are for her right now reminds me how lucky I am. And how unpredictable this disease is.

Saturday, April 2, 2016

Read a book with a character that resonates with me. Ina describes that when she became an adult, she felt like a failure because she struggled so much with balancing the responsibilities of work, life, etc., and her mother had made it all look too easy, like a superwoman. In a similar way, my mom sleeps five to six hours a night, wakes up energetic, conquers the gym by 8:00 a.m., works all day, juggles hundreds of friends, manages a household, is a hands-on mom, takes care of her parents, and is a master problem-solver. She just gets shit done and has remarkable energy and that's just not my personality. I don't have a lot of energy, I need way more sleep, I can't just go-go-go. I just feel inadequate when I look at what other people can do, but especially my mom.

Her role was to be in charge all the time. She set it up that way and wouldn't have had it any other way.

She worked inside and outside the home, more often at home as I got older, but she always had meetings out of the house. It made it seem to me that working was the normal thing to do, BUT that being there for your kid whenever they might need you was also normal. It was this ideal scenario she created where she had the best of both worlds being a mom and working woman. I admire that she will do anything for her kids. She goes to such extremes to help Micah and me that people joke about things that are "so Diane." I also admire that she was able to maintain her career and keep her work separate and her clients happy even when we as a family were going through really hard times with my health. And she has a great relationship with *her* mom.

She is a role model in many ways.

I have followed in her footsteps work-wise so far, sort of forging a nontraditional career path that involves writing and freelancing for multiple clients. I think I've also modeled my life after hers in ways I'm not really conscious of. People tell us we're similar, but in some ways we're radically different.

I decided to take another path in terms of the pace of life. I think it's important to "stop and smell the roses," whereas she just charges through life at a constant fast pace.

She did give me the best advice: Find the joy in every day. That was a good one. I've adopted the mantra "Live Happy."

My mom had lots of behaviors that growing up I said I would NEVER do when I got older. I should have written them down because now I can't remember what they are. (Seeing the past with rose-colored glasses, I guess.)

Her advice for the twenties: Establish roots (has really swayed me against traveling). Create a community (makes me more inclined to pursue and maintain friendships). Take dating seriously so you don't turn thirty and wish you were married. Live healthy.

Most important to who I am today: she taught me to prioritize love over all else.

My mom has been a huge part of my life and always will be. I think my job now as an adult is to establish boundaries, and, in a way, moving to San Francisco is the best thing I could have done. Forced to move into my own apartment that's not a thirty-minute drive from my parents' house . . . so important. I already feel like I can breathe (figuratively). It's more spacious, I'm more relaxed. When I wake up, the day is mine to take charge of and do what I want with it. I get to determine the course of my days, which determines the course of my weeks, which determines ultimately whether I have a life I'm proud of. And when I was living in LA last year I wasn't living a life I was proud of . . . I look back on that year and I'm like what did I accomplish? How did I grow as a person? Obviously, all the hospitalizations were a challenge, but even before that I feel like I was just regressing from spending so much time at home and allowing my parents to help me as much as they did.

But I don't hold any of this against my mom anymore. I used to. A letter I wrote to her in 2008 reveals how mad I was:

> *When I do my treatment is not up to you. If I choose to do it before I go out, I will do it before. If I choose to do it after, I will do it after. It is my decision. Stop treating me like a child and trying to make choices for me. It is not your right or your duty as a parent to do that; your duty as a parent is to support and guide the decisions that I make.*
>
> *You may calmly suggest, if you wish, that I do treatments by a certain time, but that does not by any means mean that I must do so. You decide to go to sleep when you are tired; I get to decide when I go to sleep. If you don't like me coming home late and doing treatment, try to remember this: if you don't allow me to go out, I can sneak out. It is impossible for you to force me to do something against my will. I have always been a good kid, I tell you where I'm going and what I'm doing. However, you seem to not trust my judgment. You seem to think you know what's best for me better than I do. But you don't.*

I realize that now that I'm an adult it's my job, not hers, to establish my independence and autonomy. Perhaps she didn't do the best job in certain ways of setting me up to be a successful adult. But she was also worried that I wasn't going to live long so I understand why my independence wasn't her top priority. She just wanted me to live. If I do have kids, a lot of the issues I faced with my mom won't be relevant, since I won't have a kid with CF.

Thursday, April 28, 2016
I remember the time when I was a kid and went to Bed Bath & Beyond to find a duffel bag for sleepaway camp. Jamie Lee Curtis was in line next to me and she asked if I was shopping to go off to college. It amused me that people thought I was years older than I actually was; I didn't realize how unusual that is for a CF patient, that most

other kids with CF look many years younger than they are. Despite what everyone said—that I would love being tall one day, that they would steal inches off my legs if they could—I wanted to be short. I quite literally would fall asleep at night fantasizing that I'd wake up short. Those critical years I spent hunched over, made worse by a lifetime of coughing, still reveal themselves in my rounded posture today.

I did not have any friends with CF growing up, and thus had no concept of the roller coaster of illness patients ride, at varying velocities. Waddington's "epigenetic landscape" model, which I first learned about in Human Biology classes in college, gives me a framework to understand the way we with CF both can and cannot control our futures. Epigenetics refers to the study of how DNA (your genes) can be modified based on inputs from the environment; genes are regulated structurally and chemically, turned on or off by processes like phosphorylation or methylation. Basically, the epigenetic landscape is a hill that marbles can roll down. Your genes dictate the range of possible end points the marbles can roll to, but epigenetic modification determines which end point the marble actually falls on.

With cystic fibrosis, I believe our genes determine the various possibilities for the trajectory of illness: how fast our lung function will deteriorate, how likely our lungs are to be colonized by opportunistic pathogens, whether our lungs or our pancreas or our liver will be the most affected organ. But within that range of possibilities, environmental factors like access to good healthcare, age of diagnosis, where we live, what family we're born into, and random chance all contribute to determining our health outcomes. I conceptualize it like this: our genes dictate the end point; our choices, environment, and chance dictate how fast we get there and the rockiness of the descent.

My CF friendships started in the hospital, in walks with masks on and in time spent sitting outside by the fountain six feet apart. To this day, I maintain these relationships through texting, phones, and social media. Having friends with my same disease satisfied my desire for something I didn't even realize I'd wanted: a confidante, someone who understood exactly what I live with day to day. My CF friends have offered strength, resilience, and unwavering support to help pull me through the toughest times. Before Melissa went on life support, lived in the ICU for nearly a month, and then had a successful lung transplant, we were talking nearly every day over text while we both did our vest and nebulizer treatments. Now, she's slowly recovering from her lung transplant. Another friend with CF died in late August last year, shattering my world and forcing me to pick up the pieces while simultaneously battling my own wildly unstable health. When I found out, I didn't sleep for days; at night, I would get out of bed, seeking a distraction from grief, and lie on the kitchen floor with Kona, listening to music.

The range of disease trajectories is huge—from people who need transplants as teenagers to people who are in their twenties with 90 percent lung function. It puts into perspective where I am on the spectrum, where it's likely I'll go, and how fast. It's troubling to see someone once healthier than me either die or progress to end-stage disease. Beyond the bone-deep ache and grief I feel for their families, I preemptively ache and grieve for mine, knowing that one day they will probably have to bury me.

People have always called me an inspiration, but I'm not. I do sweat the small stuff, just like everyone else. I just happen to also have to sweat the big, life-or-death stuff. The burden of being an inspiration is heavy, because it means you have to be positive all the time, no matter what you're going through.

It reminds me of the Stanford Duck Syndrome. Despite its cutesy name, it's no fucking joke. Here's the idea: At Stanford, students are like ducks gliding on the water. On the surface, when ducks move, no one sees their legs below the water, paddling furiously to stay afloat. Students at Stanford, from the outside, are the image of perfection; they're able to maintain straight As, intimidating résumés, and a laundry list of extracurriculars while simultaneously finding time to eat well, exercise, party, see friends, travel, and look good.

All the while *it's supposed to look easy.* Mental health issues are taboo among the student body; since everyone else seems like they're effortlessly getting by, each person struggling with their mental health feels alone. It's a vicious cycle of silence and struggle, which has driven some to suicide.

The Duck Syndrome is a dangerous phenomenon that is not quarantined to Stanford's campus—I find the same patterns all over sunny California, and despite having left Stanford over a year ago, I still find myself refusing to let anyone peer below the surface and see me furiously paddling to stay afloat when I'm going through a rough time. I want to work on that, acknowledge the ups and downs in life in a way that's devoid of self-pity and respectful of the fact that things could always be worse.

For me to be an inspiration, the expectation is that I glide, like a duck defying physics. That is what we want to see, because it gives us hope that it's what we ourselves can achieve. But when I'm in the ER and in the midst of an acute health crisis, I'm not happily greeting every single person who comes to poke and prod. I'm not thanking any sort of God for the thousands of things I have to be grateful for. When I'm really struggling to breathe, I'm not saying, "Well, I have pneumonia for the third time in two months, but at least I have all my limbs!" Sometimes I have moments when I'm very sick and also very grateful, but other times, I wallow in self-pity temporarily before I rise above it and tackle the next obstacle in my way.

I discovered that as a sophomore in college. That year was the toughest until that point, with many months spent in the hospital and on IVs and dozens of new complications. One day, I walked out of the triple I shared with Maya and Makiko and went across the hall to the lounge of my dorm, where I lay under the table and sobbed . . . being underneath tables on the floor is strangely comforting to me in crisis moments. After I was done, I headed to the ER to deal with the current crisis, but I was better able to face it having dealt with my own negative emotions and fears first.

I've found that such is the task of a writer: to help others understand

and empathize with a life experience they've never lived. Work hard at empathy, and two things will happen: First, you will feel better about your existence. Second, you will find that you're not so alone after all, and that there's always somewhere to turn to, even if it's just the blank page and the blinking cursor.

I don't want constant, unwavering happiness. Now, I want perspective. I don't want to numb the experience of pain. I want to be resilient.

I'm not an inspiration. I'm just a person, grounded in compassion, striving to achieve empathy and wanting to make my way with goodness and grace.

Tuesday, May 3, 2016

Whenever it happens, I wonder, "Will this be the time?"

Will this be the time when the blood spilling up my lungs and out my mouth will burst forth so fast that I can't breathe? The time when I'll be passed out on the floor from blood loss by the time the ambulance arrives? The time my hemoptysis isn't just a scare, but the final, swift, deadly bullet?

This isn't an entirely unlikely scenario. It's the scene that flashes for an instant through my mind whenever I cough up frank red blood in bigger-than-tiny quantities. It's the end my doctor has warned me about for years. Each time it happens, as I cough and cough and wait for the bleeding to subside, my lips a bold Marilyn Monroe red, I'm not scared—it's too common. But it occurs to me that maybe I should be. Because each time could be *that* time.

The locations where it's happened have been diverse and darkly amusing: On my high school's front lawn as we ate lunch. In the locker room of a Burton store, unclothed but for one leg stuck in a wet suit. In the ocean, while surfing. In a backyard, playing spike ball. Lying in bed, awakened from sleep. At my high school's after-prom party. At a concert, lungs irritated from secondhand smoke. At volleyball tournaments. At water polo tournaments. At swim meets. In yoga classes. In my parents' house. In my own apartment, completely alone. In front of strangers as I sat on the curb in front of my family's favorite steak house. On a bench at the gym, with terrified onlookers. In a plane going across the Pacific Ocean, where all I could do was hope it would stop. On hikes in Hawaii. In a swimming pool. Mid-kiss. The list could go on.

Often, the comically absurd nature of my parade of hemoptysis-through-random-and-amusing-locations distracts me from fear. I can laugh about it, especially when it's over and I'm in the clear. But when I reflect back on all these times, it's rattling to realize just how many times I could have died had the bleeds not stopped. It feels like luck's been on my side, and odds are that won't be true forever.

How do we live with the impending fear of a deadly event? I've noticed that as my hemoptysis has worsened, I've almost displaced my fear of death onto other, extremely unlikely situations: shark attacks, plane crashes, car accidents, abductions, armed robberies, and other subjects of a paranoid person's nightmares. Things that never scared me before now terrify me. But simultaneously, in the moment, hemoptysis events that actually could be deadly do not scare me. I can't psychoanalyze that, but I'm sure someone can.

Friday, May 20, 2016
Wednesday I went to clinic and Dr. Mohabir decided to take me off IVs! I was stunned and ecstatic. That's an understatement. I can't remember feeling happier in recent history. I was elated. Stoked. Beyond shocked. It was so unexpected. I left the clinic, it was sunny out, I discontinued my meropenem drip, went to Aunt Lissa's, did some work, and then pulled out my own port . . . (it's so nice that I can do that with the port, as opposed to the PICC line, which someone else has to remove).

Had a phone interview for a writing job at Tribe Dynamics. I explained to them that I would have to be part-time. And we talked for thirty minutes, then they said if they decided they wanted to proceed, they'd give me a writing and editing assignment as the next step, which they did! I was so happy. Very good for my ego and self-confidence as a writer.

Sunday, May 22, 2016

So much on my mind right now.

The past week was amazing, stressful, challenging, exciting, worrisome, busy, anxious, fun. SOOOO fun.

Tuesday morning I got ready and drove to Pacifica to meet Jack for our first date to go surfing. We met on New Year's Eve at Ali's pregame before we went to the Snapchat company party but didn't see each other again until a few months later when I moved up here. His friend Justin is my roommate's boyfriend. Ari organized a brunch and invited me. I sat next to Jack. He's smart, cute, cool.

We met at Nor Cal Surf Shop, rented boards and wet suits, and went down to the beach. In the water, he was so sweet, almost protective, pushing me when my arms got tired, making sure I was safe and could catch my breath, etc. There was this moment when I was looking at the houses on the hillside and talking about how beautiful they were and saying how nice it would be to just live there and write and look at the beach and take surf breaks and then go back and write more. And he was looking at me while I was talking about that and it made me feel as if he really liked me. Or maybe he was just attracted to me.

He caught a couple of waves. My arms were like lead. I needed all the pushes I could get just to paddle out and stay out of the impact zone. Finally when a good wave rolled around for me, he pushed me and I took it. It wasn't a great ride—the wave died out on me once I stood up—but it was nice to see that at least popping up still felt natural. I didn't lose that (even if I've lost all of my paddling strength).

After that ride, he caught a wave in so he could help me paddle back out, but it was bad timing, with a big set rolling through. I couldn't catch my breath since I kept having to turtle, wave after wave. We ended up just paddling in to rest and sat on the beach for a bit. We got onto the sand, and I sat down on my board and he sat down next to me on mine instead of sitting on his. We were chatting for a little, then he asked about my LXV tattoo, and I told him that it was sixty-five, for sixty-five roses, the nickname for cystic fibrosis. And when I was done, he looked at me for a second and said, "You are so beautiful," and I said thank you, and he leaned in and kissed me. I kissed him back.

For the rest of the afternoon, Jack and I hung out on the beach, lay in the sun, kissed, chatted, etc. It was lovely, the first beach/surf day I've had in so long, and the first time I'd kissed anyone in a very long time. I was so shocked by how the day developed, like it wasn't reality. I just never ever expected that would happen; even though I kind of suspected that he was into me or attracted to me, I really didn't think he would just make a move on me like that, especially in broad daylight, especially so soon. It made me happy.

This week I also had to do the writing assignment for the Tribe Dynamics job, which was a really difficult assignment since I have no experience in marketing. The editing portion was easy, actually, but the research/writing was hard. I have no idea if I did what I was supposed to do, but I worked hard, so if I don't get the job, it probably means I wasn't the right fit for it. Now that I've turned in the assignment, I'm not stressed about it, but I was super stressed while working on it. I also had articles to write and a chapter for Susan's book plus a creative nonfiction piece for a blog Natalie wants to create. So work has been nutty, but rewarding and interesting. After this week I feel proud of myself for my versatility and progress as a writer.

Friday was such a wild day. I got home at like 9:00 p.m. after ten hours out of the house. I still had to do treatment.

The next night I had another date with Jack that went really well. The museum we went to was a bit strange but very interesting, and he was fun to hang out with. It felt very, very couple-y. After the museum we went to a restaurant about a fifteen-minute walk away, a little French place. We both got burgers and cocktails. It was delicious and we had a lot of fun. He said he was thinking about coming down to LA to hang out with me before going to San Diego to see his mom. I said I thought it was a great idea. He said he didn't want to put any pressure on things or make things weird (by meeting my family). I said it would be great.

Jack says he wants to take things slowly, I think basically to establish that there's more to us than attraction. That's the reason he planned a whole date near the Caltrain station, so he wouldn't be tempted to come back and stay over at my place. I told him I respected that and was fine with taking things slowly. It seemed early to leave the city at 8:15, but given what he said about taking things slow, it made sense. I like how we're honest with each other and communicative because I feel like I know what's going on.

Wednesday, June 1, 2016

Memorial Day weekend I got to go home and see my family and friends! My plan had been to surf every day while at home, but I had fevers and learned the hard way that surfing with a fever and shortness of breath is dangerous. I asked myself the questions that come up each time I'm struck with my four classic sickness symptoms (shortness of breath, fatigue, fever, and hemoptysis): Do I need to call Stanford? Do I need to go to the ER now? Not wanting to get stuck admitted at a hospital in LA with an order from Stanford doctors not to fly back north, I didn't call anyone and got through the week. I had a secondary motive to hide symptoms—I wanted to see my friends Alex and Hannah become Mr. and Mrs. Rosenthal that weekend, the original reason for my trip to LA and a wedding I would have been devastated to miss.

Jack came to LA that next weekend and met my parents and grandparents!

I made it through the week, went to the wedding, happily dancing and celebrating the newlyweds as long as I could before needing to sit down and enjoy the night from my seat. Later that night, my fever spiked, and I knew that I would be admitted and go back on IV antibiotics as soon as I got back up north. I tossed and turned all night, hoping that I wasn't sabotaging my own body by not going to the emergency room right then.

Friday, June 10, 2016

With a burgeoning relationship, I wonder how much to divulge to Jack about the possibility that dire things could happen to me, and my fears that they will. My physical fragility and my underlying emotional anxiety. Will he run away? Will he view me as too fragile and stop seeing me as an equal, a partner? Will he want to go the long course with someone who might not be able to make it to the finish line? Or will he make up some excuse and duck out once he realizes the reality of this fucked-up, shitty, relentless, unforgiving, merciless disease?

The other thing on my mind right now is travel. We have a trip to Vegas planned in just about a month now. We're going to be flying together early Friday afternoon and coming back late Sunday night. With how my GI problems have been and my own irrational fear of exposing GI issues to a significant other (the details at least), I'm terrified at the idea of sharing a hotel room and having no privacy. I'm worried I won't sleep, I'm worried that if I'm not already sick when I go, it's 100 percent inevitable that I will leave sick. I worry about the fact that I can't just plan a trip to Vegas with a new boyfriend (I think that's what he is) and be excited about it. I wonder if I will ever be able to plan trips and feel excited again, or if I will always have anxieties, especially these particular ones that I don't feel capable of discussing with anyone (other than my parents). Can I send him off to breakfast with the other people and stay in the room and do treatment/go to the bathroom in privacy? I just don't see him wanting to leave me and go with other people. He also brought up the fact that toward the end of summer, he's going to his family's lake house property in Maine, and that he was thinking of inviting me and another couple. It's terrifying, but I'm so happy that he wants me to come.

Sunday, June 12, 2016

On June 8, when I saw my Stanford doctors, I reentered the hospital and resumed the same IV and oral antibiotic regimen I had discontinued just four weeks before. We planned for three to six weeks on the course, and a few days later, after some improvement in my clinical symptoms, the doctors discharged me and allowed me to go home on home therapy. The drugs began to work, and again, I felt a wave of relief wash over me as I resumed my daily routine of work, treatments, exercise, and evening plans with friends.

But after a week, I began to decline again, and found myself struggling with the fateful four harbingers of a pulmonary exacerbation. This time was different, though—I was already on IVs. How could I be getting worse while on antibiotic therapy? What could I be doing differently? I stayed home all week, cooked the most nutritious foods I could think of, slept a ton, and did extra treatments, but still, the symptoms persisted.

Sunday, June 19, 2016

It's Father's Day so I'm thinking about my dad. He's amazing—the one responsible for my intellectual curiosity and my philosophical musings. He's driven thousands of miles on road trips with me (with many Denny's stops along the way), he's spent hundreds of nights on a chair or cot at my bedside in the hospital, he selflessly puts his family before himself no matter what. He's my own personal lawyer, fighting to get me every drug my insurance company tries to deny.

Tuesday, July 5, 2016

By the time I went to clinic, I knew my lung function would be down (it was, by almost 10 percent) and that the doctors would want to admit me again to change the plan. Being mentally prepared for an admission helps. My bag was filled with snacks, a phone charger, my laptop, a book, extra underwear, a toothbrush, and certain medications I need that the hospital doesn't carry. I walked from clinic to the admitting desk, signed papers to appoint my mom and dad as the decision-makers for me if I were to become incapacitated, and ate dinner in the cafeteria.

Walking down the hallway to my room in the B1 wing, I greeted familiar faces that I hadn't seen since I graduated college in December 2014—my last admission in B1 was my last week of my last quarter at Stanford. Expecting a hospitalization has a strange way of making it feel normal, even though being hospitalized four times in six months at my age is so, so far from normal.

Now I'm still on B1, on day 6 of this admission. Not a whole lot has changed—I lost the fevers but gained terrible chest pain, improved a little, then got a little worse again. When I'm not walking laps around the fountain in front, IV pole in tow, I'm receiving oxygen in my nasal cannula to ease the shortness of breath and headaches. Visits make the time go by, and I'm so thankful for that. Little things like Philz coffee deliveries and fresh peaches in the cafeteria make my day. Life goes on, with work deadlines still demanding attention.

In so many ways, life in the hospital is like life on the outside. For the most part, my mind focuses on the present moment—my current treatment, my step count, chatting with friends, hanging out with my mom, reading a good book, getting work done, enjoying the sunshine sitting out by the fountain with my feet in the water. It can be easy to forget that I'm receiving big doses of powerful medications that could, one day, stop working entirely.

But then there are times that remind me of the magnitude of the situation, of the fact that these little daily/weekly/monthly challenges—and whether I win or lose at them—could determine my life-span. Today I blew as hard as I could on my lung function test, and when I saw no improvement from the week before despite four weeks of continuous IVs, a week of hospitalization, and new antibiotics on board, I wondered briefly whether all this fighting is pointless. Will it make a difference which antibiotics we use, or are they all ineffective? Will this disease ultimately do what it wants with me regardless of the weapons we throw at it, laughing at our attempts to keep infection at bay?

If a wave holds you under for too long while you're out surfing, the worst thing you can do is struggle and fight against the water; when drowning and in danger, the best chance you have is to try to relax, hold your breath, and wait until you're given the chance to pop to the surface. Sometimes acceptance and ease, rather than force and struggle, are the keys to survival.

A few hours after my lung function test today, one of the medical providers brought up for the first time the idea of placing a feeding tube. Most of the time, with CF, routines are familiar, and the pace of change with the medical regimen is slow—add a pill here, subtract a pill there, add some IVs, undergo some hospitalizations. All of that is very familiar. But when we get a new diagnosis, we have to make sense of a whole new series of reductions in quality of life. When I was found to have multiple pulmonary emboli in my lungs and had to start blood thinners was one of those times. When my hemoptysis first began to worsen, and I had to reimagine a life never lived more than an hour from a major medical center, was another one of those times.

Having to get a feeding tube, which would add complexity to my regimen and force me to cede control over another aspect of my life, would also be one of those times. The news was startling, as I look very healthy and am at a healthy weight. I told her: *I want to wait to do that until I really really need it, and I'm just not there yet.* But the provider explained that oftentimes, patients wait too long to get a feeding tube placed, until they "really really need it," and by then, it's too late—their respiratory status has declined to the point where surgery to implant the tube is no longer safe. Her explanation was informed by the knowledge and expertise she's gained working with hundreds of patients, whereas my interpretation of the wisdom of my getting a feeding tube was informed only by my own clinical history and an aversion to discomfort.

One of the difficulties with CF is that progressive decline is inevitable, but the rate at which the decline will happen is unpredictable. I could have five good years left with relatively stable lung function and weight. I could even have ten or fifteen or twenty good years. Or, my infection could rapidly worsen, my lung function and weight could both plummet, and at that point, this provider would be right, it would be too late to place a feeding tube. As patients, we have to make decisions balancing two often-disparate goals—maintaining current quality of life while extending life-span—without complete information about how much threat we're really facing. I don't want to diminish my quality of life too early, but I don't want to wait so long that getting the treatment I need isn't possible.

I recently finished a book by the late neurosurgeon Paul Kalanithi, *When Breath Becomes Air.* After working his entire life to become a neurosurgeon and ending up a chief resident at Stanford, he was hit with a diagnosis of stage IV lung cancer. His career path had been brimming with opportunity—to become a renowned neurosurgeon/neuroscientist, to do research that would change lives, and to continue operating on the very organ that makes people who they are. And then in a blink, everything shifted.

The life he had been leading was gone. The diagnosis left him facing his mortality at a much younger age than he ever thought he would have to. It forced him to consider the question of what makes life meaningful—which had long held his interest in an abstract sense—in a concrete, urgent, and highly personal way.

Lung cancer and cystic fibrosis are very different illnesses, of course, but throughout the book I found myself laughing, crying, highlighting, underlining, and saying *yes, yes, yes, yes, yes*. So much of it resonated.

With his diagnosis shining a spotlight on his mortality, he wondered how he should spend his time. "The way forward would seem obvious," he wrote, "if only I knew how many months or years I had left. Tell me three months, I'd spend time with family. Tell me one year, I'd write a book. Give me ten years, I'd get back to treating diseases. The truth that you live one day at a time didn't help: What was I supposed to do with that day?"

The question of how to meaningfully spend a life is not unique to those of us with health challenges. None of us knows if our life will be cut short. But for people with cystic fibrosis, or stage IV lung cancer, or any other life-limiting illness, there is a certainty that life will most likely be cut short to some extent. This certainty forces us to examine our values, prioritize our time, and search for meaning now rather than later. "I began to realize that coming in such close contact with my own mortality had changed both nothing and everything," Kalanithi wrote. "Before my cancer was diagnosed, I knew that someday I would die, but I didn't know when. After the diagnosis, I knew that someday I would die, but I didn't know when. But now I knew it acutely."

Kalanithi hits the nail on the head of one of the more frustrating aspects of trying to make the most of whatever amount of time we may have. "The most obvious might be an impulse to frantic activity: to 'live life to its fullest,' to travel, to dine, to achieve a host of neglected ambitions. Part of the cruelty of cancer, though, is not only that it limits your time; it also limits your energy, vastly reducing the amount you can squeeze into a day. . . . Some days, I simply persist." Some days, I simply persist; some days, I simply breathe.

A few weeks ago, on a night when I wasn't sure how to keep managing it all, I finished Paul Kalanithi's book and cried. But it reminded me of the way to move forward, the way I've been operating my entire life: "Maybe, in the absence of any certainty, we should just assume that we're going to live a long time. Maybe that's the only way forward. . . . Even if I'm dying, until I actually die, I am still living."

Monday, July 11, 2016

They told me my bacteria is resistant to all of the antibiotics. They brought the infectious disease doctors on board and overall the outlook was very bleak. My oxygen was low so I was wearing the cannula, and I was having trouble walking. I started having chest pain. My GI was not good. My weight went down to 139. But then they switched me to Ceptaz/avibactam instead of just Ceptaz, and put me on TOBI instead of colistin. A little while later they switched me to IV Bactrim instead of oral (at my urging), because the oral makes me more nauseous but probably works better. They also added oral minocycline. Day after day, nothing was really happening, I wasn't really improving.

But then I started to turn around and got discharged the next Thursday, day 8. One thing during this hospitalization made me happy. . . . Jack came to visit every day from Thursday to Monday. Then he got busy with school.

I'm scared the IVs aren't going to work anymore. They keep me on them even though we know it's resistant. The theory is that synergistically they provide some help. I just want to make it to Hawaii on August 19 with my parents, Micah, Jack, Matt, and Michelle. Haven't been to Maui in a year and I miss the sun and the warm ocean so so so much. It's painful to think about how much I miss it.

Caleigh went to Hawaii for two weeks and had the time of her life and then the day I got admitted, her mom called me from there to ask the name of the hospital I was admitted to. Caleigh had a bad bowel blockage and needed surgery but they couldn't do it there because she's too complicated. She was in so much pain. She ended up on a ventilator because she couldn't breathe, she got pneumonia, and they medevaced her to Stanford's ICU and it was heartbreaking that there was nothing we could do to help. Melissa and Emily were both checking in with me about both my health and Caleigh's. I had more info about her since her mom was updating my mom and me.

I kept picturing her in the ICU, unconscious, unable to breathe without life support. Going on ECMO—artificial life support, a way to keep her alive. Her family watching her like that, her dad and sister flying in to be with them, unable to do anything. How could they manage, how could they hold it together? How would my family deal with that? What would I want if I were in her circumstances? Or, better put, what *will* I want *when I am* in her circumstances? Because one day it will happen, that is inevitable. The when is unclear, but the fact that one day it will happen seems inevitable.

Since my *cepacia* is resistant to antibiotics, the stakes are higher, and I'm starting to see myself in Caleigh. How ironic that the writing I've been doing for Nelson Hardiman about California's death with dignity law will be relevant to my life one day soon, if I end up on a vent or suffering in some extreme way and am not able to get a lung transplant because of the *cepacia*.

Tuesday, July 19, 2016
The last two days have been madness. I've had a million things to do all at once—we're in the final throes for Susan's book, writing for Nelson Hardiman, writing for Janet, editing an app for a friend, editing Dr. David Weill's memoir about running a transplant program, writing a blog post for Emily's Entourage.

The more time we spend together, the more I feel myself falling for Jack. In the beginning I wasn't sure if we had a connection other than physical attraction, but I don't feel that way anymore. I appreciate that he feels like he can talk to me about anything, and I think I'm getting to the point where I feel more comfortable talking to him about more important things.

I'm really excited about Hawaii, which is only a month away!

Thursday, July 21, 2016

Things with my GI are as bad now as they ever were. I need to get a handle on it and wish Dr. Mohabir would let me try ataluren again because I can't fucking deal with it anymore.

Getting the infection under control feels beyond my control. They extended my IV regimen instead of taking me off IVs or admitting me. They put me back on the same regimen I'd been on three weeks before, the one that I got sick on. I need a punching bag!

I don't really feel like I have an outlet for this and I have so much anger right now. I can't talk to my parents about this or they'll force me into therapy. As I get older, the more I realize how hard my disease must be for them and how much fear they must have, too, the more I don't want to dump my anger on them. I want to be strong for them, or at least pretend to be strong. I can't talk to my friends because they won't understand. And not Jack for sure because I'm not comfortable even acknowledging that I have GI problems.

I remember asking Kari about how she discussed the topic with her then boyfriend (now husband), Brad. She said she had to tell him something, and just told him straight up what she struggles with. Apparently he said, "That's what you were so scared to tell me?" And she said something like, "But don't you find it disgusting?" And he basically said something like, "You're beautiful to me no matter what." He loved her unconditionally.

I just spent a solid twenty minutes reading old conversations between Kari and me on Facebook Messenger from 2014. Back then, I was still planning to live in New Zealand after graduation. And she was still alive. So much has changed. She was worrying about internships and job applications then. I was trying to figure out my post-college plans and career goals. I admired that she was so dedicated to working despite her health status; who knew she would be dead a year later? We were both admitted at the same time for GI stuff, both dealing with dehumanizing enemas and communication issues with the team, both wondering about the best way to disclose CF in the workplace, to friends, to boyfriends. So many of the same issues I still think about now, except I'm still here to ponder them and she's not.

My ability to talk to others with CF has waned a little bit. The main three that I always kept in touch with were Melissa, Kari, and Caleigh. But things are so different now with Melissa and Caleigh having had their transplants and Kari being gone. Melissa and Caleigh both could have died a number of times; fundamentally, they've been through things I cannot understand and have every reason to fear. They reached the end of the CF spectrum and jumped onto a completely different one—the transplant spectrum. Their lives are so different and their health status is incomprehensible to me now: I don't know the intricacies of life post-transplant, and for them, the troubles of life as a CF patient with 40 to 50 percent lung function are in the distant past. I don't think we relate in the same way anymore. I find myself not knowing what to say, thrust into the position that probably most of my friends and acquaintances are in when they hear about my health. When I try to talk to Melissa and Caleigh, I feel uncomfortable, wanting to say just the right thing but having no idea what that right thing is and fumbling with words. Melissa and Caleigh always listen when I have complaining to do, but I don't feel right about it given what they've been through. They've been at death's door, they've been on ventilators, they've had their families crying beside them, wondering if they'll make it through the night. They've had their chests ripped open, their old lungs torn out and new ones placed in, like magic, except it's not magic and there seem to be as many problems post-transplant as there were before.

Saturday, July 23, 2016

The day after I wrote that last post I started to feel much better emotionally.

Last Friday, Jack came to the city to have dinner with my parents and Glenn and Sandra, which was truly a hilarious event. He knows nothing about Judaism and it was a Shabbat dinner, so he got a full-on Jewish education, learning about the kiddush cup, the prayers, what a Seder is, the story of Passover, what a *kippah* is, etc. Sandra gave him a lot of shit and he was taking it well—apparently, she liked him a lot.

After we got home that night, we talked for a really long time about so many things. In this relationship, I'm scared I'm the one who's going to get hurt, for two reasons: (1) I wonder if part of him still has feelings for his old girlfriend, and (2) in December, he's going to move wherever he needs to be for his career, and that might not be SF. And even if it is SF, if he ultimately plans to move to the East Coast, I'm going to have to think long and hard about whether to spend so much time in a relationship with someone who probably can't be with me long-term.

For now, though, things are really good. We debriefed the dinner and laughed a lot. I like that he's so willing to spend time with my parents and family. I think Jack values family a lot. I wonder if I will meet his mom at some point? She doesn't seem to come up here often but I know they are very close. He's going on a trip with her to Oregon in September and we're still discussing the possibility of me going to Maine with him and his dad, which I keep going back and forth about.

Thursday, July 28, 2016

So much has changed in just the last few days.

Over the weekend, I started to feel more short of breath but went hiking at Lands End anyway (probably was overkill). It was a really nice day, but too intense, cardio-wise. Monday, I woke up feeling way worse. Luckily my mom was visiting, and just as we were about to pull up to the house after running errands, I felt a bleed coming on.

. . . continuing where I left off last night.

My mom pulled over on the side of the road because I told her blood was coming and I didn't want to splatter it all over the car. I grabbed a pill bottle that was inside the cup holder in between the two front seats, dumped the pills out, and started coughing the blood in there. I got myself onto the curb and the blood kept coming—at 20 mL, it was big enough and unexpected enough to be scary.

Right then, a woman from AffloVest drove up, bringing my new portable vest, something I've been wanting for five years. It was finally here, and I was bent over coughing blood on the street, too exhausted, feverish, and distracted to focus on this life-altering machine.

When the bleeding stopped, we went inside and she showed me how to set the vest up. I was shivering so I put on my fever scarf— the striped one from the Gap I got so many years ago. Hot tea, a big jacket, my scarf, chills—the telltale signs of fever. I checked my temp and it was 102.3, high but not wild high.

My mom and I got into a fight over whether to call the fellow. She sometimes thinks fellows say to come in to the hospital to cover their asses—they don't want to get sued if you don't go to the ER and something goes wrong.

My thinking is, if there's a protocol that says hemoptysis + fever + multidrug-resistant bacteria + shortness of breath = a trip to the ER, then you follow it. Because even if nine out of ten times it wouldn't matter if you waited the twelve hours until morning to go to the hospital, there's the one time it might make the difference between life and death.

We struck a compromise and told the fellow on call that if he could get Dr. Chhatwani from Stanford's CF team on the phone, we would do what she said. The fellow called us back and said he reached her and that Dr. C wanted me to go to the ER so I immediately packed my bags. I texted Jack to tell him about the hemoptysis and about the ER visit, and he called and offered to come, which was so thoughtful. He scored a lot of points with that offer.

The night was uneventful. The ER part went smoothly because I

268

had brought my nighttime IVs from home and I got up to my own room at about 1:00 a.m. I was so exhausted, feverish, and short of breath by that point that I could barely keep my eyes open while they did the admission and asked me all the same questions I answer every single time.

The repetition of things can be comforting, and it can be infuriating. The fact that things are familiar is what's comforting. But having to go over my belongings list every single time I'm admitted and having to do it not only in the ER but also again in the room is ridiculous. Having to go through every single medication is a little annoying but not ridiculous. Having to repeat the tests in the room that they already ran in the ER is frustrating and creates unnecessary expense, plus it means I don't get to sleep.

My white blood cell count was 22,000, so very high. Not surprising given the fever and how I felt. They took blood cultures, but so far nothing has come back.

I didn't realize how concerned the docs were when I first got here. I was highly concerned that I had gone down to a lesser IV regimen at home the week before, when I was already unwell, and then got sicker. I began to worry about whether the drugs would be able to get this under control. It seemed like, after getting sick so many times in a row while on IVs, with few changes to the regimen, there was little else they could try.

The next morning, we saw Dr. Chhatwani and the whole CF team. They explained how serious this was and said they were going to reach beyond Stanford's infectious disease team to *cepacia* specialists at other centers (like Toronto), and that they were going to try new things. And they did!

The next blood draw showed my white blood cell count at 17,000. A little movement in the right direction, but I was still having really high fevers. Today is the first day I don't have a high fever—the highest today has been 100.6. I've felt hot and clammy all evening but at least I'm not in the 102s. That's reassuring.

...

Wednesday I'm sitting in my room with Coach Bowie, who had come to visit. We had a nice chat, reminiscing about high school water polo days; then he went with my mom to the cafeteria and they were gonna get food and bring it back to eat in the room. While they were gone, I heard a distinctive knock but didn't put two and two together to recognize Dr. Mohabir's knock because he'd been on some sort of leave for months. He bounded in and asked if my parents were around so we could have a family meeting. I said, my mom is, and texted her to come back immediately.

Dr. Mohabir said that my prognosis is not good. People who have been on IVs for THIS long, who are incapable of being off antibiotics, don't turn around. The bacteria just don't let up at any point. He said there probably won't be a time in the future when I'll be able to stay healthy without antibiotics; he said that the antibiotics are propping my lung function up and keeping me alive. Without the antibiotics, he said, I wouldn't live for another year.

He said some people get to the point that they can't do it anymore. They go off the antibiotics, their lung function plummets, and then they get listed for transplant. But with me, it's not so easy—no center wants to transplant me. He said he's talked about me to many centers who said no. They are not excited about me as a *candidate,* were the words he used. But he thinks Duke, Toronto, and Pittsburgh are three that could still be options. He said he was going to see if they'd be willing to talk with me. According to Dr. Mohabir, the problem is that I'm in cepacia syndrome. A slow version of it. He said that when he tells the centers that I have *cepacia* and I'm in syndrome, they immediately assume I'll just die on the table. Because that's what happens when you try to transplant with cepacia syndrome. The outcomes are just not good.

Obviously, I don't want to push to get on a transplant list and expedite that process just to get a surgery I don't feel confident I'll survive. I want to prolong my life as long as possible. But at the same time, I feel like as I'm working so hard to stay alive, I need to have some kind of backup plan—I need to know that when the IVs eventually stop holding me steady and my lung function plummets, there will be a center that will list me. At that point, I'll pack my bags and be on the first plane. I don't want that to happen anytime soon, but I want to know whether it's even a possibility for my future. I want to know if there's a center that will take me, and ideally, which one.

He said that I should not expect to be off IVs for any significant length of time, and that I should not get my hopes up about transplant. He said they are still tweaking and changing the regimen to fight each exacerbation as it comes, but, looking at things on a macro scale, and based on my last year and what he knows from his experience treating others with *cepacia,* he believes that my *cepacia* is now a superbug—and it is not going to get better. The infection is going to take over. The antibiotics are slowing that process down so I will have to be on them as long as I can stand it, as long as they keep working, or as long as it's safe to . . . e.g., if I start to have kidney failure, we might need to reevaluate.

As he was saying this, it seemed like he thought there was a chance I might give up—that I might say, essentially, I can't do this anymore. I can't be on these IVs for weeks, months, maybe years more. He said other patients have just "given up" and gone home on hospice. And he acknowledged my quality of life has been shot to hell, even though my lung function is 45 percent.

Now I feel like I've sort of been living in a delusion. When I started my period of sickness one year ago, I kept thinking, for the first few rounds of IVs, that I would get better and bounce back and get back to life. In LA, I began to lose hope as the months wore on and I got worse and worse, losing more and more strength, more and more weight, and more and more reason to live. Everything was slipping away. I was completely depressed. I was anxious all the time and had no faith. No faith in my body, no faith in the doctors' ability to fix me, no faith that my life would go back to the way it was.

But when I moved to SF, even though I was on long-term IVs, it was like this dormant part of me was awakened again by the simple fact of being around friends. It was like drinking Red Bulls and taking happy pills. I felt like myself again, even though I wasn't surfing, even though I wasn't playing volleyball, even though I was on IVs, even though I was away from the beach. I reconnected with my motivated, intellectual side. I got down to business, I finished Susan's book and did other writing. And I worked out. Set goals. Made plans. Explored the city and deepened my relationships with people from my college community, people I had drifted from when I lived in LA. It was a beautiful high, a beautiful first couple of months here.

So, yes, I was living in a delusion. I thought that after a certain amount of time on IVs, I would just miraculously not need them anymore and be better. In reality, when I went off IVs, I got sick two weeks later and was back on IVs four weeks later. I did not get much time at all, and since I've gone back on them, I've been hospitalized three times. It's all becoming a blur, and that's the worst fucking part.

Anyway. Back to Mohabir's talk. He said it was time to start living my life.

This was one of the most emotional talks I've had in my entire life. My mom was bawling her eyes out. I was trying to be strong for her, and trying to hold it together, but I was crying, too.

At the very beginning, back when I was young, I used to cough up blood on the pool deck, but I was naive and excited and happy and growing and changing and trying. Now my heart breaks for that little girl because she thought she had a long future, and my current reality is telling me that I don't.

And my heart breaks for my mom and dad. They just want to keep me alive and they will do whatever they can to make that happen. I try to do my part, and I think I do my best. But I also have to live my life. And that's the part Dr. Mohabir was emphasizing. I think he was trying to explain that I might not have that much time. Because how long can one really be on these IVs? A few years, sure, maybe, that would be a long time for IVs, but a few years is not a long time to live. It's wild to think that when I'm around twenty-six, when my friends are moving in with their boyfriends or getting married or starting business school or having kids or getting promoted or doing whatever the hell they're doing, I could be packing up to move to North Carolina, Toronto, Pittsburgh, or Cleveland. That is such a mind-fuck. Picturing my mom in snow boots would almost be enough to make me laugh, if I weren't crying. And would my dad come? What about Micah?

When Dr. Mohabir was talking, he kept circling back to the idea of doing what makes me happy. And I kept thinking about people. Not places I want to go or bucket list things I want to do. It was about the people I love, getting enough time with them. Not feeling like I'm leaving them behind. Or being left behind myself, while their lives all move on. That's the problem with death. For everyone else, it's an event, it's sad and shitty and grief-inducing, but then life goes on. For the deceased, that's it, that's the end.

I'm afraid of what's to come. In some ways, I feel like nothing will change. When I leave here, I'll—hopefully—be feeling a little better. I'll be on a home IV regimen. Ideally, we'll go on a vacation to Hawaii. Whether or not we choose to take the risk and go to Hawaii, afterward, I'll come back and still be on IVs. And that could go on indefinitely. Maybe I won't be hospitalized again for months; maybe it'll just be weeks. Who knows? Nobody knows how fast this thing will progress. I think we're all just relieved that my high fevers have stopped and that, so far, there's no growth in my blood cultures. Which means that at this particular time, the antibiotics are still helping—all seven of them. It's not feasible to go home on all of them, so we'll have to figure out a way to send me home with IVs I can manage.

Dr. Chhatwani rounded the next day and told me that I need to accept more help than I've had until now. For example, I might need a home health nurse who comes and does IVs. Or have someone else who comes to help even if they don't do the IVs. Or have family live in the area to help me.

Having family stay with me aligns with my goal of having Kona up here . . . that was one of the things I realized when I started thinking about my time being limited. I want my dog in my life. Literally all I wanted to do when I was talking to Dr. M was to cry into Kona's fur.

It was an extremely dire prognosis. But it wasn't new information. Dr. M was just flicking on the lights so we could see what everyone else already had seen—that *cepacia* has taken over, and it's time to figure out a transplant option.

I realize I want to write my story.

The thing that I haven't even processed yet, and I'm tearing up thinking about it now, is that I won't have a family. I really want to have a family. I want to get married and have kids (or adopt—since I've always known I wouldn't be able to carry my own kids). I have multiple Word documents filled with names for future children. I've always loved names. And family. And the idea of having my own kids. I think it's because I'm twenty-three that this feels like an especially hard thing to let go of. It's not something I ever foresaw having to sacrifice, for some reason. Which goes to show that some part of me has always been living with the delusion that I'd live a long and healthy life.

I'm scared. And I think I'm falling in love with Jack. And I don't know if that's just because of the shit-storm I'm going through, and the fact that he happens to be there, or if it's him, but I think it's happening. It almost feels weird that we don't say the words "I love you," because our dynamic is so loving. I have to stop myself from saying "love you" whenever I say goodbye or good night. I don't know if he feels the same way, but I know he has been deeply affected by the events of this week.

The night he found out I might only have a year left, he cried so hard. I never thought I would see him cry like that, and I was so surprised, because when my mom and I were first explaining things to him, he was sort of staring off into a corner, seeming very distant and apathetic. In the middle of this my dad arrived . . . my mom had said it was urgent he come. And then as soon as my parents left the room he started crying, and I realized that he had just been trying not to cry. But once he did start crying, he completely broke down.

That's a whole long story, though, the story of that night. The short version is: He was devastated, he was crying, he said he didn't know how to be strong for me. I told him that he didn't need to be strong by not crying, he was doing exactly what he should be doing as a boyfriend by showing up and calling. I told him he's doing all the right things, and it absolutely does not bother me for him to show emotion and cry around me. In fact, it was touching to me, because it showed me how deeply he cares.

I truly did not know how he was going to react to this information. He said he didn't know if he could ever just be lighthearted around me again, if he could just go on vacation and have fun without just being sad all the time. And I kind of made the comparison that I don't know if he's leaving in the fall, and so it's similar in that I, too, don't know what the future holds, and I, too, am scared, but that doesn't mean we should back away from it.

We talked for a long time. He cried, we hugged, we laughed. The wild thing is that I had cried all that day, and have cried so many times since that day, but I did not cry one time that night. It was like my body was empty of tears. By the time he left, he said he was feeling much better, much more optimistic. He said he wasn't scared anymore and whatever happened, we would tackle it together. It was so incredibly sweet.

My mom wrote on Facebook so we wouldn't have to repeat the story over and over:

> There's no way to sugarcoat this message. Mallory Smith's long-term prognosis is not good. She has been fighting the worst possible bacteria for a very long time and it seems the antibiotic options that she's been on have run their course. The doctors are making tweaks but don't think it's likely that things will turn around.
>
> It's clear that most people don't understand the severity of the situation because Mallory looks so good and does so much. We felt it was time to let our beloved family and friends know how difficult things are for her.
>
> The doctors don't think Mallory's health can be sustained without IVs, so the plan is to keep her on

them indefinitely. Hopefully that will allow her to have some quality of life. Mallory wants to do as much as possible for as long as possible.

The Stanford team is talking to transplant centers around the country to try to find one that will consider Mallory as a candidate. But they are not optimistic because of the bacteria she cultures. We live in hope.

She has finally agreed to write her story.

Now it's 12:30 and I should sleep. I'm sure I left out much of what happened this week. There's just no way to retain all of this. And I'm pissed that I've had to take so much Ativan because it's messing with my memory.

Friday, August 5, 2016
Feeling a little emotionally numb. It's now Friday so I've been here in Stanford Hospital for a week and four days. I'm supposed to be getting out on Monday.

Today I got calls from Cleveland Clinic and University of Pittsburgh Medical Center (UPMC), from their transplant programs, to verify some information. It was shitty false hope from Cleveland because the medical director of their transplant program had already told my mom by email that they have a blanket policy against transplanting *cenocepacia* patients, and they already told Chhatwani that they wouldn't consider me. But UPMC!!!!! I'm still hopeful.

But what do you call it when the best-case scenario, the thing you're hoping for, is almost as terrifying as death itself? This week, time and again, I've thought about the fact that the road will only get harder from here. And I don't know if I should try to forget that, to distract myself from that, or if I should really reflect on it so that I can be grateful for the health that I do have now. Because on the one hand, understanding how hard things will be in the future does make me realize how lucky I still am. But on the other hand, I am scared shitless about what the future will bring, for how much I will suffer, and for how much my family will suffer.

The thing I keep thinking about, the image I keep coming back to, is a reservoir. My family's love for me and their ability to help me is this reservoir that seems endlessly deep. It always seems like it will never run out. But as things get harder and as I deplete their resources (their love, their time, their money, their concern), I know we will get to a point where we *have* to worry about running out. I don't know if we will run out of money—my parents are literally buying the apartment beneath mine in a city that I don't even know how much longer I'll live in just to be there for me—or if I will just suck them dry, until the only thing they're living for is me and they have nothing left. I already feel like I've taken so much away from them and now my mom has to uproot herself to move up here and live with me.

That's one issue.

Another issue is that I don't know what to do about my vacation— whether to go to Hawaii or not. Whether to plan a different trip.

I feel awful that I've burdened Jack with so much worry about me when he's in his second-to-last quarter at Stanford and he's worked his entire life to get here and now he's tanking his GPA. I just can't imagine the stress that he's feeling. But I also can't be worried too much about his stress because I have to worry about my own stress and, fundamentally, the one who's going through this is me. I am not minimizing what he's going through. He has to be absolutely torn about how to handle this.

He says he's on the verge of tears all the time and yet he has to go to office hours, attend class, work in his lab, etc. He has to put on a brave face in front of my friends and family and his own friends. I guess he's just picturing the worst possible scenarios in his mind and that's what's so hard for him—he says he's freaking out all the time. He's worried he'll just be walking to class and get a call that something catastrophic has happened to me. It's beautiful that he cares enough to be so distraught over what's going on with me.

But when he disappeared for a few days it was hard for me to not know if he was coming, or if I was going to hear from him. If he was having doubts, I would rather have known. I would understand. Completely. He only has one quarter left at Stanford after this, and if he wants to focus on school and friends, I would understand. Especially since he's likely going to move away anyway. I don't think he wants out because he hasn't said anything like that. I am trying to give him space but then I wonder, why? And where do we stand as a couple?

I really care about him a lot. I almost said "I love you" the other night, but then I didn't, because I didn't want to complicate things even further. Now I'm especially happy that I didn't say that, given that he's been having an awful time adjusting to what's going on with me, and that I don't know if he wants to stay together.

That brings me back to vacation. Perhaps I should make a decision about Hawaii independent of his scheduling constraints. If I do end up being able to go to Hawaii but not at a time that works for him, it will still be nice; what I want is to surf, to be in the water, etc. If I can't go with Jack, so be it. It would've been fun, especially if Michelle and Matt could go as planned. But after talking to Caleigh, who doesn't think it's a good idea for me to go, I'm second-guessing the idea of going in two weeks. It might be fine to just go to Malibu, go for some nice drives, stay in a nice house, and do some hikes.

I feel like I've given up in the fight a bit. . . . I feel so unmotivated to get back to my life, to get back to work. I feel a lack of optimism that I will ever be able to do the things I love. If I can't be the person I was, I don't know who to become. I don't know how to prioritize my health without being just a sick person. I don't know how to explain this situation to my friends, how to talk about my prognosis, how to conceive of how much time I have left, and how to prioritize what I do with that time.

Monday, August 8, 2016
Got discharged from the hospital today. But I don't feel as happy as I think I should. I vaguely remember, in my recent hospitalizations,

feeling really excited to get back to SF and my apartment. But now I don't feel excited.

It scares me how dependent I am on so many medications. I feel extremely dysphoric, just generally dissatisfied with life. And I can see logically from the outside that I have no reason to feel that way. Well, I do have some reason. I did just get news that my prognosis is horrible, and every few days I get more rejections from transplant centers. So yes, I have reasons to feel sad. But usually I can compartmentalize and still find happiness in the present moment. Today I just felt like I would never be happy again. Except when I was with Jack—I felt happy when he came over. So even if our relationship ends after this fall, I think it's worth it to be with him until then because he brings me happiness.

Later that day, Julia and Liane came over and we hung out with Tamara, who was still visiting. It was so great to have friends over! We went back out to a table by the fountain in front of the hospital. Caleigh and her mom, Lizeth, came outside at the same time, so we all chatted. It broke my heart to see Caleigh. She weighs sixty-seven pounds now and she can't eat a thing because she's nauseous and vomiting. It's just heartbreaking how much she suffers. She's so skinny, she's super fragile, but that girl just doesn't break. I wonder often how she keeps her spirits up. I think it might be her family. They seem to bring her a lot of joy.

She told me that when she was waiting for transplant but thought she might not survive long enough to get one, she started marking off bucket list items. That made me want to create a bucket list. I've been living so safely that I feel like I don't even have an adventurous spirit anymore. Caleigh found a hot-air balloon company that let her bring oxygen up in the air, somewhere near Napa. That blew my mind. I'm so much healthier now than she was when she did that, and she had more spirit than I do. It was like a kick in the ass to do things.

But at the same time, I feel like I want to protect myself, because if I can't get a transplant, then I have to keep myself stable or I'll die. Everything feels very hopeless right now and I'm trying to find a way to convince my brain to feel hope. But I can't when that doesn't seem logical.

Wednesday, August 24, 2016

I look around and see blue. Royal-blue water, turquoise farther in the distance. Blue cloudless sky. Even the boat is blue.

My back bakes in the sun and my right foot sizzles. My right arm wraps tightly around Jack—after a year away from the ocean, getting tossed off a fast-moving boat in water hundreds of feet deep would be traumatic.

My breath quickens as the wind and swell pick up. I remind myself to breathe deeply and slowly, knowing that anxiety-induced breathlessness is the one kind I can control. As I maintain my death grip on the rope and focus on my long inhale-exhales, it hits me all at once—I'm in Hawaii. In the middle of the ocean. My favorite place, and my other favorite place. I'm not in a hospital. I'm with Jack, Michelle, Matt, Ari, and Justin. Even Micah is here! It's sunny, it's beautiful. I can breathe. I'm not wearing oxygen. No one on the boat that didn't know me would think there was anything wrong with me, other than a cough. I'm happy, happier than I can remember being in a long time.

We continue on toward Molokini and I smile and smile. I wonder again if this is the last time I'll ever come to Hawaii, and then I banish that thought and look down at the water, noticing the way the boat cuts through it so forcefully yet so elegantly. It's a beautiful Wednesday.

I keep wondering: Can this be real life? I think, maybe my life can be like this again. Maybe I can walk on the beach and do long open-water swims and start surfing again. Maybe I can help with the dishes and not freak out over a bad night of sleep. Already, in just six days, showering normally has stopped feeling remarkable; maybe, just maybe, I'll stay off IVs long enough that submerging underwater will stop feeling like a long-lost vestige from my past.

I'm just so happy to be here. Even though I can't dive as deep as I could when I was a kid. Even though I can't surf at all, when just a year ago I was charging. I lugged my oxygen concentrator to the beach (or rather, Jack lugged it). Things are different now, we know that. But in some ways, everything is the same—the same peace descends each time I jump in the water, the same euphoria when a sea turtle or a reef shark swims below me. The same simple pleasure comes from eating big dinners with family and friends, from sitting on our patio with wine and cheese.

Thursday, August 25, 2016

I sit on the lanai of our condo in ninety-degree weather in a long-sleeve shirt, sweatshirt, yoga pants, and a second layer of sweatpants on top. My body won't stop shivering, so I'm searching for the warmest place I can find. Jack comes out onto the patio to get the grill ready to cook leg of lamb. I know I'll have to leave the patio when the grill gets smoky, and I wonder where I can go to avoid freezing. The bedroom is out of the question—the fan and AC keep it a frigid sixty-eight degrees. My parents' bedroom is even colder.

Finally, I drag myself up off the outdoor sofa, the bag with my oxygen concentrator draped over me cross-body style, pulling my shoulders forward. Into the bathroom I go, where I pull out the blow-dryer and start blow-drying my already-dry hair, face, neck, chest, back, legs. Anxiety begins to set in; it's completely illogical to feel hypothermic in ninety-degree heat. But when does my body ever act in a way that's logical? It's illogical to get sick while on three oral antibiotics, two inhaled antibiotics, and thirty-five other medications. Since my life never feels logical, blow-drying my entire body in a bathroom in Hawaii doesn't even feel that wild.

But a case of severe chills, for me, is ominous. When I eventually take my temperature, I have a fever of 103.3. My stomach drops.

It's a couple of hours after my fever spiked above 103, and I'm in the emergency room at Maui Memorial Medical Center. Before the trip, we'd looked up the hospital on the island to find out if it had an ICU, an interventional radiology team, and experienced pulmonologists. I didn't think I would end up needing their services; mostly, the research was meant to convince my Stanford medical team that I'd done my homework and had fully thought through my decision to take the trip.

The IV alarm blares like a siren, a foot away from my head. After five minutes of sleep, the IV antibiotic has finished, and the pump won't let me forget it. I press the call button for the nurse to come shut off the alarm so I can catch a few minutes of sleep before going to my next test. No one comes, so I fiddle with some buttons on the pump, familiar enough with how they work by now to silence it temporarily.

After a long night in the emergency room, I get admitted to the step-down ICU at Maui Memorial. Dr. Mohabir calls to check in on me at 4:00 a.m. Hawaii time, but I'm finally asleep, so he leaves a voicemail.

Dr. M tells my mom that he wants me out of the hospital in twenty-four hours. He wants me to enjoy the rest of my vacation, just with home IV antibiotics. That means no time in the water, but I'm learning that there's more to life than plan A. The particulars of plan B—R&R, good meals, reclining in the shade with a good book—sound pretty damn good right about now. Better than staying in a hospital bed for another few weeks, getting weaker, waiting for the drugs to suppress this infection.

I've quoted this saying from a fellow CF-er before, but it just hits so close to home: Reality always finds us. Being in the hospital and on IVs is my reality, as much as I would love to play hide-and-seek, staying healthy and hidden on an island forever.

Before reality found me, I got to do things that bring me unadulterated joy for six straight days. The infection caught up to me, but I have two words for it: "Game on!"

Wednesday, August 31, 2016

When I got out of the hospital we went back to the condo. Things were okay for a few days but I started to deteriorate on Saturday and got even worse on Sunday.

That night we were trying to decide what to do. We were supposed to stay until Thursday but there was news that a hurricane was coming. I started to panic about getting stuck on the island. Jack was great. He listened to me sob. It was the anniversary of Kari's death and that also rattled me. It was all crashing down on me. The future felt too hard. Jack didn't know what to say, how could he? But he listened, and he was present. And he made me feel safe. He had to get back to school and I didn't want to stay on without him.

My mom jumped through lots of hoops to change all of our tickets to get us off the island . . . clearly others had the same idea to cut their trip short. She was ultimately able to make the arrangements and we flew the next day.

The wild thing was that as we were rushing to pack and get to the airport, UPMC called to say I was approved for the evaluation. I was in the middle of treatment, everyone else was scrambling to pack up, so I handed the phone to my mom, who tried to stay calm as she attempted to capture important details about the weeklong process. She was clearly struggling to stay focused as she was processing her overwhelming joy. None of us could believe this was really happening.

The call took a long time. We were late getting to the airport and carrying so much medical gear. The hurricane was imminent, and that, combined with my high fever, made for an intense travel day. I was so relieved when we touched down, even though Hawaii had been absolutely incredible.

For a few days, being in Maui and seeing all that I could do made that prognosis I had received from Stanford seem ridiculous. How I felt the first few days of the trip gave me hope that I could reclaim my old life, my old identity. That hope felt good. Even now that I'm back in Stanford Hospital, battling the same old infection, running through the same old tiresome drill, I feel a little more hopeful.

Some might think it was irresponsible to take an IV holiday so soon after the doctors said I couldn't survive off IVs. But life is a balancing act—as patients, we have to keep our bodies healthy, yes, but also our minds. We have to know that there's life out there to be lived, however sick we get. Whatever it takes to remind us of that is worth it, in my eyes. Calculated risk-taking is the name of the game for me now, rather than cautious sheltering.

I do know now with 100 percent certainty that I made the right choice to go. And the right choice to come back, as it's pointless to stick to a vacation plan if you're so sick that being away from your doctor is terrifying. Both were such huge decisions, it was hard to know what to do. Going was enormous, canceling our last few days in Hawaii was enormous, deciding to land and head straight to the ER without unpacking or getting resettled was enormous, but my gut was telling me that I needed to be back in my second home. I needed to be evaluated.

Thursday, September 1, 2016

Two big developments with Jack!

First, his dad wants to meet me!!! Jack sent this text: *My dad wants to meet you. That's super rare. He even choked up on the phone when he told me how proud he was that I have been able to find a way to support you even though you've been going through so much. You're the real champ in my eyes, but he can tell you've made me a better person. I know your parents thank me all the time for the things I do for you, but I just want to make it clear that there is an equal amount of thanks to you for the things you do for me. In short, thanks for continuing to be awesome, everyone can see it, not just me.*

Second, he came to the hospital today (it's now Thursday, I came into the ER on Tuesday) and we hung out all afternoon and he said he loves me for the first time! He said, "I care about you so much," and I said, "So do I." And then he said, "I love you, Mallory," and I said I loved him back!

It was a beautiful moment. I'd been in severe pain all day with this pleuritic chest pain and really frustrated by the lack of coordination/responsiveness in my pain management. I'd also been feeling dejected about being back here again. But then Jack came and it perked me up, and we went on a walk by the fountain, and he said he loved me!!!!!!!!

Where I am with work/professional/creative endeavors:

I'm editing Dr. Weill's book. Want to stay on top of that and work faster but also do a very, very good job.

I need to start thinking about what I want to do for my own book. So many people have reached out to offer to get me an agent or have it read by a publisher! I need to make something of this and capitalize on the fact that I'm starting down this whole transplant road and that this is the time in my life where shit gets complicated and interesting.

My updates are scatterbrained because I'm on drugs (prescribed ones, of course).

Saturday, September 10, 2016

I'm in LA now, came to visit my grandma, who was diagnosed with end-stage ovarian cancer. It's just so sad. She and my grandpa were so much a part of my growing up.

I'm feeling sad about so many things but also worried about transplant. I hope Pittsburgh has some redeeming qualities, I really do. Something to make me think that living there for a few years, potentially even dying there, wouldn't be the worst thing in the world. I have to be able to find joy there, otherwise what's the point?

Today, I woke up before 10:00 a.m. (I've been waking up at like noon every day, so 10:00 a.m. is an achievement). I ate a normal breakfast (oatmeal, fruit, and coffee) and felt fine afterward, did treatment and worked on David's book (reedited chapter 3). I felt focused, then went to work out at Grandma's gym. (Fifteen minutes on the elliptical, thank God for supplemental oxygen, then weights, then foam rolled.) After that, I went upstairs and talked to Grandpa for a long time and visited with Grandma. Hanging out with Grandpa was really nice. I sat there with him and ate a frozen peach and listened to his stories of the old days.

Going into Grandma's room I started to get emotional. She said that now was the time she was supposed to tell everyone the last things she wanted to say to them, so she was going to tell me something. "Mallory, ever since you were a little girl, I've thought you were extraordinary," she said. "But as you've grown up, you get more extraordinary every day. I'm so proud to be your grandma, and I claim no credit for how amazing you've turned out. But I love you so much and I'm lucky to be your grandma." I started crying, because how could I not? Her diagnosis is so devastating.

Being with them was very emotional and after I left, I didn't feel like seeing anybody so I walked home (which was almost a mile, more than I've walked in a very long time). While I walked I listened to music and cried more. I was thinking about Grandma being sick, but also about what will happen to Grandpa when she dies, and what on earth he would do if we all had to move to the East Coast for me to get a transplant.

I'm also not ready to say goodbye to my life yet—my friends and my social life, Maria, Micah, Kona, Grandma and Grandpa, Northern California crisp air and trees and routines, Southern California beach days and lazy afternoons. All the little things that make up the familiar. I'm not ready to transform my life yet.

I was also thinking about how my mom doesn't deserve to have a parent die and a daughter die close together in time, so I need to live a long time for her because she deserves better than all this sadness. I worry about how my dad would survive losing me. I don't know if my parents' marriage could survive that much sadness, and I think if I were to die, my main wish would be for them to lean into each other to get through it rather than pull away from each other. I would hope that if anything ever happened to me, it would bring my family closer together, not fracture them apart.

Last Thursday at midnight, after twelve hours of travel with six medical bags and an oxygen tank, my mom and I touched down in Pittsburgh International Airport. It was supposed to be the start of our *Thelma and Louise* adventure. In fact, it was the day from hell.

Packing up all the mechanical and chemical paraphernalia that keep me alive was tough. We had to bring my vest machine, compressor, nebulizers, oxygen tank and its accessories, forty-plus pounds of IV medications, twenty-two different kinds of pills, and inhaled medications. With my foggy mind, limited energy, shortness of breath, low oxygen, and midday vomiting, it was a grueling effort. But we got it done, and Thursday morning we packed up the car to go to the airport.

People often ask why *B. cepacia* is contraindicated for transplant. The reasons are multifaceted:

1. Transplant centers need to keep their one-year survival rates above a certain percentage (80 or 90 percent) in order to stay in business: if they fall below national standards, their program risks being shut down. Transplant is a huge moneymaker for hospitals, so staying in business is a top priority. Taking on high-risk cases such as patients with *cenocepacia* can compromise outcomes.
2. Lungs are a scarce commodity. There are not enough organ donors in the United States to supply lungs to all the people waiting. Many patients die on the list. Ethically speaking, I think it's hard to give lungs to someone who doesn't have a good chance of making it when they could go to a less risky patient with a higher chance of survival.
3. Doctors are obligated under the Hippocratic Oath to do no harm. If the data shows that most patients with *B. cepacia* either die on the table or

within a year after transplant, some feel it is more harmful to try the risky procedure than not to— even if not trying means the patient will die.

4. The timing of a transplant is also complicated. There is a small window in which patients are eligible for transplant; they have to be so sick that they can't live long without new lungs, but healthy enough to survive the operation. A patient can become too sick for transplant very abruptly, losing eligibility. Right now, given that a transplant for me would require a cross-country move, I'm in the window where I need to start the process, need to complete the full evaluation. If my health all of a sudden plummeted, I couldn't just go to the closest ICU and get listed for transplant there, so I need to plan ahead.

5. The timing of a transplant involving *B. cepacia* carries an additional layer of complication since *cepacia* and *cenocepacia* can cause cepacia syndrome at any time. Cepacia syndrome is a fatal, necrotizing pneumonia that can kill within days or weeks.

When we first got the call from Pittsburgh's intake coordinator, she brought up the financial burden of transplant. The coordinator warned us that with our insurance, Blue Cross, we would undoubtedly face problems getting coverage for the evaluation (not to mention the transplant), since UPMC is not an in-network provider for them. They told us to start pushing Blue Cross immediately. It was about five weeks before the evaluation.

My mom started the process. Predictably, Blue Cross wrote us a letter explaining that they would not provide coverage for an evaluation at UPMC because it was not an in-network hospital. They recommended that I seek care at Minnesota. Obviously, they failed to understand that I have zero choice when it comes to where I get my transplant and that Minnesota had already rejected my case. Dozens of phone calls ensued as my mom struggled to get past the lowest person on the totem pole, a woman who was tasked with delivering us the bad news and who had no power to change anything. She was the wall Blue Cross put up; unfailingly polite, she said no, no, no.

Four times the coordinator would call and tell my mom that we needed to consider a particular center. Each time my mom would say they won't take Mallory. Blue Cross would then say give us five days to check. Then they would call back, say my mom was right but that we had to try another Blue Cross–approved center. This obvious stall tactic set us back weeks.

Finally, somehow, my mom got a verbal agreement from Blue Cross to issue the paperwork to provide a ninety-day authorization for me to see the transplant team at UPMC. They were not covering transplant, just the evaluation, but they confirmed that this was indeed an authorization.

When they sent the paperwork, they wrote in the name of the wrong hospital (there are many hospitals in the UPMC system). We asked them to correct it and to send the paperwork back again, and they said they would. Again, when the paperwork came in, the name was wrong—the hospital they wrote in is not even tangentially associated with UPMC cardiothoracic transplant.

At this point, our suspicions were confirmed that Blue Cross's bureaucratic obstacles were intentional stall tactics. Days and weeks were passing, and the date of my cross-country trip was getting closer and closer. We reckoned that the low woman on the totem pole was being instructed to do whatever she needed to do to prevent me from getting evaluated at UPMC.

All the while, I was in LA because of my grandma's end-stage cancer diagnosis. I was sick and did not have the energy to keep track of this ongoing battle myself. Ever since I graduated high school, I've been fiercely independent when it comes to my medical care, handling all interactions with doctors, hospitals, coordinators, and pharmacies. But when it came to insurance, I just couldn't do it. While I rested in bed, I heard my mom screaming on the phone in her office. She spent hours and hours during those few weeks fighting Blue Cross, precious hours she could have spent taking care of her own mom and dad.

Blue Cross called back and said they had done the paperwork right, and they said (over the phone) that I was approved. I was good to go. They said they would send the paperwork directly to UPMC. Everything was set, as far as we knew; our appointments were scheduled, my transplant binder came in the mail, our flights were booked, hotel rooms reserved. We had won this first battle—or so we thought.

But then, in the car ride to the airport for the flight to Pittsburgh, we were blindsided by a bait and switch so egregious it seems criminal. A woman who does insurance verification for UPMC called. She said that I had no insurance approval on file at UPMC whatsoever, and thus, that she would have to cancel all of my appointments for the upcoming week. When I told her that she was wrong, that I had already gotten Blue Cross's approval for the evaluation, she got angry and hung up on me.

My fatigue at that point was bone-crushing, as if my limbs were lead and my head were filled with bricks. My mom took over, and her first call was to the lung transplant coordinator at UPMC who had been helping us. What is going on??? This was the essence of her side of the conversation: We started this process over a month ago. How can they promise us approval, and then withdraw that approval when we're already on the way to the airport?? According to the coordinator, Blue Cross never officially sent in the authorization. They lied to us, pretended that it was taken care of when it wasn't, and waited until the very last minute to tell us that we couldn't ultimately get coverage, when it could have very well been too late to fix. My mom told UPMC that we were coming, insurance or no insurance.

Hell hath no fury like a mom who thinks someone is getting in the way of her daughter's transplant evaluation.

As I sat on the first leg of the flight, headed to Charlotte, North Carolina, I stewed. I could not live with the idea that I could potentially be going through such a grueling day of travel to end up in

Pittsburgh with NO appointments. Beyond the implications for my own health, it made me wonder what happens to the patients who don't have parents who are willing and able to draft eight-hundred-word emails, to scream at people on the phone, to threaten legal action (my dad) or a publicist's wrath (my mom)? While in many ways I'm in a position of complete powerlessness at the hands of a company that cares more about their bottom line than about whether I survive (in fact, one that would probably rather I die, because it would be cheaper), I still have an advantage that many patients aren't lucky enough to possess: two dedicated, tenacious, educated parents with the resources to fight the system.

It occurred to me in a heartbreaking moment that the patients who don't have that are the patients who die as a result of bureaucratic bullshit. It's so absurd it makes me shake with rage. When you're in need of a lung transplant, and the people on the other end of the line are intentionally trying to block you from getting life-saving care, and you're weary and you don't have parents to fight your battles, you die.

Studies show that cancer patients with bad insurance die at higher rates than their counterparts with better coverage. This sad reality is true of CF and transplant patients, too.

No one would ever write in an obituary: our dearly beloved died from bureaucratic incompetence and corporate miserliness. But if obituaries were perfectly honest, many would probably say exactly that.

By the end of that long, hard first day in Pittsburgh, and after weeks of fighting, weeks of going in circles trying to get what we needed, we heard the magic words: I was approved—not just for the full evaluation, but all the way through transplant.

Wednesday, October 12, 2016 (24 years old)
I got the best birthday present ever—UPMC officially accepted me for transplant but said I'm too healthy to move to Pittsburgh now. The evaluation had been a grueling week of meetings with doctors, surgeons, social workers, pharmacists, and financial people to make sure I met all of the criteria for transplant, and all sorts of medical

tests, blood draws, imaging. It was one of the most emotionally challenging and physically difficult weeks of my life but there was a payoff!

Monday, October 31, 2016

Jesse sent me the lyrics to her song "Clear Lungs"!! It's perfect:

I may fly lower with my broken wings
But I smile brighter every time I soar
Sometimes I worry if I dream too big
I will shatter like glass
That chasing more freedom could poison the rest

And I feel wasted
And I feel tired
And I feel lonely as I
Watch friends disappearing
And strain in these shackles
That chain me to routines
Keeping me alive
To breathe once
With clear lungs
But I'm stuck on this line

White masks surround me on every front
Make me feel guilty when I want to run
No second chances, all about percent
Every drop in that sign
Isolates me from a normal life

And I feel wasted
And I feel tired
And I feel lonely as I
Watch friends disappearing
And strain in these shackles
That chain me to routines

Keeping me alive
To breathe once
With clear lungs
But I'm stuck on this line

Don't wanna drown in myself
Sixty pills a day, 23 hours to health
Got this countdown running in the back of my mind
Hope for normal
Just wish for normal

I may fly lower with my broken wings
But I smile brighter every time I soar

So I'll feel wasted
And I'll feel tired
But I'll feel lucky as I
Live my life with meaning
And strive to be happy
Find beauty in the simple things
Most people fail to find
And breathe once
With clear lungs
Till I jump off this line

Saturday, November 5, 2016

I think I need IV iron. This severe, ongoing fatigue is messing with my head.

My brain is different. I don't know if that's due to chronic lack of oxygen, but my memory is shit now, my concentration is terrible, and I've lost my ability to juggle multiple pieces of information. My processing speed is so much slower, too. That's another thing, when I'm exhausted and anemic and short of breath and high on Marinol, I don't have a gregarious personality. I kind of just recede and watch what's going on around me since it's easier not to talk, and easier to lie or sit down than to stand up. Maybe it's the mono. I think I forgot to write that they figured out that's what's been going on with me.

Saturday, November 12, 2016

It wasn't always this way. If I was the object of others' staring in the past, I could assume it was because of my six-foot stature, so rare for a woman, people in the street would tell me. Once, in high school, I was swimming at a local community pool in Maui during spring break, trying to get back in shape for swim season in the wake of a hospitalization. A photographer there asked if he could use a photo of me swimming for a fitness magazine. I chuckled, noting the irony, but still taking my healthy appearance for granted, assuming it would last as long as I did.

For so long, while cystic fibrosis took its toll on my lungs, my pancreas, my bones, my liver, my intestines, and my stomach, the illness was invisible. It was so invisible that I could have written pieces on the difficulty of trying to get disability accommodations while looking perfectly healthy, the frustrating process of making the severity of my disease known to the skeptics on the other side of the negotiation. Those skeptics were the people who would ensure that I got through school without failing out for excessive absences and tardies; they were the people who would let me board early on airplanes, but rarely without a disapproving glare; they were the people who could either grant me the ability to work without compromising my health, or deny it.

Though having an invisible illness presents its own unique set of challenges, now I pine for the days when I could still walk down the street and blend in. I pine for the days when I could choose to hide my disease.

Now that my disease is visible, it creates walls between me and those around me. The IV pumps in my purse connected via long plastic tubing to the mediport in my right chest are an instant spectacle. The nasal cannula connected to my oxygen tank, oxygenating my blood in ways my own body can't, is another spectacle. In short, wherever I go, I am a spectacle, and it's tiresome.

On election night, I went to a party at Talia's. There were about thirty people there, packed tight into a San Francisco apartment. People stand on their feet at these types of things; that is so hard for me these days, even with oxygen. I meet people and I see the way their eyes jump from nasal cannula to oxygen tank to mediport to IV tubing, the way pity swells inside of them as they realize that this is my life. I know many are wondering—does she have cancer?

There are other signs, less obvious than the equipment to which I'm tethered, perhaps noticeable only to a keen eye. The subtle thoracic kyphosis, which worsens by the year. The edema in my ankles, a sign of mild heart failure. My disproportionately large rib cage and upper torso compared to my chicken legs and noodle arms. Clubbing, common in CF, characterized by curved and bulbous fingertips and toes. My pale skin, a trademark of the iron-deficiency anemia my doctors are too afraid to treat because iron can feed the infection in my lungs. My labored breathing, so loud it can't possibly be ignored. My periodic winces, from pleuritic chest pain or stomach cramps or migraines. The dark brown staining around my teeth, a result of the enamel being destroyed from months of frequent vomiting. The bald patches on my head, which became noticeable only after I'd become anemic and malnourished. Blue nails, deprived of oxygen. The blank look in my eyes when I can't follow a conversation because of the Marinol pills I have to take for appetite stimulation and nausea. The coughing spells that often hit when I laugh, which are painful and sometimes lead me to avoid laughter altogether.

Soon, I may have to get a feeding tube, a gastrostomy-jejunostomy tube (G-J tube). The tube bypasses the stomach and feeds liquid nutrition directly into the small intestine, ideal for patients with a lot of nausea and vomiting. I can't eat enough to keep up with my body's nutritional requirements. It will be yet another piece of medical equipment, surgically implanted into my body, just like my mediport. It will help save my life, but it's yet another way my previously invisible illness is rendered visible.

All of these identifiers are walls that separate me from meaningful interaction with the people around me. People do not know what to say. I don't blame them; I wouldn't, either, were the roles reversed.

I pine for the days before those walls existed. I pine for the days before I had to tug my leash around, the twenty-five-foot tubing connecting me to my home oxygen machine. I pine for the days when I could play a beach volleyball match, and people would just assume I had a cough or a cold. I pine for the days when I could swim, surf, hike, even just *sit* there, *comfortably*. I pine for my invisible illness, now that it has turned visible.

Sunday, November 13, 2016

This past week has been super hectic. Today is Sunday. On Wednesday, I went to clinic at Stanford. We discussed lots of problems: newfound swelling in my feet (possibly a sign of a blood clot, which we ruled out via ultrasound, or heart problems), continuing fevers, round-the-clock oxygen use. We talked about when to move to Pittsburgh, my weight, and their desire for me to get a G-J tube. The one thing we didn't discuss is that I think I have a partial obstruction. I wasn't as certain about it then as I am now; now I'm almost positive. At clinic I didn't want to tell them my concerns because I thought they would immediately test and treat me, which would mean an admission since I haven't been able to resolve blockages at home. And it was important to me to stay out of the hospital because the next day was Jack's birthday.

As it turns out, on his birthday I had a fever so we stayed inside while I drank hot tea and curled up with a blanket. I gave him his gifts: a North Face reversible flannel shirt-thing, Birddogs shorts (his favorite), and a framed picture of the two of us. He genuinely loved the gifts, which made me really happy.

We had a really intense conversation that night. He cried. He told me that his dad said to him, "You know this relationship is going to have a tragic ending, right?" I don't know if his dad was referring to us breaking up when Jack gets a job, or to me moving to Pittsburgh, or to the pain of watching me get sicker, or if he was talking about me dying. He could have been referring to any of those possibilities. I didn't ask because I didn't think he would want to say aloud, "He was referring to the fact that you will probably die at some point and that will be tragic because of how much I care about you."

It's at times like this that I realize how much he cares. The fact that sometimes it seems like he doesn't care is a function of compartmentalizing; he cares so much he can't NOT compartmentalize, otherwise he wouldn't be able to function. And to some extent, I do the same thing. I'm not constantly tormented about my disease; I wouldn't want him to be, either. I need to realize that when he does not seem the most empathetic, it's not for lack of caring but rather for lack of experience dealing with tragedy and hardship, and an inability to figure out how to comport himself in times of crisis/sickness.

At a certain point, a person breaks. My mom is having to do everything for me while I'm just trying to exist. I'm toxic to the people around me and my body is toxic to myself. I thought about what it would be like to just not exist anymore. Not to kill myself, obviously; I would never do that. But I just thought, *What if I did have some kind of heart problem and just went to sleep and didn't wake up?* That thought was even more stressful to me than the idea of living with sickness because of what it would do to my family.

So I will persist. But something needs to change, something needs to improve, if not with my actual health, then at least with my palliative care to keep me more comfortable as I struggle. Marinol is a good first step, but I'm sure there are other things that could be helping.

Thursday, December 1, 2016
Need to write about what happened after reaching the glorious acceptance by UPMC. A viral infection pushed me off the summit. I free-fell into the deepest abyss of illness I've ever faced. A spate of complications drove me to panic: severe fatigue (which fourteen hours of sleep a night couldn't reckon with), complete loss of appetite, incessant nausea and vomiting, respiratory distress with any

amount of exertion, and oxygen saturations plummeting into the seventies when I changed clothes or walked to the bathroom (they are supposed to stay above 90 at all times). When I went to the emergency room on October 28, I collapsed in the waiting room walking to the check-in desk. A week later, when I got discharged, I hardly felt better.

Then Jack's birthday, which I wrote about.

Then Sabrina came to visit from Philadelphia, and I spent most of the time asleep. I accrued more worrisome symptoms: strange lumps that I worried were tumors and swelling of the legs and ankles (edema with pitting). My heart thrashed around inside my chest, feeling like a fish trying to escape a fisherman's hook.

Stanford told me to come in for an echocardiogram, which showed mild heart failure. They wanted to admit me right then, that Monday before Thanksgiving, and told me I should not plan on going home (which meant I'd miss both Thanksgiving and Mallory's Garden, our annual fundraiser). Thanksgiving is my favorite holiday and I was desperate to be at the fundraiser so my mom suggested we call UCLA and ask for a direct admit—which Dr. Eshaghian was willing to arrange. We left straight from the echo test at Stanford, flew to LA, and then my dad picked us up and took us straight to a room at UCLA Medical Center in Santa Monica, bypassing the ER.

I spent the week there but was discharged in time for our twenty-first annual Mallory's Garden. There, we announced our departure and said emotional goodbyes to our community. But then, three days later, we got another call from the coordinator at Pittsburgh, explaining that the team there had changed their mind. Once they put all the pieces together in their transplant meeting—the mono, the heart problems, the timeline of my decline—they realized that if mono was causing most of these problems, then when the mono went away, I might be too healthy to be ready for transplant. They did not want me to move all the way to Pittsburgh just to get healthy again a month later and have to turn around and go home.

More important, they couldn't list me for transplant with mild heart failure without listing me for a heart AND lung transplant. No one wanted to do that, since I had a perfectly healthy heart up until I contracted the mono. The Pittsburgh doctor's decision was that I should wait until the mono cleared and until the heart function improved; at that point, we would determine if it was still the right time for me to be listed.

By the time I heard the news of their change of heart, two days before Thanksgiving, I'd ridden an emotional roller coaster trying to come to terms with the idea of moving to Pittsburgh. And I finally had. In fact, I'd done such a good job of coming to terms with it that when I found out they'd changed their mind, I was devastated; I'd actually wanted to go to Pittsburgh, I realized. In order to get better, in order to get a transplant and live the life I want to live, I have to get worse. I have to pay my dues. I have to move to Pittsburgh. I was ready for that next step. But it was a false alarm.

Friday, December 2, 2016
I feel like people with CF are privy to secrets it takes most other people a lifetime to understand. How lucky we are to be alive. How lucky anyone is who has their health. How we should be appreciative of anything that's in our control, since our health is not. That we can leave behind a legacy when we go that will impact others. That simple things are often the most beautiful. That love and happiness are the most important things to strive for. That ultimately, we shouldn't give a damn what other people think, because everyone's making their own way and everyone's facing different struggles that others aren't aware of. CF has given me my value system and ultimately, no matter how hard it is, I'm grateful for it.

Saturday, December 3, 2016
New Year's is important to me. Not New Year's Eve; I've never liked that night as far as holidays go. But the new year and the weeks leading up to New Year's always force me into a state of reflection that I generally don't get to at any other time.

So as the new year approaches, I find myself reflecting. This year has been monumental. Colossal. As far as change goes, who I am and what my plans are for the future changed weekly this year, whereas in the past, they changed over the course of months or years. My resilience has been challenged and my ability to adapt has been called upon. "Mind over matter" has never been more important.

Questions that have been prominent: those of identity; what matters to me now and in the future; who matters to me now and in the future; how I can keep my mind stimulated while my body deteriorates; how I can accept the fact that my body is deteriorating; how I can be happy while feeling like absolute shit.

I don't have the answers. It's a struggle. There have been many low points. But I realize that as time goes on, what I define as a low point will keep changing. For example, at UCLA hospital in January, I was traumatized by having to use the commode inside the fishbowl of the ICU room. I demanded to walk to the bathroom in the hallway each time I had to go, which was frequently, because I drink so much water. When I was too sick or unstable to walk to the bathroom, it felt like defeat. It was crushing, humiliating, and dehumanizing. Now, in my most recent hospitalization (again at UCLA—coming full circle this year despite lots of Stanford admissions in between), I requested a bedside commode because I literally couldn't bring myself to walk the five extra steps to the bathroom in my room. I voluntarily embraced the bedside commode, something that a year ago was unfathomable to me. I call this progress.

It's sad that I have to come to terms with these things, but transplant is going to test me in ways I can't even imagine now. Being on a ventilator in the ICU and having to have my butt wiped in the bed by some male nurse assistant is going to be my reality, either pre-transplant or post-. There will be pain beyond what I can tolerate right now. I only hope my pain tolerance adapts and that I don't wilt under the force of all the hardship.

Another thing to get used to is my diminishing brainpower. I used to be smart. I didn't know what it would be like to be less smart—but now I do. I don't remember things. I don't draw connections in the way that I used to. I don't understand complex concepts.

I can't focus on books, and thus I've lost an entire world I used to have as an escape. Not one world—many worlds. Being smart was a part of my identity that I took for granted because I didn't think that would change. I heard a quote recently about books that was something like, "Though I remember nothing of the plots of the books I've read, nonetheless, they've made me." And that is so true. Books have taught me compassion. They've taught me to see beyond the bubble I was raised in. They've shown me other experiences, other lives, other worlds. They've awakened in me a spirit of adventure, which now lies dormant. They're like friends that I've pushed away, but now I miss them.

Thursday, December 8, 2016

Today was my first day of pulmonary rehab at UCLA. It inspired me to take more action to control what I can with my health. And where that starts is with exercise (and nutrition, but I'm already working on that).

I feel like my body is a foreign object, one I don't understand. The CF rules I've learned my whole life and biology I learned in school do not apply, because something more complicated is going on.

I'm giving myself a goal and that's to be able to walk on the beach on hard sand for twenty minutes by the time Jack comes and we go to Malibu. I just have to have something concrete to work toward or I will languish.

In some ways, I struggle so much more than any twenty-four-year-old deserves to. But in some ways, I'm privileged beyond belief. I wish those two things canceled out to make me feel somewhat normal. Instead, I just feel the deepest lows of CF misery, and the incredibly fortunate highs of having the family and friends and resources to live as well as possible despite that. Having the most incredible house in Malibu offered to us by Walter and Hildy for Christmas vacation? Unreal. It's unbelievable. Having Jan buy me a really great coat for the Pittsburgh winter, even though we're probably not even going this winter anymore? Also unreal. I just have to do my best to keep those feelings of gratitude at the forefront. And that's easy when I'm feeling well; it comes naturally to my healthy self. But it's like I have a split personality. When I feel sick, everything feels terrible, and my future feels so bleak, and I can't stand the idea of being around anyone, and I can't stand the idea of being alone—it's a catch-22 that leaves me stuck in a trap of unhappiness, which I recognize from the outside as being absurd, but it's like a nightmare I can't wake up from. While I'm in it, I don't have the ability to change the channel away from self-pity so I can only do my best while I am healthy(ish) to bolster my sick self through the sick times by coming up with strategies to remind myself of how lucky I am, even when I feel like absolute shit. When I feel good the world is filled with endless possibilities.

I'm so conflicted about whether to stay in LA or go back to SF in January. There are pros and cons to each.

The main thing I worry about up there is loneliness. But it's funny because the main thing I worry about in LA is also loneliness. CF is just an isolating disease but I don't do anything to try to combat that; I just get tired and watch TV alone. I think I would benefit from therapy but I don't go. Except that there's no one else to talk about my issues *with*—other CF patients deal with their own issues and it's really hard to complain to people who are worse off, and those who are better off don't understand; healthy friends don't understand and often don't say the right thing. They say things like, "I'm sure it will be fine," "I'm sure you'll get better," "Stay positive," all platitudes that don't really help. With Jack, for some reason it just doesn't feel natural talking about my problems; I minimize things. It kills my mom to see me sad so I don't want to burden her with that when she and my dad are going through their own struggles as my caretakers.

I'm starting to think therapy is the only option because in my own head I just go in circles, and with others, it's not working well. And I need to be so mentally strong before transplant. I need to be at peace with the idea of death while also fiercely wanting to live; it's hard to feel both at the same time.

Thursday, December 22, 2016

Wednesday morning, I woke up to tragic news—a blog post by Caitlin's mom (a girl I met when I was in Pittsburgh for my evaluation). They had been there for two and a half years waiting for transplant. She worked so hard and did everything right. But then her health crashed, and she ended up on life support (ECMO and ventilator). She was having all sorts of problems and I was following the updates from her mom on the blog. Because I've been working on David's memoir, I have more insight into transplant than I otherwise would. And as I saw how sick she was getting, I kept wondering if Stanford would have already removed her from the transplant list for being too sick. But UPMC didn't, and after a couple of dry runs with lungs that weren't viable, she finally got lungs, perfect lungs.

But she was still in critical condition. They couldn't close her chest because of swelling, and even though Maryanne made it seem on the blog like that was normal, I knew that if they cannot close the chest, the likelihood of the patient making it is slim. She was having more problems, though; her blood pressure was too low, she had rising lactate levels, which signified dead tissue somewhere, and they didn't know if it was in her leg or her liver or her bowel. And her liver started to fail, and maybe her kidneys, too.

The next day I read that she had died. It was devastating. I immediately started bawling and could not control myself. I let myself cry for ten or fifteen minutes, thinking about her family, thinking about how hard she fought, and how futile it all turned out to be. All that struggle, all that uprooting, and now she's just dead. Gone forever. It felt like my heart was being squeezed by a vise grip.

Wednesday, December 28, 2016

I find myself thinking about Caitlin, her family, and how tragic her ending was. It reminds me to be grateful for the health I do have.

Saturday, December 31, 2016

My anniversary card to Jack:

Jack,

I can't believe a year has come and gone already. When I met you on NYE 2015/2016, I never could've guessed that you would become one of the most important people in my life, in one of the most important times of my life. I'm so lucky to be with you—you're caring, smart, funny, so fun to be around, so handsome, and so, so, so good to me. Ever since the day you charmed my grandparents—two weeks into our relationship—I knew you were a keeper! Time and again, though, you've surprised me with your willingness to jump into this wild life of mine. It amazes me, but it also doesn't, because you're amazing. I know this distance thing we're doing is hard, and we don't know what will happen in the future. But whatever does happen, I want to thank you deeply for an incredible year with you and for the best relationship I've ever had. Paradise really is anywhere I'm with you (although I do hope for more times in true paradisiacal places in the future). :) Love you so much.

Mal

2017

Tuesday, January 24, 2017

In the hospital at UCLA Santa Monica. Been struggling with the usual symptoms.

We are likely going to Pittsburgh in two weeks. Mom started crying today when she talked to Dr. Eshaghian about the fact that then she has to leave me to go to SF to pack up my apartment, and then we're going to Pitt soon after that. It made me so sad to see her cry. She always puts up such a tough and strong front, but I know that there's so much sadness and fear underneath that she rarely lets anyone see.

Thursday, January 26, 2017

Today is a better day. My lungs are clearing out and I didn't wake up at 6:00 to bring up floods of mucus. I'm no longer using morphine for shortness of breath or lung pain. And I'm not having fevers, which is the other biggest thing!! The fevers would prevent me from being listed because it would show that we don't have the infection under control. Pitt wants them under control.

Sounds like we're going to Pitt soon. Wouldn't be surprised if it was end of next week, which would be ironic because I think a few people are coming to town to see me that weekend. Don't remember, though, because my memory is shit.

Friday, February 10, 2017

The past week was hellish. I kept spontaneously bursting into tears. Talia had a going-away party for me on Wednesday night so I could say my goodbyes at one time instead of trying to see everyone separately. There was so much back-and-forth about me going/not going/going/not going so in the end, I only had two days at home between when I got out of the hospital and when I had to be across the country for UPMC's clinic. It was stressful trying to pack up my entire life to move across the country while (1) battling end-stage lung disease with fevers and an acute infection, (2) spending my last two days with Jack before being long-distance, (3) saying goodbye to my grandparents, who will be dead most likely when I'm back, (4) saying goodbye to my dog, which feels like abandoning my own child, and (5) saying goodbye to Maria.

Yesterday, I took the biggest leap of my life into the scariest chapter of my life. UPMC has given me reason to hope. Dr. Pilewski is my hero for being willing to gamble on high-risk cases like mine—and for giving me a second chance at life.

I left California so I don't become a life-expectancy statistic or a sad case study written about in a medical paper. I left to chase the dream of a better and longer future. A four-hour flight across the country was the beginning of the journey. My mom, dad, Linda, and Dr. Monvasi, a doctor from Tampa that David recommended, flew with me. It was the last nonstop American flight from LA to Pittsburgh before they discontinued the route. It was so nice to have help moving.

I still can't believe we're in Pittsburgh for good (temporarily for good, oxymoronic as that may be).

Monday, February 13, 2017

JUST GOT THE CALL THAT I'M LISTED!!! I was in bed at our hotel taking a nap, then woke up and was on the phone with Sabrina. Got a call from a 412 number and should have answered but ignored it because I hadn't talked to Sab in so long and didn't want to cut her off. Then two mins later my mom comes busting in with the biggest smile on her face, on the phone, and tells me that it was UPMC and that I was listed!!

We thought the call might come tomorrow but I didn't want to get my hopes up. And then it came early! Such a relief. But it also means we're now on call 24/7 so I can never turn my phone off again and I should have a hospital bag packed so that I'm always ready.

It's surreal.

Stanford had said that no one would give me a transplant but now UPMC is doing something miraculous. I don't think it ever really sank in that I WOULDN'T get a transplant, but there was enough doubt to know that this is a huge moment. Huge huge huge moment!

Right after I got the call, Jack texted me to pick up his FaceTime and I did and then my mom brought in a bouquet of a dozen roses. They were from Jack for Valentine's Day!

Saturday, February 18, 2017

The past few days have been okay. We rode the high of me getting listed for a couple of days, which was great, before settling back into our new normal. It could take months or a year or more to get the call, so we have to straddle the line to be ready at any moment but also prepared for a long wait. It's a bit of a mind-fuck.

The thing that scares me is my persistent fevers. If I got the call today, what would I say? Whenever I don't take Tylenol or Advil on the dot of six hours, I start getting chills and a fever. I don't know how high it would go, because I'm continually suppressing. I can't go into surgery with active infection. But I ALWAYS have active infection, which is why I need to be on IVs.

Caitlin's mom and dad are in Pittsburgh to pack up for their move back to Boston. They did what we did—moved here to get listed since their own hospital in Boston wouldn't transplant Caitlin because of *cepacia*. They invited us to a party given by their neighbors. It was a chance to say goodbye to all the people they'd gotten to know in the two and a half years they were here.

I was going to go but wasn't feeling well so my mom went without me. After the Advil and Tylenol kicked in, I finished treatment and was hungry so wanted to get dinner. We were still in a hotel so I texted my mom to find out if she had eaten. She asked if I wanted to come to the party and so I went. Everyone was so nice, especially the hosts, Ralph and Mary. My dad had already gone back to LA so my mom was ecstatic to make friends in a city where she knew no one. And everyone was so welcoming and sweet.

It was tragic to see Maryanne and Nick. Apparently my mom was crying when she arrived and Nick (Caitlin's dad) gave her a stern talking-to, basically saying something like, "We're not doing this. You have one job now, and that's to take care of Mallory. You have to be on it, and right now you're a blubbering mess."

When I arrived and looked at him sadly, he said (very nicely), "We're not going to do this, I already told your mom." He was so nice and gave me Caitlin's old oxygen carrier that she made with her boyfriend. I think Maryanne was having a harder time by the end, and she did cry when she said goodbye to us. I didn't know what to do, what to say, how to act. That was why I was worried about going in the first place, because they're grieving the loss of their daughter while I represent the beginning of the journey, and what are they supposed to say? "I hope it goes better for you than it did for Caitlin"? They did basically say that. She said, "I'm so happy you're even taller than I remember. You're not going to have to wait like Caitlin did—she was too small to receive most donor lungs."

I'm happy I went. Ralph and Mary invited us back again on Sunday for a pasta party, and we're going to go. Stacy will be here then to help my mom move us into the new apartment. Today is our last day at the Fairmont so I'm going to try to muster the energy to foam roll at the gym and use the sauna, just to take advantage of it for the one last day.

Tuesday, February 28, 2017
Since I last wrote, every single day (until yesterday and today) I had a fever pattern that was the same every day. I would start shivering madly around 1:00 p.m., after Tylenol and Advil, and as the fever

went up I would feel like shit—shortness of breath, tachycardia up to 140 bpm at rest, nausea, the works—and then the fever would spike up to 102 or 103, or some days even higher (one day it got to 103.7), then it would go down. When the fever would finally break, around 4:00 or 5:00 or 6:00, my appetite would come back in full force and I would eat a ton to make up for having not eaten for hours.

This pattern was unsettling. I kept thinking we should tell Larry, my transplant coordinator. The day I spiked up to 103.7 I packed my bag for the ER; it did not occur to me in my wildest dreams that they would tell me to stay home. But they did! And then a few days later—Sunday, to be specific—I just didn't have a fever that day. I was exhausted, for sure, but no fever. It was miraculous. It might've been the right call not to go to the ER, but the day I called I was so anxious. I was bawling in bed and thought things were going to end in tragedy for me and for my family. I was terrified. The fevers reduce me to this scared, shriveled, sick, anxious blubberer with no sense of control over any part of my future. The fevers are the hardest thing for me right now. When the fevers are gone, life feels manageable.

I need a long-term kind of project to occupy myself with while I'm here. Maybe take up a musical instrument? Or start my book? That's what my mom thinks I should do but not sure I'm up for that yet. I guess it can't hurt to brainstorm.

Oh, to dream about what it could be like . . . it makes me wilt a bit. To think about all the girls who, in the exact same position that I'm in now, were filled with so much hope, and dreamed about all they would do post-transplant, working so hard to stay alive to get to that goal, who then didn't make it in the end. Caitlin, I think of her so often. Her mom sent me a blog post that Caitlin wrote where so much of it hit close to home about the experience of coming to terms with being listed for transplant and coming to recognize it as a beautiful opportunity to have so much GREATER of a life than what we've had for years. It made me want to cry, though, because she wrote it only about a year before she died, and she had no idea how terribly it would all turn out. No one did. It wasn't fair. And it won't be fair if it happens to me. Transplant scares the shit out of me.

Sunday, March 5, 2017

I never wrote about Bakery Living! It's the apartment my mom and I live in here in Pittsburgh. It's amazing and cozy. The lobby is like a hotel with coffee every day and bagels on the weekends. They have a gym we work out in and monthly activities that create community. Freddie and Samir are the first two people I met.

Tuesday, March 28, 2017

Had another massive bleed. I need new lungs. Apparently the amount of hemoptysis I had this time has a 50 to 85 percent mortality rate without embolization. I just keep wondering what happens if the bleeding doesn't stop in time for them to embolize. Last night, lying in bed, I found myself replaying the scene in the ER but with an alternate ending. I pictured the bleeding going and going and not stopping until I lost consciousness and my pressures dropped and I inhaled the blood and then died. And I mainly just pictured my mom and dad crying, and it made me cry just thinking that that could have happened.

Monday, April 3, 2017

A girl, a CF patient, who was treated at Stanford, Monica Harding Wood, died sometime this weekend. Or at least I found out this weekend. She had been completely fine and her death came out of nowhere. She had advanced disease and was close to being listed for transplant, but she was totally stable and there was no indication that she was near the end. She went in for a port placement and G-J tube procedure and somehow died in the process, no idea how. It's so tragic and so terrifying.

My mom went to LA last week to be with my grandma. She comes back today and my dad leaves tomorrow. I'll miss him a lot. But I do think it will be good to have my mom here again because she does things for me and for the apartment that I don't have to ask her to do. The apartment is always clean, I get three meals a day, there are always groceries, the laundry gets done frequently, etc. Pidge needs more sleep, plus he has to work for his job. He just doesn't move as quickly as she does (no one does) so not as much gets done. But it was SO nice to have him here, to be able to spend quality time together. We watched movies, talked about books, and had a lot of good meals. I'm sad he's leaving.

My mom is bringing our new dog tonight!! I'm hoping and choosing to believe that having Cooper here will turn things around for me emotionally at a time where I could either go back to "normal" or fall off an emotional cliff.

Thursday, April 20, 2017

On post-transplant life:

I found myself fantasizing a little earlier about being back on a surfboard on a sunny day, then coming back onto the beach and toweling off. And then I remembered that the likelihood of skin cancer is about a zillion times higher post-transplant, and I realized that I'd have to adjust my image of myself doing that to include a rash guard and a face full of that funny sunscreen that doesn't rub in. I was also picturing myself in Hawaii, and then I realized, I don't know if I can go back there post-transplant. It was a devastating thought.

I'd wanted to go to South Africa sometime in my life.

I also want to have a kid, and I was thinking to myself about Jack and whether I see us in the long term. And (1) I started to feel conflicted because I don't know if I see us as long-long-term compatible, but he told me he wrote seven pages about me while sitting in his conference in Boston today and that he got teary-eyed while the rest of the people talked about software, so I just can't gauge if we're on the same page about futures, and (2) I realized that I'm freed by the fact that I can't have a biological kid anyway, so I could theoretically have a kid later in life since if I did have one I would adopt and I don't have to worry about fertility and all that. So that was kind of liberating to realize that this timeline that other people are on, to find a partner early enough to get married and have kids before the fertility years are up (this is a real concern that I know people have, as anti-feminist as it sounds to say), I don't really have to follow that timeline.

That being said, I do HOPE to not be in my mid-thirties still looking for the right person. I hope that if it's not Jack, it's the next person after Jack. If we do break up, the number one thing I want myself to remember is to NOT choose my next person based on looks/physical attraction. Obviously that has to be there, but the person needs to be kind, needs to be down to support me through health stuff, needs to want the same things as me long-term, etc. All those things are much more important than someone being hot in their twenties; that kind of hotness doesn't last anyway.

At the same time I'm also terrified of starting over, and I know that leads me to overlook certain concerns I have about my compatibility with Jack. I just don't know if our goofiness aligns, if that makes sense. Like, everyone is goofy in a certain sense . . . but in different ways. And people's goofiness and weirdness and quirkiness have to align for them to be compatible, I think. And with Jack I just don't know if we laugh enough. But also, it's unfair to compare him to anyone else I've ever been with, because the entire time we've been together I've been so sick and had so much on my mind. So I haven't really had the ability to be an independent, confident woman in the relationship like I have been in other ones.

Also on post-transplant life—I might want to work with animals. I don't know if that's allowed, though, shit. Ugh. I just remembered that post-transplant patients can't pick up dog poop, and can't have certain types of pets, so I assume that would render me unable to have a career in animal welfare or conservation or something like that. But I love animals. When I think of things that bring me unadulterated happiness, animals are one of those things. And one of the things that makes me so sad that I would want to help prevent/reduce/fix animals' suffering.

I'm at that point with my nails that they get in the way of my typing, so thus my slow typing gets in the way of my thoughts. My typing is clunky so my thoughts are clunky. This was all much more clear in my brain somehow.

Friday, April 21, 2017

The day started out the way mornings have been starting out for the last few weeks: with fatigue, nausea, an attempt at breakfast, vomiting, some chills, nausea meds and fever suppression, and thoughts about a nap. But Talia was in town, and I was determined to make the day a good day.

I was doing my breathing treatments in my bedroom while she was having breakfast in the living room. My mom was out walking the dog. The phone rang with the Pittsburgh area code, 412. When we first moved to Pittsburgh in February, I would always jump at those calls, thinking they were about lungs; eventually, when time and again they were just hospital administrators confirming appointments, the home health nurse, or medication refills, I stopped getting my hopes up.

"Hello?" I said.

"Hi, Mallory, this the Cardiothoracic Transplant Program at UPMC."

My heart started to beat faster. The Cardiothoracic Transplant Program does not usually call me.

"I'm calling because we have a potential set of lungs available for you. But I have to ask: Are you willing to consider lungs that are on EVLP?"

I immediately said yes. EVLP, which stands for *ex vivo* lung perfusion, is an investigational procedure/machine used to keep lungs in good shape while they're transported from the donor to the recipient. Not everyone says yes to lungs that are on EVLP because it's new(ish) and experimental, but for me, it was an automatic yes. On EVLP, lungs can be manipulated to better determine their quality, and keeping the lungs perfused with the machine can prevent swelling or other complications that would render them nonviable for donation.

The woman said she would call back in an hour or so with more information. As soon as I hung up with her, I dialed my mom and yelled into the phone that I got the call. "What call?" she asked. "THE CALL!!"

Talia stood by me as I started crying, feeling the implications of this moment all at once. My mom came bursting into the apartment frenzied, tears in her eyes. By 4:00 p.m., we got the go-ahead to pack up and get to the hospital. By 5:00 p.m., we were in registration, watching TV and making silly videos to pass the time until we could get into our room.

There are many points along the way after getting the call for lungs at which the surgery can be called off. We had always known that at any point from the death of the donor to the time they remove the lungs of the recipient, surgery can be called off because the lungs are not good enough.

After a short wait in registration, I was put into a room on 9D, the lung transplant floor. Two nurses collected seventeen vials of blood—blood type and screen, as well as a slew of tests to determine whether I was healthy enough to undergo surgery. One tech came to do a bedside chest X-ray, and another came for an EKG. They took vitals, my weight, a urine sample. At that point, we settled in for the long wait.

We were itching for someone to come talk to us who could give us more information about the viability of the lungs and the timing. Finally, a cardiothoracic surgical fellow, a mellow Chilean man, arrived. He told us that the "donor time" was set for 2:00 a.m. However, the donor was in a category called DCD (Donation after Cardiac Death); this means that he or she did not meet formal brain death criteria but had suffered irreversible brain injury and was near death. The family had decided to discontinue life support systems; once that happened, they would wait for the heart to stop beating. Only after cardiac arrest would organs be harvested. When the dying process takes more than about an hour, the lungs become nonviable, because as the body struggles, the lungs can become damaged. DCD lungs are often (maybe always) put on EVLP in order to improve quality and increase the chances that the lungs can be transplanted. But the likelihood of a transplant actually happening from a DCD donor is a bit lower than from a typical donor that meets criteria for brain death.

Listening to the fellow explain what would happen at 2:00 a.m. at the donor hospital—the pulling of the plug, the waiting to die, then the eventual harvesting of organs—I was struck by the two completely different experiences that were happening at the same exact time. One family undergoing heartbreak they would forever grieve. Another family celebrating the possible rebirth of a sick loved one who has suffered too long. The first person's tragedy had the potential to become the second person's lifesaving miracle.

My survival is dependent on the death of someone else, another human being with memories and goals and loved ones and, often, no expectation of dying. This is the twisted reality of being on the waiting list. How do we, as transplant patients, come to terms with the idea of "waiting" for someone to die, with hoping it happens quickly enough for the organs to be allocated and not wasted? I expect I will grapple with this question for years to come.

When I got summoned to the hospital by the cardiothoracic department, we called Gaby to come. She was in DC, so it was a quick flight. Throughout that evening and overnight, Talia, Gaby, and my mom helped keep me calm when my nerves were practically bursting through the seams. I was a wreck of wired, restless energy and tempered hope. At some point, Talia and my mom left to go sleep at the apartment while Gaby got comfortable in the (terribly uncomfortable) recliner chair that so many hospitals carry for guests to sleep in. I suspected I wouldn't sleep a wink. I was right.

For hours, Gaby and I sat there chatting, laughing, passing the time. It felt like two girls having a sleepover. It did not feel like we were in a hospital—I was not hooked up to an IV pole or a heart monitor, no nurses were coming in and out, no vitals were being taken by a nurse's aide, and no medications or breathing treatments were given. We just waited and waited but no news.

I finally turned off the lights and rolled over to try to sleep but it wasn't happening. I lay there, thinking, wondering what was happening at the donor hospital, what the timing would be, when they would tell us if the surgery was a go or not. I checked the clock every ten minutes until I realized that if I didn't turn on a movie, I'd crash and burn from adrenaline by the morning. My neck and back ached, and I had rock-sized knots in my back, neck, and shoulders from the tension.

I had thought that at around 4:00 a.m. they would come in and tell me whether the lungs were looking viable. Four a.m. came and went, as did 5:00, 6:00, and 7:00. Alarms and code announcements outside the room jolted me awake anytime I got close to falling asleep (the "Condition F" fire alarm seemed to last forever and was immediately followed up by a "Condition A"—cardiac arrest). The sun came up. I mixed and infused my morning IV antibiotics. I was fatigued, my optimism waning. I called for respiratory therapy to administer a breathing treatment, to help with the chest tightness and cough that had been doing its part in keeping me up.

Then, at 7:30 a.m., a man came to my room with a gurney to tell me he was taking me to the pre-op area. "Does that mean the surgery's happening?!"

"As far as I know, it's on," the guy said. "But I'm not the one who would know."

"That's abrupt," I said.

In the pre-op area, I finally found out some details about the timing from the anesthesiologist. The lungs, at that point, were still on EVLP and would need one to two more hours of manipulation to determine if they were viable. While we waited, he talked to us in detail about the anesthesia during the surgery, the sedation post-surgery, and a bit about the difficulty and risks of the surgery itself. He assured me that they would not bring me out from sedation after surgery until they were certain that I would not be in pain—this was very comforting to me, because the idea of being hooked to a ventilator and possibly ECMO, in pain, immobile, and unable to speak, was unfathomable.

Jack had been in Boston for the past week for a conference, so he got on a 6:00 a.m. flight to Pittsburgh to try to see me before I went into surgery. He arrived around 9:00, in time to hear some of the conversation with the anesthesiologist.

Finally, we met the man we've been waiting to meet ever since my first evaluation in Pittsburgh last October, Dr. D'Cunha. He is the lead transplant surgeon with the most amazing reputation. Unfortunately, he came in that morning to tell us that the lungs were good but *someone else* was going into surgery. I'm happy for that other person, but it came as a complete shock.

What we did not know until this moment was that UPMC will sometimes call in two patients for the same set of lungs to ensure that they don't get wasted. If they only called in one patient per set and then the lungs didn't end up being a good fit (because of size or other reasons), it would be a tragic waste of precious organs that too many people die waiting for.

I had assumed that once I'd made it to the pre-op area, I was the only candidate for the particular set of lungs that had just been harvested. What I found out later is that the entire time, those many hours of waiting, I was actually the backup candidate, which would have been helpful to know at the beginning (for the purpose of managing expectations).

The only good thing about the experience is that we got to meet Dr. D'Cunha. The stakes had been high, emotions fraying, nerves unraveling. When he told us I wasn't getting the lungs, it was like he stuck a needle into an overfilled balloon of anticipatory stress. I was sad that I wouldn't be getting my rebirth that day, but also a little bit relieved that I wouldn't have to be sawed open down the chest just yet.

When my mom asked how I was feeling about it all as we left the pre-op area, my answer was: "Definitely disappointed. But also a little relieved. Mainly starving. Can we go to Starbucks?"

Those twenty-one hours, from 1:00 p.m. Friday to 10:00 a.m. Saturday, were emotional, wild, and definitely hazy. My anxiety levels have never swung so wildly, so quickly. But my crew of First Responders—my mom, Talia, and Gaby there that first day and Jack the second—eased the bumpiness of the roller-coaster ride that it was. After the hospital, we left and got Turkish food at 11:00 a.m. Warm bread and olives, soft-boiled eggs, halvah, jams, Turkish coffee, kebabs of various meats and rice, and pickled cabbage and salads, all after a day of fasting and an all-nighter, have a way of soothing the heart and providing some distance from the disappointment.

Sunday morning rolled around. Jack left. Talia and Gaby and I planned a normal day, hanging around in the morning and then going to lunch in the afternoon. At 4:00 p.m., in the car on the way home from lunch, I got another call from the Cardiothoracic Transplant

Program, from the same person who had called me on Friday. There was another set of lungs for me, I was told, and this time, there were no other recipients being called. The donor was not DCD, and the surgeons were not planning on using EVLP on the lungs. This sounded super promising, and she said to get to the hospital quickly. It was more stressful this time because my mom had been sick and vomiting the entire day—probably from stress and exhaustion—but we made it to the hospital in a much shorter time frame since my bag was still packed from the previous trip two days prior. After getting to the hospital at 5:00 p.m. Sunday evening and waiting in the ER for five hours before getting registered, by 2:00 a.m. we were in pre-op, and a surgeon was coming to tell us that the lungs had been deemed nonviable in the donor surgery. After two and a half months of no calls, in one weekend I got two calls that turned out to be two dry runs.

Two dry runs in one weekend is absurdly comical for someone who's healthy enough to wait a bit longer, like I am. But for those who are at the very end, who might not live another day or another week or another month, having more people signed up to be organ donors is the difference between life and death. My friend Caitlin fell on the wrong side of that divide, simply because she had to wait too damn long to get lungs, and by the time she did (almost three years after being listed), her body had just been through too much. My heart still breaks for her family.

This process is wild. And exciting. After a weekend of sleeplessness, I have nothing profound to say about it. My sentiments can be summed up by: holy shit. Here's hoping the third time's the charm.

Friday, April 28, 2017

Jack is here visiting! We're having a really good time so far. He got in super late last night at like 1:30 a.m. so I didn't see him until this morning at 11:00(ish) when he woke up. We had a lazy morning and had sex and had a big brunch, and then took Cooper out for a walk and went and sat on the bench swings by the blue building. It was super relaxing and felt like a warm summer day.

We had a really good talk, too. Talked about how hard the

320

distance has been. About what we're worried about. He's worried that it's going to become too hard for him at a time when I'm going through a lot. I told him that I never want someone to be with me out of pity, I'd rather get dumped than have someone be with me out of the fear of hurting me when they'd rather be out of the relationship. I was wondering when he was going to get sick of all this. And it's only going to get harder. I told him that, that basically it's hard enough now how little we see each other, and how is it going to feel when I get the transplant and everything is changing so rapidly and he's hardly here.

So we'll see what happens. One day at a time. Tonight we're going to eat in, he's cooking filet mignon my mom bought and we're going to open a bottle of wine.

Wednesday, May 3, 2017

I feel good about things. I've had a good feeling the past few days. Maybe because things are so good with Jack. I have the strength and stamina to walk around with my O_2 backpack, which makes me SO much more mobile and independent and makes me feel like my recovery would be quicker if I got the transplant in this current condition. I like that I have a steady stream of friends visiting, with at least a day break in between. I feel so loved.

I'm really sad about my grandparents, though. They are not doing well. My mom's voice sounds so grave on the phone (she's back in LA because it's the end with her mom) and she's eager to hang up, which is not her normal. I miss Grandma already and she's not even dead yet—but this is what I knew would happen. I knew I wouldn't really be able to keep in touch with them from afar because Grandma would get so sick. Now Grandpa is in a ton of pain from a fall, but his needs are kind of secondary to hers so I think his pain is not really being addressed. It's all terrible.

Friday, May 5, 2017

Grandma died today. I don't really have words; I've been feeling run-down all week but all the symptoms really hit me hard today, and that, combined with the complicated emotional experience of grief, has left me completely drained. I can barely muster the energy to talk out loud.

I don't really know how to grieve her and honor her memory when I couldn't be there with her at the end. I don't know if there will be a funeral but regardless, I can't go. It just feels unnatural, like tomorrow will come around and I'll forget about it until something reminds me of her and I will have to remember that she's gone.

My mom flew back to be with me last night, Aunt Meryl was with Grandma and called to say it was the end, so my mom spoke to Grandma on speaker. It was sweet to listen to; they talked about memories of her, said they loved her and would miss her but that everyone would be okay. My mom was on the couch having this conversation, and I was at the kitchen table, bawling my eyes out.

After Grandma died, my mom jumped into action. But she was crying, so I hugged her. I feel powerless to help and guilty that my mom flew back here last night and missed the actual end. My mom said Grandma wanted her to be with me so I guess I understand.

We spent a long time going through photos of Grandma and family to find ones for my mom to post on Facebook. I helped a lot with that.

Sunday, May 7, 2017

So much on my mind. This has really been a weekend of highs and lows.

Friday night is the last time I wrote, and I was feeling really unwell and morose. Then Sabrina arrived and they came to my door with her friend Mark and the guy in my building Seung, who lives with his roommate, Bryan, with their husky puppy. They're some of the first people I met in the building but I never saw them enough to become actual friends, but it turns out they're the people that Sabrina's friend/her ride to Pittsburgh was coming to see! Sabrina's friend/her ride was this guy named Mark who just recently broke up with Olivia Jew. He was so sweet, so good-looking, but also so smart and funny, definitely a 10/10. If I were single and if we lived in the same city, I would've been very into him.

I got more energized when Sabrina arrived, and she came in and ate some food and I sat with her and we chatted for a couple of hours until I was ready to go to bed. The next day I woke up and we had breakfast, then right after, Mark asked Sabrina if we wanted to go to brunch and we said yes so we got ready. We were all slow to mobilize so we left at like 1:30 or something.

I have been coughing up blood in small amounts intermittently all week, but I keep not resuming treatment because it just keeps happening! So my lungs are starting to feel worse, and I was coughing up a storm when we were at brunch.

It was really fun to go out with all of them, though. They had another friend in town visiting them, too, named Connor, who Sabrina ended up making out with later that night when they went out to bars (when I went to bed). Brunch was hilarious, we laughed a ton. We went to Urban Tap on Highland, which I've passed a million times but never been to. I told Seung and Bryan about how my mom thought they were gay (because they said their vet thought they were a gay couple, and I was like, "Oh my mom did, too!"). Everyone thought it was hilarious. I did cough up some blood at brunch, though.

We stayed at brunch for a few hours and then got back to the apartment around 4:30. I was energetic till we got back into the apartment, then I kind of crashed so I tried to take a nap but ended up just lying there listening to the Harry Potter audiobook. I find it so strangely soothing, it's bizarre. Sabrina studied while I slept. It's good for her that I sleep so much because she needed to study, and it's good for my sleep that she had studying to do so I didn't feel guilty leaving her alone all those hours in the morning and the afternoon.

That night we had dinner in the apartment, my mom made a delicious chopped salad and then we had strawberries and chocolate. It's so nice to be able to eat good food and big meals without vomiting (for now—don't want to jinx it). Around 9:00 p.m. we went to Bryan and Seung's apartment on the third floor to "pregame"— I put it in quotes because they were pregaming to go out but I knew I wasn't going to come out so I was just hanging out. I wasn't planning on drinking anything because I'd had half a drink at lunch and with the bleeding didn't think I should drink more. But I ended up pouring a tiny bit of rum into my ginger beer and I think it was fine. We hung out for a while just talking and listening to music and them drinking, and then we started playing stack cup, which I haven't played since I think my Manhattan Beach days . . . it was really fun. I wasn't drinking (a) because I didn't want the alcohol for the bleeding/because of my meds and (b) because I can't drink beer cuz of gluten and (c) because I didn't want to drink out of glasses other people had drunk out of cuz of germs. So I got to just decide who would drink for me each time I was supposed to drink.

It was the most normal I've felt in a really long time. For short periods I would forget that I was wearing oxygen, forget that I'm here for a transplant, and it just felt like I was a normal twenty-four-year-old. So it was really fun to have that. I felt like myself again. Part of it is not taking the Marinol anymore really (for a while every time I drank I felt like a zombie and I couldn't form sentences because I would be high and drunk at the same time). So having like one half or one drink was perfect to have fun without any negative effects. I don't think I'm supposed to drink on Mestinon, though, which is my new motility drug, although I don't exactly know why and the GI doc didn't say that, I just saw it online.

When they were calling Ubers to go out they were counting us and I told them not to count me in because I wasn't coming, and that was the first time I felt my disease kind of insert itself in my night. I did want to go, and I wasn't tired, but I knew I would regret it and probably want to leave the minute we got there, and I would be tired for days and would be punishing myself emotionally and feeling guilty. Especially cuz of the hemoptysis. I also hadn't talked to Jack all day and I felt guilty about how attracted I was to Mark, so I felt like I should go home, let them go out and get more drunk, and I would eat a snack and talk to Jack and then go to bed on the earlier side. Which is just what I did.

Sunday I woke up and felt pretty good at first. Had breakfast—French toast—then went outside with Sabrina to sit in the sunshine on the lounge chairs outside near the pool. It was lovely. I ended up venting a lot about my concerns with my relationship with Jack and filling her in on our recent conversation that we had during his visit—where we were both honest about our fears and worries and where he voiced the possibility of breaking up. We lay out there for an hour or so, then came up and had lunch. Then at 2:30 I walked her downstairs and said goodbye to her and Mark, and traded numbers with Bryan.

By the time I got back up to the apartment I felt sort of feverish and exhausted. Planned to shower but was too wiped, so I just got in bed. Decided to call Jack. Had a conversation that didn't feel right to me. It made me feel emotional and upset. I can't even write why because I had the hour-long conversation, which wasn't even serious, it was mundane, but it opened up such a can of worms that when my mom came in the room I started crying and cried about it for like an hour while we talked. And by the end of that talk I felt like we should break up, but I knew I should not act in a rash way because I might regret it. He's leaving for Europe later this week and I feel like maybe I need to just take some space while he's gone to see how much I miss him.

I was just really not in a good state of mind. But I think it's not fair to judge him when I feel sad/exhausted/physically unwell/depressed because I'm way overly harsh. But on the other hand, I think I let things slide when I feel well that I probably shouldn't, so maybe it averages out in the end. I'm starting to think I'm pretty positive that he's not my person for the long term, but he is a really great boyfriend for now (Mr. Right Now instead of Mr. Right). Except he might not be a great bf for now once the transplant happens, so we'll see. It's just a matter of whether he brings me more positive than negative, and it's always skewed more positive but I'm starting to think that could change.

Saturday, May 13, 2017

On Monday I had a call with a Penn med student who is writing a story for *Slate*, about gender and wait times for organ transplants.

Apparently, women wait longer. I hope to continue advocating for the issues surrounding transplantation.

Jack left for Europe on Thursday with his mom. His Wi-Fi on the riverboat is shitty so between that and the time change I don't expect we'll talk much over the next couple of weeks. It'll feel weird to not catch up at the end of each day. I've gotten used to that.

I got a Fitbit gift in the mail yesterday! It was a great surprise from Emily. She is SO thoughtful.

Sunday, May 21, 2017

Things have been pretty good lately, all things considered. Stable!! Went to see Dr. Pilewski in clinic last week and didn't have much to talk about, which is a first! I LOVE him and the three women he works with.

Jeremiah and Marla got married this weekend in Cleveland, and I went! Micah and Dad flew in from LA so the four of us could drive to Cleveland together. First family trip without friends or boyfriends or girlfriends in literally YEARS—maybe even a decade? It was nice to spend the alone time with Micah. I feel like we never really got quality time together when I came to LA from NorCal because we were always in big groups or with people we were dating or at large dinners. So it was nice to have sibling time and actually catch up on each other's lives.

Thursday, May 25, 2017

I'm in the hospital. I coughed up lots of blood on Tuesday, the day after coming home from the wedding. At 4:00 p.m. I had a big bleed that led me to call an ambulance, but the small bleeds had started at 2:00 a.m. I'm thankful that the bleeding didn't continue and that they didn't have to embolize. Knock on wood.

Today has been hard. Things started out badly when my mom heard from the transplant coordinator that Dr. Hayanga, the surgeon we met with during the eval, is leaving to start up a new transplant center in West Virginia. The volume of transplants will go down, but I didn't realize how much this news affected her until she recounted the information on the phone to my dad and started crying. She seems like she's losing it a bit, between hearing this news, the hospital staff giving her shit yesterday for blocking the door while I took a nap (then ratting her out to Dr. Pilewski), and the pharmacy staff messing up my meds. Normally, she handles so much without cracking that I don't know what pushed her over the edge this time. It could've been the hemoptysis (bigger than usual), or maybe it's the aftermath of grief from her mom dying, or maybe it's sleeplessness. All I know is she seems down.

I get it. Transplant scares the shit out of me, so for the first time in my life I'm choosing to be ignorant rather than research what's to come so I can prepare myself. I don't want to know about the vent, don't want to know about ECMO, don't want to know about chest tubes. I know I'll somehow put my head down and get through it, and on the other side I'll be grateful that I did and be stoked to be living life again.

Saturday, June 3, 2017

Sometimes it feels like there's a hand inside my chest, taking my heart and squeezing it tightly so that it becomes hard to breathe for reasons completely unrelated to my lungs. And my heart will start to race and I'll feel this sense of panic. And I know this anxiety is new, and it's a growing problem. I'm just not sure what to do about it. I don't want to keep taking Ativan because, first of all, if I'm dependent on Ativan that doesn't look good to the transplant team. And second of all, I think if I use Ativan a lot, then when I don't use it, I'm more irritable (I think that's a thing?). So I just try to relax and let it pass, sometimes I cry, sometimes I watch TV, sometimes I write in this journal, I guess? But I feel like that just solidifies that this is my narrative—that I'm anxious and struggling and miserable. When really that's not true most of the time; it's just that the times when it is true have a disproportionate impact on my perception of my life experience.

I think my own hang-ups are going to ruin my relationship. Because when I feel that death grip on my heart and the crushing anxiety (which has no immediate cause to address), I can't talk to Jack about it because he has nothing to say, and I know myself, I just push everyone away. That's just how I am.

And I swing wildly back and forth in what I think about it. Sometimes my feelings toward Jack are very tender, and I get a rush of love and appreciation for him. But then sometimes I feel super bitter and resentful, even contemptuous maybe? And I do think contempt is the death of a happy relationship. And my feelings about it are so complicated and there are so many of them that I've kept to myself for so long, feelings about him as a person and him as a partner, that I don't know how I can talk to him about it without having a SCRIPT in hand so that I don't just start talking myself in circles and making no sense. Because when you try to talk to something else and say some distortion of the truth, usually to avoid hurting the other person, then you end up just saying things that don't make sense.

So I wonder, what would I say? Would I say: I don't think you know how to support me emotionally? Your future is too uncertain and I don't see how I fit into it? I don't think you understand what I'm going through and it's too hard for me to be in a relationship where we're so distant and disconnected? I feel like I'm supporting you right now instead of the reverse, even though I'm the one going through a life-and-death situation? I am worried that we don't have the same values in life and that that would ruin us down the line so maybe we should just quit now since it's so hard to be together anyway? Maybe we should transition to just being good friends, because then I won't have so many expectations of what you should be doing to be there for me. My worry about that is that then I would start to think that he was just meeting girls and hooking up with them in Hermosa and it would probably just make me uncomfortable to think about that if he came to visit . . . and would we have sex? I tried to do that with Shawn, the transition to being just good friends, and then we had sex anyway when we saw each other when he came to stay with me in November 2015 when I was in the hospital, and it made everything very mucky and messy and confusing.

Part of me wonders if a big part of my issue with Jack is just that

I have loathing for MYSELF, and I'm projecting that unhappiness onto him somehow? There are just so many things I despise about myself right now. As much as I hate to admit that, it's how I feel. I hate my appearance (hair, skin, teeth stains, skinny flabby body shape with enormous midsection), how my body feels all the time (weakness, tightness, tension, shortness of breath, nausea, fatigue, etc.), my GI problems (which are ENDLESS and now I have to deal with incontinence and I'm just completely perplexed and disgusted and have no idea what to do about it and, not to sound dramatic, but I can't imagine a life where that's a problem I continue to have), my inability to follow through on any goal I set for myself (to write anything interesting, to work on my Spanish, to teach myself ukulele, to read more books, to get in better shape, to follow the news more closely, to keep in better touch with friends). Nothing feels right. I feel like I'm living the wrong person's life, and it makes me wonder how did I get here??? And then I hate myself for caring about all this shit, because so much of it should be insignificant, and it's stupid to be so concerned about it all when I should just be grateful that I'm stable and focus on trying to stay alive.

Part of it is also that the post-transplant life, which I used to imagine as idyllic, is starting to seem worse and worse. My perfect picture of it is disintegrating as I watch Caleigh and Melissa struggle so much, and as I learn more about all the weird side effects and stuff you have to deal with. I mean, yes, it's better than dying, but it feels so unfair that those are the only two choices. And yes, I know LIFE IS NOT FAIR. People always tell me I'm "inspirational" because I don't wallow in self-pity but that's exactly what I'm doing. But it feels like I have a right to do that sometimes when my only options right now are (1) to continue living in Pittsburgh and being on IVs until I get a transplant and then hope the transplant succeeds and I don't die, (2) to go off IVs and hope I don't get too sick for transplant and die, or (3) to not get a transplant and leave Pittsburgh and definitely die.

I think I want to go to temple when my dad is here. That sounds like it would be really nice for some reason. I think it would ground me. And it would remind me of happier, simpler times, of being young, and at camp, and part of a community, and not separate and isolated, and not struggling with life-and-death issues. Of being plugged into something larger than myself, even if that thing is community, and NOT God, since I don't believe in God.

Tuesday, June 13, 2017
Thursday night Jack came to town! I heard him come in at 1:30 a.m. and I hadn't been to sleep because I was lying there, tossing and turning. So I went into the kitchen to have a snack and say hi, and I scared him so badly, he jumped about five feet in the air! It was hilarious. We had a really good visit. It felt like things were back to normal with us after our heavy conversation. I think it was the fact that I'd finally unloaded the things that I was feeling upset about, and we talked through it, and then he got my anniversary card, which was really sweet, and he was very grateful about that and he really realized he needed to step up. And I know part of it was just that I was in a vicious cycle of anxiety where resentment was building and I was too scared to bring it up, and that made me more anxious, which meant I was even more sensitive to things he would do/say and make me more resentful and doubtful about our relationship.

So when he was here it just felt like we could have fun again and add good memories to the bank. Friday afternoon we got massages together, then we went to the patio to lie in the sun. I realized I really do love him and hope we have a future—and that a lot of my doubts are because I'm so unhappy with my situation.

Saturday, July 8, 2017
Caleigh got rejected from Stanford for a second lung transplant. So now they're looking into coming to Pittsburgh. I hope so badly that it works out for them. I got a bad feeling about it when they suddenly discharged her from the hospital two days after telling her she'd have to stay inpatient until the next transplant. It seems as if they're giving up on her and they want her to spend her last days outside, enjoying herself. She has so much will to live, and I hate when

centers are so utilitarian in their thinking; that's what led everyone to reject me, too.

Monday, July 17, 2017

I've been having a lot of small bouts of hemoptysis recently.

Because I've had to skip so many treatments lately, post-hemoptysis, I feel more short of breath and have had more tachycardia. My last blood work showed I'm low on vitamin A and now I'm wondering if maybe I'm low on vitamin K, too, and that's why I keep bleeding day after day?

Thursday, August 3, 2017—Mallory's mom (Diane)

At 8:30 the other night, I parked in a handicap space across the street from Millie's Homemade Ice Cream so we could get dessert—one of the simple pleasures Mallory can still enjoy as she is tethered to oxygen and at the end stage of her battle with cystic fibrosis.

When we were coming out of Millie's I saw that a tow truck had my car on it and was ready to drive away. I ran across the street and told the driver that my daughter was at Millie's and I needed to go get her as it's hard for her to walk because of her medical situation.

The driver said, "I don't care what your daughter has—you can only have your car if you give me $200." I said I didn't have that much cash on me so he told me I'd need to pick up my car at their impound lot. I told him I wanted to call the police because she has a valid handicap placard and the proper paperwork but more important, if he took my car I wouldn't be able to get my daughter home and her oxygen tank was running out.

The driver was beyond nasty and again said he didn't care what my problem was. He started to get in his truck to drive off, so I opened my car door and straddled the seat so he couldn't move without hurting me. I called 911 and explained the situation.

The nice police officer who answered said to stay put and tell the tow truck driver that the police were on the way. I started crying when I was on the phone because I felt helpless. Mallory was with me by now, standing to the side, visibly upset about what was happening. She was connected to O₂ with two IVs running simultaneously. Anyone seeing her could only feel pity. That the driver ignored her and her situation left me stunned. And PISSED.

And then the driver just let my car down and drove off. I said thank you. But then three women and one man who were standing off to the side—a group I had noticed but not thought anything of—approached me. One said, "Don't thank him, we paid him to leave your car." I was STUNNED. I didn't know these people. I was deeply distraught and unsure what to do and they stepped in to help. They said they gave him $100 to go away and then refused to take any money from me, saying they know how many expenses we'll have after transplant and to use the money for my daughter.

I asked the woman who actually paid the driver what her name was and she said Jeanette Ware. I was in shock that people we'd never met before would do that for us. She said, "Welcome to Pittsburgh."

Tuesday, August 15, 2017

Feeling really good about things:

1. Even though UPMC only has one surgeon now, there's a chance I could get double-listed at Tampa—thank you, David!! And my health is stable right now, so I am in a position to wait awhile (fingers crossed it stays that way).

2. Jack came to visit this past weekend and it was wonderful. It was just the two of us, with neither of my parents here until my mom arrived late Saturday night. It was super low-key. Friday we had to stay in all day to wait for oxygen deliveries because my concentrator was broken, but it was lovely. Then in the late afternoon I tried to take a nap while he went to Whole Foods, and then he cooked an incredible dinner for us. He made rosemary duck, golden beets, yams, and tomato

avocado salad. The next day was also really low-key, but we did get to take a walk and watch people play kickball at the park nearby. Things with us are so good right now, very loving and tender.

3. I'm on a mission to introduce new things into my life now that I feel like we're really going to be here for a while. I went to a yoga class for the first time in eleven months last night! My last yoga class was on Union Street in SF, last September, the morning before I went back to LA because my grandma got diagnosed with cancer.

4. I'm going to try really hard to make the most of my time in Pittsburgh. I don't want to waste any days that I feel good. I want to have lists of things I love to do ready, so that on any day I feel good enough, I can do something!

Friday, August 25, 2017

I GOT ANOTHER CALL FOR LUNGS!!! It was 7:00 a.m. and for some reason my phone didn't ring so they called my mom.

It's so funny because we had been despairing lately about how it felt like it was never going to happen and how we could still be waiting a year from now. And then the call came!! The lungs were increased risk and had to be on EVLP. Dr. D'Cunha reassured us that they don't use lungs if they're subpar.

I wonder if this call has anything to do with my score going up two days ago in clinic? You never want to decline, but when you're waiting for lungs, the sicker you get the more likely you are to get lungs.

Jack happened to be in Boston for work, again, which is an amazing coincidence. His going there has turned out to be my good-luck charm! He said he would come here instead of going to Maine with his dad!!! Liana is coming tonight, too, so my mom won't have to wait alone. She doesn't want my dad to fly in until we're sure it's a go.

My mom took FOREVER to get ready. We got to the hospital four hours after they called us—the time you're allowed to take. Her reasoning was that the last two times we raced over they kept us waiting for more than ten hours and she hadn't properly prepared the house (whatever that means). This time she wanted to throw out trash, get laundry done, clean the house in case it's a go. By the time we were in the car, on our way to the hospital, we got calls from four different people, all asking where we were. One was a coordinator who was really nasty on the phone.

We didn't even go to a room on the floor this time, probably because we were so late. We just went straight to pre-op and they did the testing there. Everything was rushed and frenzied.

Jack showed up from Boston shortly after we got into the room. Everyone was talking over each other, and there were about five people surrounding me the whole time.

Eventually they took me into the OR so this time, I actually had to say goodbye to my mom and Jack for real. I was stressed out in the OR. They gave me two doses of Versed. A nice doctor, a cardiac fellow, put old episodes of *Friends* on her phone for me to watch. Eventually, Dr. D'Cunha came in and told me that the lungs were no good. I don't really remember what he said besides that. But he had talked to my mom and Jack for a long time about it so they shared the details.

It was a very young donor, a drug overdose. The lungs looked good and would've been a perfect match other than being hep C antibody-positive but when they opened him/her (they don't tell you the gender) they saw the person had aspirated, and when they stress-tested the lungs, they started leaking fluid, which made it a no go. I guess EVLP is a good thing to rule out bad lungs.

Sunday, September 10, 2017
We got another call!!!!!

TRANSPLANT

Monday, September 11, 2017—Mallory's mom
Nine-eleven is an inauspicious date for transplant but after twenty-four hours it's a GO!! Hoping God, karma, science, or a medical miracle will help Mallory to the other side. Surgery could take twelve hours.

After a long night and a seemingly even longer day, Mallory's surgery was deemed a success by Dr. D'Cunha, who said her new lungs are pristine and the procedure went well. The next twenty-four to forty-eight hours are critical as that's when she is at risk from a surgical perspective. After that, the big concern is cepacia, *as this deadly superbug can still colonize the new lungs. We are cautiously optimistic!*

    As Mal lies heavily sedated on a ventilator, and we dare to dream about a new life for her, we shed a tear (many, in fact) for the selfless person who gave our daughter the gift of life. We aren't allowed to know who provided the lungs so we throw our eternal gratitude into the universe and hope it finds its way to the family and friends of our beloved donor. We can't imagine their grief but will remain forever grateful.

Tuesday, September 12, 2017—Mallory's mom
Twenty-four hours post-op—Mal is stable and doing better than expected. Vital signs look good, no fevers, minimal sedation, less O_2 needed

than anticipated, and, most important, tolerating the ventilator! Tomorrow she will go back to the OR so Dr. D'Cunha and his team can close her chest (left open so the lungs settle in). Hoping that by end of day tomorrow we will be over the surgical hurdle. Jack arrived late tonight!

Wednesday, September 13, 2017—Jack
Diane texts me the room information. "CTICU Rm 18." That's cardiothoracic intensive care unit, room 18. Mallory's dad, Mark, meets me at the elevators.

It is 2:00 a.m. when I see her, the first time since I left two and a half weeks earlier after the third dry run. Diane and Mark are exhausted so I'm on the night shift until 6:30 a.m., watching her.

She is sleeping soundly, faceup, about two dozen lines running across her body. The data lines run to an LCD screen behind her head, giving a full ten-second visual readout of seven body measurements. The rest of the lines pump in medicine. She has a ventilator hooked up to her lungs; a tube the diameter of a quarter goes in through her mouth. She won't be able to speak until she has it out.

She'd written short notes on a clipboard in order to communicate.

Her first question: "What medicine am I on?" She always likes to be in charge, especially of her own body.

I sit down and take it all in, getting used to the feeling of wearing a full-body medical gown, gloves, and face mask. Here we are, just us, in a moment we had both dreamed about—me since I met her, Mal for a lifetime.

The whirring of the medical devices makes the room strangely peaceful.

I'm beginning to doze off when her eyes flicker awake. She blinks a few times, slowly tilting her head to see if anyone is in the room. I stand up to put my face in her field of vision. She sees my figure in front of her, her eyes beginning to focus. She reminds me of a sloth waking up from a nap, but one who is also extremely high.

The recognition hits. Her eyes bug out and get huge, her arms rise up and start swinging about in the air. The LCD health monitor lights up in protest. Alarms blare and red warning lights flash.

"Whoa, whoa, whoa, heyyyy, hi, yes, calm down. Chill, chill, chill . . . CHILL!"

Her heartbeat has jumped to 185. Her blood oxygen level starts to drop, her minimal energy stores used by all of the effort she is expending. She motions with her hands for me to get her pen and clipboard with paper.

"I have SO much to tell you!!" she writes.

I had thought she wouldn't be fully lucid for a few days. That clearly is not the case. I guess she is overachieving even now. So typical.

We catch up, our progress hindered by her lack of muscle memory for writing combined with her memory fog, which causes her to forget the topic of a sentence halfway through writing it.

I can't stop smiling.

She is alive, breathing, and the proud new owner of two lungs she was not born with.

"What does my chest look like?" she writes.

I tell her, "I could describe what it looks like, but there's a lot there, you sure you want me to describe it?" Her chest is still very much open but covered by bandages and her gown. She can't feel that part. Yet.

"Wait, describe what?" she writes, then stares blankly. She can neither remember nor see what she has just asked.

The sun rises and my shift ends as Diane comes back to take over.

Wednesday, September 13, 2017—Mallory's mom

Mallory had surgery midmorning to close her chest and is now recovering in ICU. Watching her still sedated and connected to the ventilator, with tubes everywhere. I can hardly believe she's on the other side and that things went so well. Dr. D'Cunha (the AMAZING surgeon) and Dr. Pilewski (the INCREDIBLE head of CF at UPMC) say she's surpassed expectations!! Still a long road ahead, but now that her chest is closed we can work toward the goal of getting her off the vent. It's been a VERY difficult few days in terms of pain.

Wednesday, September 13, 2017—Jack

I wake up in the apartment around 3:00 p.m. and make my way over to the hospital. Diane tells me it has not been a good day for Mal.

Now that she is recovering well, the doctors want to wean her off pain, nausea, and anxiety medication, enough so that she can control her own lungs for the first time—without the ventilator. The only problem is, when you take away the medications that make you not able to feel things, you start to feel things.

It's been hard but might get a whole lot worse before it gets better. I settle in for a long night on my second watch.

She has pain, nausea, confusion, nightmares, hallucinations . . . it's overwhelming for her.

"Do they have all of their knives? There might be one that got stuck behind my left lung."

No, Mal, they have all of their knives.

"My whole body feels like a squid."

I know, Mal, I know.

"Is there someone standing behind me?"

No, Mal, no one is there.

"Is the ceiling leaking? It's dripping all over me."

No, Mal, the ceiling is fine.

"Is my skull bleeding? Did they operate on my brain by mistake?"

No, Mal, your noggin looks great.

It's a long night. She calms down when we hold hands.

Somehow, we fall asleep.

Sometime later, she shakes me awake, asking for her pen and paper. With the most concentration I have seen so far, she writes a note that I will never forget.

"You have so far exceeded my expectation of what is possible for love."

I have gotten into the practice of reading the words aloud as she writes them, slowly, so she can rewrite words that end up being illegible. The full weight of the sentence does not hit me until she draws a heart.

I look up from the clipboard and into her eyes as she gazes back into mine.

Amid all of the chaos that we have become accustomed to, despite all of the hardship, Mal and I have survived, we are here, as a team, in the middle of the greatest battle Mal will ever have to fight, hopefully.

Red lights flash and alarms blare.

"WARNING! THE FOLLOWING LIMITS HAVE BEEN EX-CEEDED: HEART RATE, BLOOD PRESSURE, OXYGEN SATU-RATION, BREATHING CADENCE," the screen reads.

Shit . . . shit, shit, shit!

Panic sets in. I realize I need to calm her down.

"I forgot to tell you, Cooper had a really big poop today." Cooper is her nine-pound dog, comprised primarily of white fluffy fur and love.

Her lips smile around the ventilator tube.

"Nice," she writes.

One by one the alarms flicker off. A nurse has rushed in, ready for anything.

"We're okay. Totally fine. Stellar, actually," I say.

The nurse looks skeptical, then leaves.

Mark comes to relieve my shift midway through the night, but I stay, unable to leave Mal.

Friday, September 15, 2017—Mallory's mom

MIRACLE—Mal got the ventilator out and is breathing on her own!! There aren't words to describe the moment you see your baby girl breathing with new lungs.

Saturday, September 16, 2017—Jack

Now that Mal is off the ventilator, new sensations have begun to dominate her attention.

The first is thirst.

She is not allowed to drink but can suck on small sponges soaked in water. Swallowing is still too dangerous as she has a feeding tube inserted. It's much smaller than the vent tube, but aggravating to her throat, which is still tender. Though her hydration levels remain perfect, the sensation persists.

Finally, she has had enough.

Instead of asking for another soaked sponge, she asks me to come close. Talking is still challenging with such a tired throat, so all she can manage is a whisper.

"No. More. Sponges . . . Need. Drink. From. Bottle."

I tell her that's not allowed, that it's too dangerous. She grabs my medical gown with all her strength and pulls on me. Her eyes look manic.

"NEED IT. PLEASE," she whispers angrily.

I tell her that she will be okay, that we will get through this together. Mal glares at me, releases my gown, and slumps back into her bed, defeated.

Sunday, September 17, 2017—Mallory's mom

Mallory's pain is unbearable, which tempers the joy we're all feeling now that she has new lungs.

Sunday, September 17, 2017—Jack

More pain and discomfort continue despite Mal's progress.

It gets worse and worse through the day.

"Why did I do this?" Mal asks, out of the blue.

"What do you mean?" I say, confused.

"Why did I agree to a transplant?" she asks.

"Well, let's remember why," I say. "You had hours of treatment every day, treating but not curing a sickness that was only getting worse month to month, which was slowly but surely taking away your ability to live a happy and normal life with your family and friends. We knew a transplant would be hard—we knew it would be painful. But we also knew that the pain would be primarily condensed into your recovery period, resulting in the reward of a longer, healthier, more fulfilling life. Does that still sound like a good trade?"

I wait for her to think about it as she stares vacantly into the distance.

I feel thankful for a lot of things. Pride, joy, and exhaustion best describe the week.

But transplant inflicts trauma. Mal has endured so much. Good thing she won't remember most of it . . . or so they tell us.

Tuesday, September 19, 2017—Mallory's mom

UPMC transplant team continues to amaze! Two issues Mal was dealing with—vocal cord paralysis from intubation during surgery and a feeding tube that was stuck in the wrong place—have been resolved. Each mole-hill feels like a mountain until Drs. D'Cunha and Pilewski (and their stellar colleagues) work their magic. While pain is still unbearable for Mal, she continues to surpass everyone's expectations in terms of milestones. Today's victory—Mallory walked!!

Thursday, September 21, 2017—Mallory's mom
Mal had her first hair wash in ten days, thank you, Eileen! HUGE smile, followed by tears when she realized her vocal cords still aren't working properly. Feeding tube can't come out until she can swallow, so she is now working with speech pathology and ENT. Also acute and chronic pain teams are trying to find a regimen that will work. Today's activities include walking, swallowing, and breathing exercises. I have to take mandatory training to learn about post-transplant care.

Friday, September 22, 2017—Mallory's mom
Yesterday started with the expectation that things would continue to improve, but it turned out to be a very difficult day. When Mal felt she was at the breaking point, I reminded her that she has tremendous inner strength, a strong will to survive, and more love/support than she could possibly imagine. And to keep looking at the photograph of her diseased lungs to remember why she agreed to this traumatic surgery.

Saturday, September 23, 2017—Mallory's mom
Today was GREAT! We heard blood cultures were clear (after they hadn't been), that her vocal cords are closing as they should, that Mal's walk was 175 feet!! We watched her blow 1,000 on her incentive spirometer (first days she couldn't hit 250) and her pneumothorax is improving.

Sunday, September 24, 2017—Mallory's mom
Mal is still dealing with vocal cord paralysis and a chest tube still culturing positive for cepacia. The feeding tube and chest tube, which continue to cause major pain, should come out soon. The good news is Mal more than doubled her step count today—she walked a half mile!!

Monday, September 25, 2017—Mallory's mom

Today was all about swallowing. Mal continues to improve but can't get her feeding tube out until she can eat and drink. They say practice makes perfect.

Tuesday, September 26, 2017—Mallory's mom

Each day brings new milestones—today Mal's feeding tube was removed and she walked stairs. Marveling at the MIRACLE!

Wednesday, September 27, 2017—Mallory's mom

Sixteen days after Mal's transplant, they are preparing for discharge (will take a day or two to get the home meds set up). Exciting but also terrifying as Mal still has a "swallowing disorder"—temporary, we hope—and is immunosuppressed, still with chest tubes, still in pain. They can't do a bronchoscopy to check for rejection because they don't want to risk stirring up cepacia. Continue to think it's a miracle or a dream that I don't ever want to wake up from.

Thursday, September 28, 2017—Mallory's mom

Final chest tube cleanout, final PICC dressing change, and final instructions. Vitals and clinical assessment are good so Mal is cleared for discharge!! Still a long road to recovery—and a whole new set of meds—but getting out of the hospital is a major milestone. Used to sing "Somewhere over the rainbow, there are lungs, and the dreams that we dare to dream really do come true." Now we sing "Somewhere over the rainbow, there WERE lungs." Mal, our dream came true.

Monday, October 2, 2017—Mallory's mom

Still so much pain but every day seems to be a little better. Mallory still does not have much of a voice yet and swallowing is still an issue. Hosted a dinner tonight for her friends in the lobby, which got her up and out of the apartment. Tomorrow we head to the hospital at 6:30 a.m. for post-transplant tests. Crossing our fingers that the last two chest tubes come out as that will help with the pain. Mal washed her own hair for the first time today. When she was changing her clothes she noticed her chest was much smaller and asked if I thought they had cut out some ribs. Hadn't heard that they did but wondering if her discarded/diseased lungs were swollen and infected, making them enlarged. One more question for the team tomorrow.

Friday, October 6, 2017—Mallory's mom
This week's activities for Mal included transplant clinic, blood transfusion, magnesium, potassium and antibiotic IVs, physical therapy, CT scan, X-rays, dressing change, and blood draws. Still lots of pain from the last two chest tubes but we continue to hope for improvement. They say all of this is part of routine recovery and she's doing well given that she's twenty-six days post-op, twenty-four if you count from date of chest closing.

Saturday, October 7, 2017
I haven't written anything since my transplant on September 11. Typing with errors because I'm wearing a pulse ox.

Want to remember getting the real call, Gaby coming in, sitting in the hospital for twelve hours. I told my mom while we were waiting that if this wasn't the time, I would need a break. She looked at me with conviction and said it WILL happen and you WILL get through it. I wasn't serious, of course, but it was reassuring to see her so confident.

Night of surgery

Saying goodbye to Maria on the phone, crying. UPMC cameras recording everything so that they can share my story.

Heading into OR, extreme anxiety. Not knowing if I would come out alive.

Will continue later, too tired to cover so much at one time.

Pillboxes are wild hard. Need to update the list:

Post-transplant pillboxes
1. Domperidone QID
2. Calcite 900 mg BID
3. Misoprostol 200 mcg QID
4. Prednisone 15 mg QD
5. Bupropion HCL XL 150 mg QD

6. Ursodiol 250 mg or 300 mg BID
7. Voriconazole 200 mg BID
8. Bactrim (sulfamethoxazole) DS 1 tab TID
9. Biotin 1,000 mcg QD PM
10. Prograf (tacrolimus) 4.5 mg BID
11. Levaquin 750 mg QD
12. Colace 250 mg BID
13. Simethicone 180 mg QID
14. Dexilant 60 mg BID
15. Mestinon (pyridostigmine) 60 mg TID
16. Minocycline 100 mg BID
17. Aquadeks 1 tab BID
18. Famotidine 40 mg QD PM
19. Melatonin 3 mg QD PM
20. Amitiza 24 mcg BID
21. Lopressor (metoprolol tartrate) 50 mg BID
22. Coenzyme Q10 100 mg TID
23. Senna 2 tabs BID
24. Gabapentin 300 mg QD PM
25. Dulcolax 10 mg QD PM

NOON
1. Domperidone
2. misoprostol
3. simethicone
4. Mestinon
5. Bactrim
6. magnesium 2 tabs

EVENING
1. Domperidone
2. misoprostol
3. simethicone
4. CoQ10
5. magnesium 1 tab

Monday, October 9, 2017—Mallory's mom
Mallory taped two TV segments today—ABC and CBS—about her journey. The simple act of cleaning up is a major milestone after you've been so sick that washing your face is a huge effort!! Each day seems to bring improvement, so clinging to the idea that slow and steady wins the race.

Sunday, October 15, 2017 (25 years old)
On my twenty-fourth birthday in 2016, I got the phone call from UPMC that they would accept me into their lung transplant program when I became sick enough to need one.

One month and one day after transplant surgery, I celebrated my twenty-fifth birthday with Pittsburgh friends and then spent the rest of my birthday weekend with Jack. But the recovery from this surgery has been more harrowing and more painful than anything I've ever experienced before, and it's a good thing I don't remember the worst of it. What I do know is that I had angelic family and friends who stayed by my side when I was on the vent, disoriented, in pain, and panicking, who reminded me why I chose to put myself through this: for the hope of a better life.

I never knew if I would live to see the other side of transplant, if any program would take a chance on me, but UPMC doctors did, and here I am. This year, instead of wishing for something else, I just sent my deepest gratitude to my donor, whose selfless choice to donate organs gave me the chance at a new life. My primary aim will be to make him/her proud.

Friday, October 20, 2017—Mallory's mom
Five weeks and five days after Mal's transplant they removed the final two drains and took out the remaining staples from the surgical site. Immediately after, Mal said, "Today is the best day of my life!"

Wednesday, October 25, 2017—Mallory's mom
Oh, what a difference a day makes! A day after being out with friends, we are in the ER with Mal about to get admitted. Double-lung transplant is

not easy to recover from, so we're hoping it's just a bump in the road, but Mal is still struggling with pain, nausea, loss of appetite, fever, speech, and swallowing issues. Just had a CT scan, which revealed possible pneumonia; next will be a bronchoscopy to look for rejection.

Friday, October 27, 2017

Need to remember to write about these things:

Chest open, ventilator, million lines. ICU, writing notes, banging phone on bed—when the ICU kicked my dad out for shift change and I was terrified. Called my mom but couldn't talk because of the vent so I banged the phone on the bed rail to communicate my distress. She put Jack on the phone and he calmed me down until my mom could track down my dad and he came back. Subsequent fight with hospital personnel about insane rule of kicking families out of ICU during shift change, the time nurses are least able to be responsive because they are distracted giving reports to the next shift.

Indignities in ICU. Chest closing, starting to be lucid. Moving to second ICU room, then to transplant floor (7?). Blood infection, infected pleural fluid, infected port.

Extreme thirst. Fear, anxiety, panic attacks, worst pain of my life, wishing I were not alive for parts of it.

First time sitting in a chair. First walk. Difficulty of getting to the bathroom with four chest-tube receptacles and IV pole and me unable to walk or lower/lift myself onto/off the commode.

Stacy visiting, then Eileen and Don, Natalie, Danielle, Maya. Kyle and Dave coming soon. Increasing step count each day. Being fed through nasal tube. Surgery on my vocal cords to plump them up so they can close, but failure. Thickened liquid diet with the threat of aspiration if I drink thin liquids.

Writing notes. Amazing doctors—Pilewski, D'Cunha, Kates, Harano, PA Marissa, many more. Great nurses.

Going home. OVERWHELMED. Wasn't ready at all, wild pill organization with lots of help from my dad and Barb. Crying to Maya about how this was the hardest thing I had ever experienced, sleeping through most of her visit. Birthday and birthday dinner. Chest tubes staying in FOREVER. No showers. Scary weight loss, down to 110 (BMI less than 15). Forgot to write before, Sabrina's visit in ICU but too drugged to remember.

Pain management issues, nerve block solution for a while. How opioid epidemic is making it harder for legit patients to get what they need.

Strange reality of me feeling closer to Jack post-transplant because of how amazing he was, and him feeling more distant cuz I couldn't talk on FaceTime/phone as much cuz of fatigue/my voice being weak/being overwhelmed/having visitors.

Physical therapy and walking, speech not improving. Hope for 2018—travel, lots of time with friends and family, being healthy and hospital-free, and writing my book!

Lots of visitors—Talia and Ronit, Becca and her mom Nancy, Ali and her parents, Nancy and Alan. Running around, lots of activity, fancy nice dinners to try to fatten me up, Ralph and Mary hosting us for cocktails, then fever on October 25 and trip to ER and admission. Current insomnia. Tomorrow thoracentesis to culture and possibly drain the pleural fluid and make sure there isn't an empyema. Then later on a bronchoscopy with biopsy to check for rejection/culture any infection that's there?

Saturday, October 28, 2017—Mallory's mom

After having a good day yesterday, Mal spiked a high fever late last night, the hallmark of cepacia syndrome and cause for great concern. Drs. Pilewski and D'Cunha explained the challenges they face treating both infection and rejection.

Anyone who knows Mal knows she's got more inner strength than most, but it's hard not to be scared. On a happier note, Jack came today. If only love could heal!

Sunday, October 29, 2017—Mallory's mom

The highs and lows of this weekend are indescribable. Simplest explanation for what's happening is that Mal has a worsening pneumonia, not surprising given the cepacia *that's still stalking her and the immunosuppressants needed to keep rejection at bay. Treating for both is proving to be impossible. We check Mal's temperature multiple times a day as she can go from a high fever that leaves her listless and in pain, to seemingly fine within the span of hours. There's reason to be hopeful as Mallory's O_2, BP, and HR are good.*

Tuesday, October 31, 2017—Mallory's mom
Mallory is facing post-transplant pneumonia with tremendous courage as cepacia *continues to wreak havoc on her fragile body. UPMC is using every weapon in its arsenal to attack the moving target of symptoms. Feeding tube is back in, antibiotics are layered on, and ancillary service providers come to help with PT, swallowing, and walking. Pulmonary, transplant, and infectious disease docs confer and round daily as Mal's case is "complicated."* Cepacia *is so resistant and virulent that no one is talking about rejection. The silence is deafening.*

It's been an exhausting week for Mal as she struggles to recover. The days blur together with mornings incredibly difficult and afternoons much better. Many medical minds worked together to devise a cocktail of drugs that will keep the cepacia *at bay. Morning vitals were cause for great concern.*

Tuesday, November 7, 2017—Mallory's mom
Mal isn't getting better. Since there is no hope left from traditional, approved medicine, Mark asked Mal's doctor if he would help us pursue phage therapy. Dr. Pilewski said, "YES, but if we're going to do this, we need to do it now, as we're out of time." We are now working with UPMC, Adaptive Phage Therapeutics, the US Naval Medical Research Center, Texas A&M, UC San Diego, AmpliPhi Biosciences, the University of Michigan, and the University of Alberta to find an appropriate phage treatment.

Thursday, November 9, 2017—Mallory's mom
One week ago we had NO options left to treat Mal's pneumonia since her cepacia *is resistant to every single antibiotic on the market—the same* cepacia *that was in her old lungs is back in her new, pristine lungs. But*

now we have hope as Mark is working with the doctors to get phage therapy for Mal. If I wasn't a witness to what transpired this week between so many doctors at so many institutions, I would never believe it could happen. Isolates have been sent to various labs and phages are being tested in different parts of the country and Canada. While not a sure thing, it's the single most promising treatment we can try to get.

Mark also found a drug made by the Japanese pharmaceutical firm Shionogi (not yet approved in the United States) that might be active against cepacia. We brought it to the attention of our team at UPMC, who told us they'd been actively trying to secure it but there wasn't inventory. Danny knows someone at the company so he is putting us in touch. But UPMC said we didn't need to activate this connection, as they had just secured a full treatment course for Mallory!!

In the span of five days we went from feeling hopeless to hopeful. It's been a totally overwhelming week with an endless cycle of multiple teams rounding, IVs, RT treatments, PT, swallowing therapy, procedures, and showering (a BIG deal). One of the hardest parts is getting those darn compression stockings on. Such a relief that Linda is here and took on that job!! I am so grateful she is here!!

Friday, November 10, 2017—Mallory's mom

Things took a turn, Mal is much worse, we're in final throes. Dr. Pilewski will do what it takes to keep things going. Starting the new drug today (Herculean efforts were taken to make this happen!) and hoping it will work or act as a bridge until they find phages. At Dr. Pilewski's urging, we are asking family and friends to fly in.

Friday, November 10, 2017—Jack

Today is my birthday.

I wake up with a jolt to the sound of my alarm.

A single notification is displayed on my phone, showing that Diane had called me not even five minutes before and left a voicemail.

I shoot up in bed, fearful that something bad has happened.

I hit the voicemail playback button and Diane's voice fills the room.

"Jack . . . if you're going to come, come now. . . ." (click)

Fearing the worst, I call her right back. It's time.

On the way to the airport, Mal checks in with a text. "Good morn-ing!! I hope today is wonderful and that this birthday is the start of an amazing year. And I hate to put a damper on the day but I'm getting moved to the Intensive Care Unit." She ends the text with a sad-faced emoji. Even as she was struggling for her life, she was thinking about others. Quintessential Mallory.

When I ask Diane why the urgency to come, she explains that Mal is at the end and it is time to call anyone who needs to be there. By 8:00, I'm in the room, along with thirty others who have flown in to be with Mallory.

Saturday, November 11, 2017—Jack

Things are scary, as Mallory isn't turning around. Diane arranges for all of us to stand outside Mallory's ICU room and take a picture smiling. Intubated and drugged up, Mal scribbles: "Can't talk at all (sad face) but so grateful that you are all here for the hardest part." She smiles, so re-markable in light of what is happening. She is writing notes to everyone, thanking them for visiting. At one point, she gets tired and tugs on my sleeve, pointing to the paper and motioning for a pen: First she writes, "Can we be alone." I squeeze her hand and indicate yes. Then I ask the others to give us a moment. She continues writing: "Is everyone here be-cause they think I'm going to die?"

This is a hard question to respond to. I steady myself and answer as calmly as I can. "We knew this situation was risky, so everyone just wanted to be sure," I say vaguely, knowing how stupid it sounds. But I am trying to follow Diane's lead. Her mandate, in fact. She has very clearly and unequivocally instructed all of us to stay positive. She has chosen to ignore the advice the doctors have been giving for the past week, which is to let Mallory know she is dying. Diane feels strongly that since Mark is on a mission to get her phage therapy, there is still hope. And Mallory needs hope to hang in there.

Mallory looks into my eyes, searching for the truth. After a moment that seems to stretch far too long but in reality is only a slight pause, she shrugs her shoulders, tilts her head, and nods.

Sunday, November 12, 2017—Mallory's mom

Things are spiraling out of control. I continue to insist that no one tell Mallory she is dying. Mark and I agree that we want her to take her last breath thinking she is going to sleep and will awaken when the phages have done their job. She is terrified of dying and my response as a mom is to try to take away her fear.

Monday, November 13, 2017—Mallory's mom

UPMC is working its magic to keep Mal stable. One of the labs in Maryland has confirmed that they have at least two active lytic phages that should be ready for delivery (expanded AND purified) by Thursday. Mark is in high gear coordinating additional phage preps to maximize Mal's chances. Dr. Pilewski said she won't make it to Thursday. Mark thinks we should have the phages delivered and administered in whatever state they are in. Mark called Dr. Robert (Chip) Schooley, the one guiding us through the phage therapy journey, to ask about stopping the growth/purification process and using whatever phage prep is now ready. Jack came up with the idea to split the not-fully-mature existing culture in two, so one could be ready to administer and the other would continue the growth/purification process.

Mark texted this new idea to Chip. Chip liked it, and passed it along to APT.

Mark and Danny talked to APT, who gave us an ETA of 4:00 p.m. Tuesday for the first phage preparation.

I sent urgent emails to Drs. Pilewski and D'Cunha asking if we could use the UPMC chopper since they use them for organ procurement. They said yes!!!!

Tuesday, November 14, 2017—Mallory's aunt Meryl

It's the early-morning shift and I'm sitting alone with Mallory, who rests fully sedated. It's not clear what she absorbs in this state but Diane thinks, as do I, that she knows we are there, so I keep my hand on her leg and believe she feels the presence of family. When I remove my hand to take photos of Mal's vitals, I explain to Mallory that I just need my hand for a minute to use my cell phone, that her mother loves her so much, and she likes to see the machines' readings.

I take photos every hour per Diane's request and send them to her, so that she can know the status of Mallory's O_2, the most important number she's tracking. Diane is trying to sleep in the apartment but hasn't been able to during this critical time. I hope the good numbers enable her to doze until it's time for the next set.

Tuesday, November 14, 2017—Mallory's mom

Just got word that the helicopter can't fly in current weather so they're sending Dr. Harano to Allegheny County Airport to fly by plane to Frederick Airport, the airport closest to APT's lab. APT will be waiting to hand off the phages and then Dr. Harano will fly back to Allegheny and be met by an ambulance to deliver the phages. Dr. Abdel-Massih will be waiting at Mallory's bedside to prepare the phages for administration.

Tuesday, November 14, 2017—Aunt Meryl

With the phages on their way, everyone is whirling about in such a frenzy of excitement that I am terrified the excess energy will affect Mallory's numbers. There has been a great deal of conversation about keeping Mal's room a calm, meditative space because noise and excitement appear to cause her numbers to go wild. So as everyone else bounds back and forth at her doorway, bringing status reports, racing off to watch the helicopter that is delivering the phages to the hospital roof, I stay in the chair by her bed, and hold her hand. My voice is steady as I deliver a very long monologue, reminding her of the beautiful days to come after the phages do their work. And I try to describe a medical process I barely understand. People come in and out. I feel like a drill sergeant, reminding them to keep their voices low. "The phages are coming," I say, we all say. "The phages are coming, Mal. They're almost here."

Tuesday, November 14, 2017—Mallory's mom

We need a miracle.

5:10 p.m.—Dr. Harano is on the plane with phages in hand. Turns out he will be met by a helicopter to bring the phages to the hospital by

6:00 p.m. The plan is to deliver them into the trachea. Everyone in the ICU is on standby. . . . Dr. D'Cunha was instrumental in securing transport, Dr. Pilewski will deliver the phages through a bronch. My new favorite quote: Some superheroes wear capes, others wear stethoscopes!!

5:55 p.m.—THE PHAGES ARE HERE!!! Dr. Abdel-Massih takes the cooler to the lab to prepare the first doses.

6:00 p.m.—Dr. Abdel-Massih brings three syringes into Mallory's room, and delivers them to Dr. Pilewski. Dr. P empties one through a bronchoscope into Mallory's right lung, and then a second one into Mallory's left lung. He then administers a microdose intravenously. I ask Mark how long it's supposed to take, and he tells me that Tom Patterson woke up from a months-long coma and recognized his daughter seventy-two hours after the phages were administered. Now there's nothing to do but wait for them to work.

Wednesday, November 15, 2017—Mallory's mom

Mal started desatting around 7:00 a.m. UPMC docs paralyzed her chest to keep her from expending energy fighting against the ventilator.

Mark, Micah, Maria, Jack, Meryl, Danny, Eileen, Stacy, Cindy, Ron, Jesse, Marissa, Mich, Natei, and Tyler are here for Mal, with Susie fetching food for all of us as we stand by in a minute-by-minute race with time.

Wednesday, November 15, 2017—Jack

I have to fight to wake myself up when I first hear the phone ring.

It's Eileen. "You need to come to the hospital now."

I throw on some clothes and run straight to the hospital. At the entrance to Mal's room, I gown up and join Diane and Mark, who are stroking her hands and speaking softly to Mallory. Her playlist of favorite songs is on in the background. They see me, then step aside to give me time with her.

Mallory is on her left side, her body angled to encourage the flow of blood to her left lung, the one that isn't completely overtaken by pneumonia. The right lung is completely saturated.

I sit beside Mal, holding her hand, squeezing it hard. Her vitals are terrible and visibly dropping.

"Mal . . . I'm really glad I met you . . . I want to thank you . . . for making me a better man. . . . I love you, Mal . . . always."

I break down in the moment. I had only cried once this hard before, the night that Mallory's Stanford doctor had said she'd have a year to live. Now here we are, fifteen months later, powerless. We had fought so hard—and she had come so far—but now she is slipping away.

When I leave the room to give others their chance to sit with Mallory, Dr. Pilewski takes Mark, Diane, Micah, and me aside. In the staff room, he informs us, in clear, simple language, that irreparable damage has been done to her brain due to lack of oxygen. Mallory's identity—her endless wit, fierce love of others, and inner spirit—is gone.

In that moment, we know it is time to let her go. She has endured enough. Diane doesn't want to tell Mallory she is dying and makes the decision that our last words will be ones of hope.

Diane is resolute: "If anyone deserves to rest in peace, it's Mallory." Micah is sobbing. Mark is distraught. We walk back to Mallory's room and join Meryl, who had stayed with Mal while we left to confer with the doctor. Everyone else is in the waiting room so it's just family for the final moments. Doctors begin switching off the devices working so diligently to keep her alive. One by one, the whirs of each machine vanish.

Together we hold Mallory, so she feels our love, each of us taking a hand, her head, a leg. We speak to her, saying, "It's okay to sleep. You have the phage, it's going to work."

Wednesday, November 15, 2017—Mallory's mom

Despite everyone's heroic efforts, our brave, beautiful, loving Mallory passed peacefully today at 4:52 p.m., surrounded by Mark, Micah, Jack, Meryl, Danny, and me. The phage therapy we got for Mal couldn't be administered in time to save her but she will provide a lung biopsy so that researchers can learn from her case. Our hope is gone but Mallory's memory will be a blessing forever.

AFTERWORD

by Jack Goodwin

After Mallory died, a heavy fog settled over her community.

Maya was the first person I called to share the news that Mallory had passed. I'll never forget her desperate shrieks of terror as they rang out over the phone, each word growing more distant after she had dropped the phone from her ear. Despite knowing that death was always a possibility, we shared a sense of shock as the foundations of our former reality crumbled into the past.

The morning after Mallory died, her family, her friends, and I got on a plane in Pittsburgh to go back to LA. We had left Mallory's body at the hospital so that an autopsy could be conducted for research before it would be cremated and sent home to her parents.

Plans for a celebration of life had already been set in motion. As someone who finds comfort in getting things done, Mallory's mom, Diane, turned to our squad and asked if we wanted to hold it that coming Saturday, the same day as Mallory's annual CF fundraiser, which they'd held since she was a child. Or, she suggested, we could wait a few months, which would give us more time to prepare. The vote for Saturday had been unanimous, leaving us seventy-two hours to prep.

The day came, and more than a thousand people arrived to show their united support at Mallory's celebration of life in her hometown of Beverly Hills. Mallory's family and closest friends all spoke, filling the air with poignant and humorous stories of her abundant spirit and wisdom. As the newest member of Mallory's inner circle, I spoke last. It was a moment I had feared since the day I fell in love with her. But surrounded by her community, her family, and her love, I found that the words came easily.

Mal didn't just bring out the best in me; she brought out the best in everyone she knew.

I spoke on the subject of titles in our relationship, and how time spent with Mallory as a mere "somebody" and then "boyfriend" had made both those titles, as well as my strength and character as a man, grow.

When Mallory and I were first courting, Diane had called to check in on Mallory during one of her routine hospital visits to ask who was coming to visit her that day.

"Becca, Michelle, Ari, and . . . somebody," she said.

I started out as *somebody*. Humble beginnings.

From there, I became "the new boy." Or, for short, "the boy." Then, finally, I made it to the title of *boyfriend*—a title that I was honored to hold. And yet, after about a year of dating, I came to realize how I hoped to one day trade all those titles for new ones: fiancé, husband, father. Titles that were never meant to be for us.

However, I knew it was not the rank or privilege of those titles that counted—they're just words. It's what you do with them that matters. And no matter the title or outcome, I would choose to fall in love with Mal all over again.

Several months after the memorial celebration and subsequent gatherings, the Shader Smith family, a few of Mallory's friends, and I flew out to Mal's favorite place in Hawaii to make good on her final farewell wishes. In an entry found in her journal, "When I Die," Mallory had asked for a celebratory paddle-out into the ocean and for her ashes to be spread at sea. Mal wasn't just an earth-to-earth, dust-to-dust, ashes-to-ashes sort of gal. She was a full-on stardust-to-stardust woman. In her mind, her love for and connection to the planet we call home was the same bond she felt for the universe she was born into. Despite the constant assault on her body by sickness and the attacks on the planet by mass pollution, Mal recognized how precious and wonderful her life was while she was alive.

In the deep blue waters of the Pacific, near Maui, the petals of sixty-five roses became our ceremonial substitute for Mal's ashes. Diane and Mark were not yet ready to let her go, electing instead to spread her ashes over time. We all donned floral leis and set out in what became a small armada of outrigger canoes and surfboards, using our paddles and hands to push our disparate worries behind us as the gentle kiss of sea spray welcomed us to a future without Mal but still filled with sunshine. Out on the water, I breathed in deeply, the scent of flowers and sea salt filling my lungs with peace as Mallory's spirit danced around us.

Everyone has their own journey of processing grief. As a type A person, I started by telling myself I'd be over Mallory within three months. Boy, was I wrong. Three turned into six, which quickly turned into twelve. I immersed myself in my work as a satellite engineer to distract myself, envious that I could command my satellites to carry out their missions so easily while I felt so lost without a mission of my own. Throwing myself into the ocean at sunset alleviated part of my frustration, allowing the waves to soothe my grief and give me more direction than my compromised mind seemed able to. Over time, hope returned steadily, but for a long time, it was hard to feel anything but lost.

Reading Mallory's words in what would become *Salt in My Soul* forced me to accept my new reality and gave me the courage to ask for help now that I needed it. As someone who'd grown up witnessing the societal stigma surrounding men and therapy, I was apprehensive to jump into getting to know *me* better. Knowing that Mal had gone to therapy and was a huge proponent of building a better relationship with oneself as well as others gave me the final push I needed to give it a go. The experience was raw, expansive, and wonderful in a way that allowed me to become a stronger man than I could have otherwise been on my own.

Sixteen months after Mallory's death, *Salt in My Soul* came out. A week later, I gently lifted a copy from a bestseller bookshelf in Terminal 4 of the Los Angeles International Airport, seeing her book in the world for the first time. Another airport-goer already had the book in hand, casually turning the pages to chapter 2. I was unsuccessful in hiding my smile as I returned the book to the shelf, waiting for whoever its rightful owner would be to pick it up and welcome Mal's story into their life.

Readers around the world loved Mallory's story, and, boy, did they have questions for me. Born out of equal parts respect for my privacy and curiosity about what dating Mallory was like, the main questions usually took some form of the following: *Why did you choose to love someone you knew was going to die soon? Wouldn't you fear falling for someone who would likely die before you did? Who might require care and experience stress and life upheaval far beyond that of a healthier partner? Why would you willingly choose such chaos and uncertainty?*

These questions were natural to ask; I had thought about many of them, too.

When I began dating Mallory, I had wondered what a relationship with her might look like. Sure, I feared the realities. I feared how they would affect my life, and ours. And yet even during our earliest visits and interactions and flirtations, I feared something else far more: not having Mallory in my life. There were many reasons for this, many things that made my net attraction to Mallory greater than the sum total of my fear. One stood out above the rest: Mal's goal in life was to "prioritize love."

My first understanding of the duality of Mallory's sickness and personality happened when she coughed up blood in front of me for the first time. At a house party, while playing a lawn game, Mal dove rapidly for a well-placed shot I had hit, and she fell hard on the ground. I'll never forget watching her eyes widen in fear as she scrambled to pick herself up and sprint inside to the bathroom, clutching her chest. Five minutes later, she came out smiling, teeth still slightly bloodied as if she'd just been punched in the mouth. I was at once terrified and impressed by her response to the chaos CF and superbugs brought to her life. This girl had a warrior spirit, and if she could take a punch like that and still come up smiling, I could only imagine how much farther her spirit would take her, let alone how far it would take me.

In 1992, when Mallory was born, the average life-span of someone with the CF gene mutation was twenty-five years. When Mal found out she had the superbug *B. cepacia,* however, that added complication chipped away at her average nominal life-span even further. Double-lung transplants, first-world treatments for superbugs and cystic fibrosis—all could prolong Mallory's life, though each with seemingly insurmountable odds. While the exact nature of her life remained uncertain, an early death was all but guaranteed.

Though the hard facts of Mallory's physical infections were immutable and intimidating, they were transcended by the far more infectious nature of Mallory's character. Mallory had been in a battle to reject the status quo of her body for her whole life. Thousands of hours of treatment, missed birthdays of friends due to sickness, days spent recovering indoors while hooked up to burdensome machines, feeling ill and nauseated, all gave her every excuse to be a bitter, hurtful person. And yet Mal had the courage to say, *You know what? I don't just intend to love my life in spite of its limitations. I intend to love fully and completely for every second I can, for as long as I can.*

Mal feared death just like everyone else, but as long as she lived, she didn't want to settle for living, or loving, half well. Mediocrity in life and love equated to giving ground to the fear that one day soon she might die. So when she did have enough control over her health to be master of her fate, she was going to use it to love with her whole heart. This approach to intimacy and love gave Mallory the confidence to live life to the fullest, granting others around her the contagious permission to do the same.

A few months into our dating, Mal's doctors told us that they were out of treatment options and that they hadn't found a transplant center that would take her. They promised to keep trying, of course, but said she might consider going off IVs and on hospice to live out her days as best she could. If she did that, they said, she might have a year to live.

At first, I panicked, creating distance from Mal in an effort to protect myself. As a competitor in all things, I humbly admit that some champion-level panicking was achieved. But I soon recovered and found the strength to look in the proverbial mirror and start asking the tough questions. I started with the wrong ones:

What if I stayed with her for a year and she died? What if I stayed with her for a year and she lived, but with a restricted life? What kind of relationship am I okay with?

These were dark and negative questions. I didn't like them. As an aspiring astronaut candidate at the time, I turned to President John F. Kennedy's 1962 speech about putting the first humans on the moon (which can be applied more generally to taking on any major challenge in life): "We choose to go to the moon. We choose to go to the moon in this decade and do the other things, not because they are easy, but because they are hard, because that goal will serve to organize and measure the best of our energies and skills, because that challenge is one that we are willing to accept, one we are unwilling to postpone, and one which we intend to win."

I certainly wasn't the president of the United States, and I definitely wasn't weighing whether or not to go to the moon (yet), but I saw the value in acknowledging that taking on certain challenges in life can be extremely difficult, but doing them anyway can bring even greater joy and triumph. With this attitude in mind, I soon found the right questions to ask:

What if the outcome is greater than I could ever imagine?

And, most important, *What kind of man do I want to be?*

Did I want to be the type of man who loves someone only when it's easy—or when it's hard? And not just when it's hard but *especially* when it's hard.

The answer revealed itself, and three days after learning that she might have only a year to live, I told Mal my decision: I wanted to be the type of man who stayed.

I knew staying on its own wouldn't be enough, however, so I

came back with an attitude: I was going to be the greatest partner of all time! Romeo and Juliet? Trash. Cleopatra and Mark Antony? Hot garbage. My goal was to raise the bar.

And yet . . . I was quickly humbled because Mal sat me down and said, "Jack, I know you are doing your best, but I need you to do better."

She was right, of course. I was trying to be both a good PhD student and a good partner, but I was failing at both. So I decided to drop out of my PhD program, knowing that my dreams of pushing humanity closer to the stars would always be there for me—while Mallory might not be.

Mallory's and my shared belief in a happy life together made sacrifices worth it for the outcome we got together in return. This remained true right up until the moment when Mallory's blood oxygen levels dropped below those needed to sustain her brain and she wasn't with us anymore. Soon after, we said our goodbyes and let her go.

When Mal died, I felt a natural relief that someone I cared deeply for was no longer experiencing pain, but also an unexpected and overwhelming sense of pride. When we started dating, I had wondered if I could stay strong when times got tough. Feared that I might tap out—call it quits—or make decisions that I would regret. When she died, I finally had the answer to the question of whether I could stay true to our love: the answer was yes.

I could never picture what death brought to Mal—could never imagine the dark void of nothingness that enveloped her. Instead, in every whip of warm wind through tall mountain grass, every shout of children as they ran toward their next adventure, every glimmer of a rainbow, I would feel Mal with me. Our sun is one of more than 100 billion stars in the Milky Way galaxy, and for a long time, I believed I would love Mal until the last star burned out. When it did, I would love her in the darkness.

And yet, as the moon waxed and waned and the seasons turned anew, I came to accept that all of life's long walks under a canopy of trees, belly laughs with friends until the wee hours of the morning, and nights spent staring up into the eternity of the stars are ones that I think are full of breathtaking beauty not because Mallory and I would have enjoyed them but because *I* enjoyed them. I was ready to move on. Somewhere, somehow, I knew Mal was there supporting me when I did.

It's been more than six years since I lost my best friend and partner, but every day, I try to be the man I became during our time together. I try to be a little less judgmental—a little more gracious and grateful for the small moments in life—a little more persistent in my pursuit of the truth. More than anything, I try to help build a world in which Mallory would have been proud to raise our children.

WHEN I DIE

By Mallory Smith

When I die, the most important thing I want my parents to know is that everything I am (and all the things I've been able to do) is because of them. As a daughter, a granddaughter, and a sister, my relationships have always been lopsided, because I can never give as much as I take. I wish I could repay them for everything they've done for me. Everything my parents and grandparents have done since I've been born was with the single-minded purpose of keeping me alive and well and happy and motivated, no matter how much it meant sacrificing themselves. I've never felt like I could express how much it meant that they were willing to give and give without expecting anything in return; I'd write cards, buy gifts for the holidays and birthdays, but no gesture comes close to being big enough.

The tiniest moments have stuck with me in the most profound ways: that time my dad slept on a springy cot in my hospital room for the eighth night in a row, in hospitalization number twenty-something, and told me about how he felt when his own dad died (lost and lonely, like he had come untethered, all of a sudden lacking roots or a home); all the times my mom put my needs over hers and didn't pursue the illustrious career she, as such a smart and hard-working woman, could have had; the times my brother offered to do my errands because I hadn't slept or wasn't breathing well; the hours Grandpa and I spent listening to symphonies and chamber music string quartets, bonding over Bach and Beethoven; sunny days spent sitting on the beach with Grandma in Hawaii throughout the years, joyous because we were together and by the water; lazy hours passed in the kitchen with Maria, debating the merits of Catholicism and the existence of God, knowing that despite our wildly different upbringings we would always be connected.

The most important thing they must know when I die is that none of these moments are forgotten, and they all contributed to me becoming a person who feels the world is a good place. I could have been a bitter person, might have felt cheated by getting stuck with a chronic terminal illness, if I weren't born into a family that surrounded me with fierce love and unwavering support from my very first breath.

I hope to be remembered as a kind, honest, good-hearted person who worked hard and put others before herself whenever possible.

I would like to be cremated, and hope to be celebrated on the water, where I always felt most at home, and for my remains to live on there.

A big funeral party would be good, too, for those who are unable to paddle out or are not comfortable on the water. Overall, I want people to celebrate my life with joy for the time we had together, rather than mourning my passing.

CURRENT STATE OF PHAGE THERAPY

By Diane Shader Smith

When it was clear Mallory's bacteria was fully resistant to all available antibiotics and antifungals, Mark tried to get a little-known treatment called phage therapy for her. It was extremely difficult because phages weren't part of mainstream medicine. The primary phage centers were in Eastern Europe, operating without FDA approval.

Herculean efforts on the part of the US Navy, a start-up company called Adaptive Phage Therapeutics, researchers around the world, epidemiologist Steffanie Strathdee, and Dr. Joe Pilewski at UPMC led to Mallory receiving an initial dose of the treatment, but it was too late to save her.

Mallory's autopsy did show proof of concept. To paraphrase the conclusion of her report: Phage therapy is ideal to treat bacterial infections because phages are very specific and only kill the target bacteria, so they aren't dangerous or toxic. If Mallory had gotten phage therapy sooner, she could have lived.

Since Mallory passed away, there has been tremendous progress. At the time of this writing, five phage centers have opened at major universities, and many more institutions are doing work with phages in a less formal way in the United States and abroad. The biggest obstacle to bringing this treatment to market is lack of funding. There's also a lack of awareness of the need to address antimicrobial resistance. Mallory's story and her writing have reignited interest in this on a global scale.

There is an urgent need for action. CARB-X and the AMR Action Fund, among other groups that support medical advances, now support several phage companies in preclinical and early clinical work, including phage libraries and custom engineering of phages to help prevent and treat many bacterial infections. Congress is currently considering passage of the PASTEUR Act to encourage innovative drug development targeting the most threatening infections, improve the appropriate use of antibiotics, and ensure domestic availability of antibiotics when needed.

In the meantime, rigorous randomized controlled clinical trials have begun, to enable subsequent requests for approval from the FDA and the European Medicines Agency for phage therapies. Mallory's Legacy Fund, housed at the California Community Foundation, an independent 501(c)(3) organization, made the inaugural grant to support the first clinical trial using phages in the United States. The trial is now also being funded by the National Institutes of Health, co-led by Dr. Chip Schooley at IPATH. All profits from this book will be donated to support phage therapy research and clinical trials.